UNEVEN

Sam Mills is the author of *The Quiddity of Will Self*, *The Watermark* and *The Fragments of My Father*. Sam has written for a number of publications, including the *Guardian*, *Independent*, 3 AM and *London Magazine*. She is also the co-founder of the independent press Dodo Ink.

UNEVEN

Nine Lives
that Redefined
Bisexuality

SAM MILLS

Atlantic Books
London

For L. K.
and my dear Andrew Gallix

First published in hardback in Great Britain in 2025
by Atlantic Books, an imprint of Atlantic Books Ltd.

A CIP catalogue record for this book is available from the British Library.

Hardback ISBN: 978 1 83895 683 7
E-book ISBN: 978 1 83895 684 4

Atlantic Books
An imprint of Atlantic Books Ltd
Ormond House
26–27 Boswell Street
London
WC1N 3JZ

Printed and bound by CPI (UK) Ltd, Croydon CR0 4YY

www.atlantic-books.co.uk

MIX
Paper | Supporting
responsible forestry
FSC
www.fsc.org
FSC® C171272

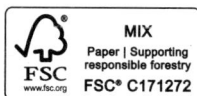

Contents

Prologue

I remember my first kiss with a boy. I was fourteen years old, dressed in khaki and surrounded by a circle of onlookers who watched us with wide eyes. We'd found a secret patch for our game. The moonlight shone soft on the grass and metallic on the roof of the ammunition hut that shielded us. I still had mud on my boots from the morning exercise, which had dragged us from our beds at four. My hands were rough from dismantling a rifle down to its vital organs. My uniform made me feel dull, its camouflage blending away my individuality, and I surreptitiously pulled my hair free from its band, letting it flow around my shoulders.

If we'd had a bottle, we might have spun it; instead, the bossiest member of the group played Eros-compere. She paired us off, clicking the stopwatch on her watch. She pointed at me; she pointed at Stefan. She demanded ten seconds of contact.

Stefan was a beautiful Black boy with an afro. Before this evening, I'd barely spoken to him. Now I hesitated. Was this the right setting for my first kiss – no chaise longue, no fancy Cadillac with leather seats? A first kiss had a butterfly life, could not be repeated once lost, and wouldn't it be better to wait for the perfect setting? He was stepping closer, pupils bright, leaning in—

Many of the romantic books and films I'd read had promised a kiss as neat punctuation: the full stop on a date, played out against the poetic backdrop of a glorious sky. There was the rapturous kiss in *A Room With A View*, where Lucy's repressed Victorian nature unravelled in a field in Italy, a terrace bathed in light and beauty, abundant in violets that beat against her dress in 'blue waves' as George 'stepped quickly forward and kissed her'. The punctuation of that kiss is like a dash, its illicit nature made more delicious by its abrupt end when Miss Bartlett enters the scene, dressed in brown like a theatrical killjoy, calling sharply for Lucy. Then there was *Les Liaisons Dangereuses*, where the French word for kiss, *baiser*, is rarely used, where the embraces described have the feel of ellipses, made even more seductive through what is implied rather than what is said. And *Sweet Valley High*, the trashy high school series about two identical twins (of course, they are distinguishable by morals: one a good girl, one bad), where kisses only took place between characters who were obscenely beautiful, kisses as cartoonish as an emoji.

All these had layered my desire and made it idealistic. Because I went to a girls' school, boys were elusive. They were like wild animals we saw through cage bars, glimpsed on buses, street corners, wondered how to tempt and excite. That was why I had joined the teen Army Cadets despite being a member of Greenpeace. I had no interest in learning how to fire an L98 rifle, or dragging myself through an assault course, or forcing my hair under an itchy beret. That morning we had been taken into the woods and forced to lie down for several hours, guns idle between our hands as the cold seared into us, and our sergeant advised us to piss through our trousers into the mud if we got desperate. I had saved precious Saturday-job money to endure this torture, but it had felt worthwhile when, on one previous camp, I had *nearly* been kissed. His lips had awkwardly missed my mouth and landed on the edge of my lips before he ran away. And now I had this opportunity, this opportunity to kiss Stefan, but I wasn't sure whether to be brave or flee, whether to wait for a setting where life could match art.

Our lips touched.

Ten seconds went by, then twenty. Sixty. We were separated by the leader, who looked a bit cross. Stefan and I smiled dreamily at each other.

Looking back as an adult, it's easy to project awkwardness onto the scene. But, once the magical kiss had begun, I was no longer worried about the imperfect setting, the gap between life and art, and I wasn't embarrassed by having an audience. The group around me didn't feel like voyeurs, because they knew as little as I did about sex. I was grateful that I wasn't paired with anyone but Stefan, that we got to kiss for a second time that night.

Some weeks later, a boy walked up to me on an evening meeting at Cadets and asked if I wanted Stefan's phone number. Suddenly my feeling for him made me vulnerable. I laughed uncertainly and lost the moment.

A few more weeks on, and I heard that Stefan and a group of others would be attending a fair. When my mother told me I wasn't allowed to go, I wept and begged, but she was anxious that I was too young. And so I had to spend the evening writing about him, giving him life in my imagination. I never saw him again.

*

I remember my first kiss with a girl. I was seventeen years old. It was around three in the morning; I was squashed onto the back seat of a car, dance music reverberating. As I was dropped off at my house, my friends waved and blew kisses. We were still fizzy from an evening of clubbing; bubbles of cocktails, flirting, dancing, hilarity were floating inside me. Amelia, my best friend, got out of the car. I assumed we were going to hug and I opened my arms—

She planted a kiss on my lips.

We'd seen the film *Basic Instinct* a year earlier, on a ferry, on the way back from a school trip to France. We'd felt such a thrill when we succeeded in talking our way in to see an '18' film in the onboard cinema, the boat lurching and rollicking as we watched. Sharon Stone was as glossy and cool as a Hitchcock blonde, beautifully dressed and always poised, lighting her cigarettes with languor, telling Michael Douglas's cop that he was 'in way over your head', as though she was a cliff-face and he was about to drive over her edge. While some actors are known for their alter egos, becoming Sherlock, Fleabag, or an Agatha Christie detective, some characters become the shadows of their actors. Stone's charisma shone so brightly that I can't even remember the name of the character she played, a writer who may or may not have murdered her ex. She had a female lover, also blonde, who emitted a snarling, predatory energy, angry about having to share Stone with Douglas. The film was loathed by the critics but loved by audiences, who devoured it as a trashy delight. Madonna was so impressed by it that she made a film called *Body of Evidence* that was practically a *Basic Instinct* remake, in which Madonna effectively played Sharon Stone mark II.

Madonna was one of our first insights into the world of bisexuality. A queen of metamorphoses, she suddenly swerved into her sexy phase in the early nineties. Her infamous book, *Sex*, shocked us all. Her music shifted from the religious controversy of 'Like a Prayer' to the erotic controversy of 'Justify My Love'. I saw the banned video that accompanied the song late one night on *The Word*, my parents asleep upstairs. It is a beautifully shot black-and-white affair which begins with Madonna slinking down a hallway in a shiny black mackintosh, entering a secret room, embracing several lovers, male and female, cis and trans. The song has an eerie, smoky quality. Madonna doesn't shine in movies, but in pop videos her acting comes to life beautifully, and the end shot of 'Justify My Love' left an afterburn in my mind: she leaves the secret room and hurries away down the corridor, laughing in guilty ecstasy, ashamed, savouring her shame. What has now become the norm in female pop videos was Madonna's innovation. She suffered a visceral backlash, and we admired the way she stood strong, proud to be a woman exploring her sexuality.

At that time, I had only ever once seen two girls kissing in real life. It happened at a teenage house party; it felt like a spectacle. The girls had boyfriends and the moment their lips touched, heads turned and whispers rustled. Their kiss concluded with viperish smiles; they seemed to relish their transgression. That memory is definitely flavoured by Sharon Stone and Madonna. They framed bisexuality as something daring, dangerous and cool. And so when my best friend kissed me outside my house that night, I interpreted it as affectionate. She was grinning. Her eyes were sparkling with happiness. There was nothing edgy in her behaviour, which I had come to regard as a signifier of female seduction. We had bruised each other in netball, shared a double bed on holiday. We were always hugging, tactile in the way that teenagers at a girls' school are. On our school exchange trip to France, we walked around a square holding hands, amused by French passers-by who did double takes and whispered that we were *lesbienne*. I thought the kiss was an exuberant celebration of our friendship; maybe. I never mentioned it to my friend, though I never forgot it.

I cannot remember the moment when I first knew that I was bisexual. I feel it ought to be accompanied by a lightning flash of revelation, but there was none. I don't remember being conscious of it at Oxford University, a dry place that was all work and no play, where everyone around me seemed far too busy making contacts in their quest to become the next prime minister to have time for romance. All I know is that some time in my early twenties, I had various crushes on famous women. It seemed safer to be attracted to fantasy icons than real-life women, perhaps; a cautious way of tiptoeing into this newfound sexuality. Kiera Knightley; Kate Moss; Saffron Burrows; Zadie Smith: all women I was wild about. I discussed these crushes with a male friend. It was very bonding to agree on how we thought Kate would be a good laugh to go for a pint with, and how exquisitely delicate Kiera's features were.

In contrast, I refrained from mentioning my crushes to female friends. I think I was afraid that it might introduce awkwardness to the friendship, that hugs might become stiff, that they might begin to reinterpret jokes, overanalyse things I said. I was careful to compartmentalize it in this way, so that my sexual identity was not necessarily secret, but certainly private, and when I first dated a woman in my late twenties hardly anyone knew about it. My mother died without ever knowing I was bisexual; none of my present family know. Even recently, when I joined a dating site and clicked on 'bisexual' and then added 'sapiosexual' for the hell of it, laughing at such a pretentious dating term, I felt anxious when one of my female friends spotted me on the site, someone who had known me for years, and cried, 'Oh, I never realized you were . . . !' It was not that I felt judged by them, nor that I felt our friendship would suffer, because we had known each for years; more that it felt odd to have a label pinned on me. Which, it turns out, is something many, many people feel.

*

In recent years bisexual chic has come into fashion again. 2019 was hashtagged on Twitter as #TwentyBiTeen. At the Grammys, St. Vincent and Dua Lipa shared a sexy duet as they sang *Masseduction/ One Kiss*; Ariana Grande released the bisexual anthem *Break Up With Your Girlfriend, I'm Bored*; Desiree Akhavan's *The Bisexual* premiered on Channel 4, where the main protagonist, Leila, angsted about her bisexuality, declaring that it 'makes you seem disingenuous, like your genitals have no allegiance'.

As teenagers, my friends and I thought Sharon Stone and Madonna had invented bisexuality. We naively assumed we were creating culture anew, that society had been governed by a hang-over of Victorian prudishness up until the point that Madonna overturned it. We loved Madonna for shocking the world in the same way that David Bowie sparked a cultural revolution during the 1970s. Picture him in 1972, bounding onto the stage as Ziggy Stardust: a bisexual androgynous alien rock star come to save the planet, sporting flaming red hair and a Lycra bodysuit, radiating glam and glitter. In his iconic *Top of the Pops* performance, he put his arm around his guitarist Mick Ronson; choreographer Michael Clark reminisced on how revolutionary this was: 'It was the only physical contact I had seen men do apart from punching each other. It seems ridiculous now that a small gesture like that could be so meaningful, but, for me, it was.' Bowie's sexuality might have been characteristically mercurial (in his press interviews, he was provocatively 'gay', then 'bisexual', then a decade on 'a closet heterosexual'), but nevertheless, he gave a voice to all those who were gay or uncertain about their sexuality. He brought queer culture into the mainstream. Headlines about 'bisexual chic' ran in magazines such as *Time* and *Newsweek*; Bowie was rumoured to be lovers with Mick Jagger. We loved Madonna in the same way that audiences in the 1930s adored Marlene Dietrich for challenging accepted ideas about femininity, playing femme fatale roles and glamorizing gender-crossing haute couture. 'I am at heart a gentleman,' she declared, and the famous Dietrich silhouette was emphasized by the masculine cut of her trousers. Dietrich was daring at a time when the Golden Age of Hollywood perpetuated illusions of heterosexuality and arranged marriages of convenience, though many of its stars were bisexual: Marilyn Monroe, Joan Crawford, James Dean, Judy Garland, Cary Grant, Errol Flynn. This was preceded by a period of bisexual experimentation in the 1920s, when the Bright Young Things took pleasure in rejecting fusty Victorian values and bobbed their hair.

The history of bisexuality is discontinuous, of course, and expressed differently across cultures. If we jump back to sixteenth-century

Japan, we find the practice of *shudō*, where *samarai* warriors would train younger men, known as *wakashu*, for battle. It was expected that teacher and pupil would become lovers, until the young man was old enough for marriage. Further back still, in Ancient Greece, young men were expected to have relationships with older men of a higher status in order to gain wisdom and experience before growing up into heterosexuality and wedding a woman. The Roman Emperor Hadrian had numerous female and male lovers. His favourite was a young Greek slave, Antinous, who was exceptionally beautiful. One day, the emperor and his entourage were sailing on the Nile, when Antinous fell into the river and drowned. He was deified by Hadrian, a city named after him, his exquisite features stamped onto coins, his form immortalized in busts and statues – around 2,000 of them. It is harder to find evidence of female bisexuality, because men were writing history, and women were the property of men. For Roman men, however, it was socially acceptable, suggesting that bisexuality is something that has existed in society in cycles, celebrated at times, frowned upon in others, banned and outlawed now and then.

The meaning of the word bisexual has fluctuated over time. An interesting early appearance occurred in 1859. Robert Bentley Todd, a physician, used it to describe a hermaphroditic species having male/female sex organs. Darwin and his contemporaries also adopted it. In nineteenth-century evolutionary theory, 'bisexual' was a term that described how humans begin life in a state of primordial hermaphroditism; men were seen as more evolved than women because they had developed further beyond that primitive state. This formed the basis of that Victorian phase of classifying sexuality – sexologists such as Richard von Krafft-Ebing saw homosexuality as a deviation because it suggested the person had suffered an arrested development. Bisexuality was seen as a state of potency from which homosexuality and heterosexuality developed. So it was for Freud too, who developed bisexuality as a psychological idea, manifesting in each individual as a blend of masculine and feminine traits. It was only in the second half of the twentieth century that 'bisexual' came to commonly refer to sexual orientation. However, it is a mercurial term, one that is vital but whose subtleties and nuances have differed from decade to decade. Due to its historical roots, it is often muddled with androgyny; it overlaps with this meaning even in modern times: in 1989, Milan Kundera declared that 'All great novels, all true novels are bisexual. This is to say that they express both a feminine and a masculine view of the world.' In 2009, the American sociologist David Halperin listed thirteen different definitions of the term bisexuality. Academic Carol Berenson notes that during the 1990s, many women chose bisexuality not as a positive term they embraced, but as a conclusion that evolved from what they were *not*: not gay, not straight. It's an invisible identity, scientists claim; it's for those of us 'who choose not to choose', says Udis-Kessler; and, as Marjorie Garber poetically sums up, it's 'not an identity, but a narrative.'

One smart, warm and inclusive definition of bisexuality, by activist Robyn Ochs, is favoured by many bis (although note that, once again, bisexuality is qualified here by what it is not as much as what it is): 'I call myself bisexual because I acknowledge in myself the potential to be attracted – romantically and/or sexually – to people of more than one sex and/or gender, not necessarily at the same time, not necessarily in the same way, and not necessarily to the same degree.'

We live in an era now when defining yourself by your sexual identity, adding it to a dating profile, a social media biog, listing it in a website summary, is the norm. In modern times, we like to label ourselves. But it is an elusive term. What does it mean to be bisexual? Does it denote how you feel, or what you do? Can you be bisexual if you are attracted to your same sex but never act on it, if your desire remains solely in the world of fantasy – like Brett Anderson, lead singer in Suede, who famously said, 'I'm a bisexual man who's never had a homosexual experience'? If you once experimented, but have now flipped to being hetero or homo? Does it also imply that if that you settle into monogamy with one gender, you cannot ever be truly satisfied, secretly longing for another?

The very ambiguity of the word makes it vulnerable to criticism; ironically, for a term with so many overlapping meanings, it can also be seen as too exclusive. Bisexuality undercuts and undermines the binary (male/female, gay/straight), yet due to its prefix, it appears to reinforce it. It is often wrongly deemed to imply 'attracted to men and women', when its actual meaning is far more fluid: that you are attracted to more than one gender – if, for example, you like men and nonbinary people, you can be bi. As a result, in recent years, the word 'bisexuality' has suffered a misguided backlash. In a Netflix episode of the teen comedy series *Big Mouth* a character called Ali introduces herself as pansexual. Nick, a classmate, asks her if this is the same as bisexual, which is condemned as 'so binary'. After a Twitter backlash from upset viewers, the creators apologized. There is a misconception that the term excludes trans people, that bis have recently been forced to rebrand their label and throw off its prejudices. In fact, during the early days of bisexual activism, it was more ambiguous than that. In 1991, the *Anything That Moves* bisexual manifesto stated that: 'Bisexuality is a whole, fluid identity. Do not assume that bisexuality is binary or duogamous in nature: that we have "two" sides or that we must be involved simultaneously with both genders to be fulfilled human beings. In fact, don't assume that there are only two genders.'

Still, the prejudice lingers, and some prefer to opt for pansexuality these days. Is there a difference between the two terms? It has been argued that bisexuality means that you're attracted to more than one gender; pansexuality means you're attracted to *all* genders. However, many bis feel that they fought so hard to see the term included in LGBT+ that they don't want to see it die and be replaced with another.

People can also mistake bisexuality as a term of evenness: on the scales of attraction, your predilection for each sex should achieve a median balance. In my own life, I have had far more relationships with men than women, though I cannot be sure if this is due to inhibition and social circumstances rather than my own preferences. Once someone asked me how my bisexuality 'functioned' and I replied, 'I'm unevenly bisexual.' It seems the best way to sum up my sexuality, which doesn't fit into any neat stereotypes or absurd ratios or percentages: my attraction to various genders is ever-fluctuating.

Bisexuals are the world's largest sexual minority. In a recent Stonewall survey of 16–75 year olds in the UK, 84 per cent identified as straight, 5 per cent as bi and 4 per cent as gay/lesbian. We are also the fastest-growing sexual community. In a 2021 Gallup Poll, US adults self-identifying as LGBT reached a new high of 7.1 per cent, a doubling since 2012, and 57 per cent of them identified as bisexuals. The shift is generational, too, for 15 per cent of Gen Z (born 1997–2012) say they are bi, compared to nearly 2 per cent for Generation X (1965–1980).

Women are more likely to be bisexual than men, especially those who are younger and well educated; their number is rising rapidly. But there is still a wide gap between those who are openly bisexual and those who practise it in private. Only 19 per cent of bisexuals have told the most important people in their life about their sexual preference. This compares to 75 per cent when it comes to gays and lesbians. Bisexuality, then, is not only an ambiguous sexuality but, more often than not, a secret one.

To be bisexual is apparently to be furtive – and anxious. The Bisexual Resource Centre notes that bi people have statistically 'higher rates of anxiety, depression and other mood disorders'. They are more likely to self-harm and attempt suicide. They are also 'less likely to be comfortable with their sexuality'. Research shows there's a link between these mental health issues and the phenomenon of bisexual invisibility or erasure. During the course of researching this book, I have been surprised by how many icons I thought were gay were actually bisexual: Freddie Mercury, Oscar Wilde and Gore Vidal. Vidal's editor, Jason Epstein, said that 'he wasn't unhappy about being gay. He was unhappy about being wrongly classified.' This is the trouble with bisexuality: it is often seen as a phase, an ambiguous place occupied by someone who is indecisive, experimenting, finding a path. That – as Freud once argued – it is a state of immaturity before someone makes a final, grown-up decision to be either gay or straight. Geographically, bis are seen as 'on the fence', looking down on both sides, as though precariously balanced and ready to fall. As actress Sandra Bernhard said, 'lots of people think that bisexual means cowardly lesbian'. Then there is the issue of hypersexuality, the assumption that bisexuals cannot be monogamous or are inherently promiscuous, that they are greedy. To be openly bi still has a sense of playfulness and transgressiveness about it. Will Self caused a stir when he recorded a dream about Owen Jones on his blog, describing how he dreamt that he followed him into a Gothic revival church on Gloucester Road – 'I try to reach the young man, who I find attractive' – but was thwarted by young Japanese tourists with Hello Kitty satchels coming in the opposite direction. Self was at the time married to journalist Deborah Orr.

And what about the power dynamics of bisexual relationships? Before I first dated a woman in my late twenties, I had an idealistic view that women would be easier to date than men, though I also feared they might be less exciting, that a certain friction and frisson might be lacking. In past centuries, women were forced to occupy very narrow roles in their romantic relationships. During the Victorian era, they were expected to be 'the angel in the home', devoted wives and mothers, chaste and angelic. Men had power, through ownership of property; the law allowed them to be more complex and flawed. Female adultery was grounds for divorce, male adultery less so. When I read about the writer Colette, for example, I saw that power was a central theme in her relationships – a contradiction she struggled with. Born in 1873, she was only twenty years old when she married Henry Gauthier-Villars, who was fourteen years her senior, a successful writer and a libertine. Soon Colette was writing books that were based on her experiences but published under his name. The *Claudine* series became hugely successful but all the royalties went to her husband. Colette was furious. Eventually, she took him to court and divorced him. Yet she also relished the power dynamic of their relationship, the master/submissive undercurrent.

By contrast, the affair she had with an aristocratic woman, Missy, gave her more independence and liberation. Homosexuality was not outlawed in France, as it was in Britain, for after the Revolution all victimless crimes were abolished. But its social acceptability was still ambiguous. When Colette and Missy performed on stage and shared a kiss, it caused a riot precisely because it was deemed *genuine* rather than a show for male titillation. After her divorce, Colette ended up with a new husband, and a third later in life – for bisexuals of the past, it was often inevitable that if they had to make a choice, they would settle with the opposite sex, given that it was impossible for them to enter into same-sex marriage.

We all want to love and be loved; early on in life, we often nurture a fantasy of finding our ideal partner, of experiencing a great love affair, whether in the form of a passion or a more stable relationship with a family. As Elton John said in 1976, his tone rather wistful: 'I'd rather fall in love with a woman eventually because I think a woman probably lasts longer than a man. But I really don't know . . . I haven't met anybody that I would like to settle down with – of either sex.' He would eventually find happiness with David Furnish. I too hoped to find love, but I was never sure whether it would be with a man or a woman.

The bisexual figures I want to examine in *Uneven* are Oscar Wilde, Colette, Bessie Smith, Marlene Dietrich, Anaïs Nin, Susan Sontag, David Bowie, Jean-Michel Basquiat and Madonna. This book is not a comprehensive account of their lives, but rather a look at how attitudes to bisexuality shaped their relationships, and how these icons challenged and championed new ideas about sexuality and gender in society in their lifetimes. I have found in these figures many parallels with my own love life on my journey in search of that elusive perfect partner. And so this book is a hybrid: a blend of memoir and biography, from my first love affair with a woman to my experience of a threesome, an exploration of my own struggles with identity, androgyny and creativity.

1

Oscar Wilde

Oscar Wilde lounges languidly on the corner of Adelaide Street. I passed by him for many years, seeing him without seeing him, as I hurried from Charing Cross station into St Martin's Lane, until one day I found myself eyeing the black marble block from which his head looms. Was he meant to be lying in a bath, I wondered? Or was it supposed to be a coffin, his head rising up ghostly? The sculpture, *A Conversation With Oscar Wilde*, designed by Maggi Hambling, was unveiled in 1998 and it provoked a mixed reaction. It captures Wilde as a social being – the nonchalant, witty dandy – for he seems to be in mid flow, epigrams dropping from his lips as his fingers curl around a cigarette; you can imagine a group of young male disciples forming a circle around him, listening in earnest awe. As I came to work on *Uneven*, I felt a little hurt when I saw how often people discarded their rubbish across him, haunted by my research into his final years when his surname was replaced by the prison designation C.3-3 and he was locked away in his cell in Reading Gaol, the light frail, his genius decaying with his health.

But this sculpture captures Wilde on top form. His face is clean-shaven and his locks are long, rendered in stiff black curves. This was unusual in the Victorian era, when beards were in fashion. You can find pictures of Victorian gentlemen with beards so ebullient they look like small animals. As someone who has sometimes suffered from beard envy, I admired them. Penises I did not covet, but beards were an object of lust: they could be pleasurably tugged when you were thinking deeply, gave age and profundity to a face, layered wisdom onto a chin. Being kissed by a man with a beard was also enjoyable; the sensation of prickle and tingle, the aftermath of a stubble rash, graffiti on my skin. Victorian facial hair reflected an age which celebrated the patriarch, the man as head of home; women, meanwhile, forced themselves into corsets that damaged their health or wore bell-hoop skirts that made it so hard to sit comfortably in a train carriage that travel became undesirable. Oscar Wilde boldly defied the fashion of his day. Picture him in 1882, stepping off the SS *Arizona*, arriving in America to give a lecture tour about the arts, already famous for being famous. He is greeted by flashing bulbs and questions from the press. His outfits include silk breeches and a bottle-green coat trimmed with otter fur, fashion like a blast of fresh air that guaranteed him column inches. This was Wilde as a flamboyant dandy, practising kaloprosopia – the act of living your life as a work of art. He was just twenty-seven years old.

A friend warned me that if I wrote about Oscar Wilde's bisexuality I would offend people. That I would corrupt his status as a gay icon. But Wilde's own grandson, Merlin Holland, has publicly declared that as a gay icon, Wilde is 'flawed', asserting that Wilde married for love, not as a smokescreen, and that his sexuality is complex: 'If it was a black-and-white story of Oscar just being homosexual from the year one and concealing it and finally coming to terms with it, it would make a much less interesting story.' In fact, the negation of his bisexuality is frequently tied into historic prejudice against bisexuals. Take these words from Eve Kosofsky Sedgwick, queer theorist, in 1991, for example: 'I'm not sure that because there are people who identify as bisexual there is a bisexual identity . . .' The interviewer goes on to summarize that, 'In questioning whether bisexuality is a potent identity, Sedgwick points to historical figures the gay and lesbian community claims as lesbian and gay (Cole Porter, Eleanor Roosevelt, Virginia Woolf, Walt Whitman, Oscar Wilde)—who would actually be classified as bisexual', to which Sedgwick concludes: 'the gay and lesbian movement isn't interested in drawing that line.' To acknowledge that Wilde was bisexual does not mean that his gay inclinations are halved or half-hearted, or that his tragedy is diluted. It does not diminish the cruelty of Victorian society in condemning him to spend two years in a dark, freezing cell picking oakum apart, his health corroded, his mind suffering a slow shattering, his genius going to waste simply because he did not conform to their narrow idea of what sexuality should be.

Oscar Wilde was in court in 1895 for one of the first 'celebrity' trials in the country. It began with a libel case, after his lover's father left him a facetious card with the scrawled accusation that he was posing as a 'somdomite' [sic]; and evolved into Wilde's own prosecution for 'gross indecency'. The sudden shift in his fortunes accentuate the shock, the vertigo of his sharp fall: like a Shakespearean hero, Wilde suffered a tragic loss of potential. His life was cut short just when he was soaring the highest, with two plays, *The Importance of Being Earnest* and *An Ideal Husband*, the talk of the West End. In his twenties he'd been a poor poet penning derivative verse; now he was ripening into a superb playwright. We know there might have been dozens more plays that we will never see; we are haunted by ghost novels, might-have-beens, lost witticisms, glorious epigrams. The rich insights of *De Profundis*, the philosophical letter to Lord Alfred that he penned in Reading Gaol, might have been reached outside prison, with a maturity of vision and wisdom that comes with age, rather than being whipped into being through penal degradation. There is in the story of his downfall too that sense of Greek tragedy, of forces from within and without coalescing, forming a fatal concentrate that led to his toppling, his life smashed into pieces.

In the Victorian era, there was a collective social unease as to what sort of man a homosexual might be: the criminalization of homosexuality went hand in hand with attempts to classify it. When we picture Wilde now, we imagine him as a glorious dandy, and we tend to stereotype dandies as queer. But earlier in the nineteenth century, the dandy – that intellectual, sophisticated, detached aesthete, who wore beautiful, foppish clothes and strutted about twirling his cane – was associated more with asexuality. His love of exquisite tailoring reflected his vanity rather than his effeminacy. Wilde's trial helped to shape and define the persona of gay men, the influence of which lives on.

Because Oscar Wilde has come to represent the homosexual martyr, the gay Christ who was persecuted and crucified by ignorant masses, his sexuality has been simplified. In reality, it was complex and went through various shades and phases. In order to make the simplification hold, his marriage to the Irish writer Constance Lloyd, mother of his two sons, has sometimes been rewritten as a sham, a façade that concealed his true sexuality. But this does not fit well with Wilde's behaviour, for he was no great concealer and his masks frayed; he would often flaunt his sexuality publicly, testing the boundaries of Victorian acceptability. The journalist Neil McKenna claims that Wilde's marriage to Constance Lloyd was 'passionless', that it was based on 'emotional and sexual indifference'. This is wrong. It was a rich and fulfilling relationship for a time, and when attraction faded Wilde began to explore another dynamic in his sexuality. In his landmark biography of Wilde, Richard Ellmann tries to explain what forces 'turned' Wilde's 'reorientation' from heterosexual to homosexual, without considering a more obvious answer: he was bisexual.

Before his male lovers were female ones: women whom he loved, whom he was attracted to, made love to, wrote poems for, was a warm friend to, helped in their careers, cherished and cared for. As Lord Alfred Douglas – his lover and nemesis – observed, women loved Oscar. He felt this was because 'although he was expected to talk brilliantly, he really did a great deal of listening.'

*

Oscar was born in Dublin in 1854 to an illustrious family. His father, Sir William Wilde, was a leading Irish surgeon and eye specialist. An oculist to the Queen in Ireland, he was knighted in 1864. Oscar's mother, Jane Wilde, published nationalist poetry under the name Speranza, and made the flamboyant claim that she was a descendant of Dante. She organized regular salons at their home. And so Oscar, along with his two siblings, grew up in a household alive with creativity, buzzing with intellectual conversation and ideas.

After shining as a star pupil at Trinity College, Dublin, he won a place at Magdalen College, Oxford. It was there that Oscar, influenced by Walter Pater and his theory of aesthetics, began to indulge in kaloprosopia. Coined by the writer Joséphin Péladan in the late nineteenth century, the term originates from the Greek καλός (beautiful) and πρόσωπον (person): transforming your personality by living your life as a work of art. It is a term that feels applicable to life in the twenty-first century, as we filter our Instagram pictures and compress our concerns into tweets, conscious of that gap between projected persona and true self. However, kaloprosopia in the modern era is a quite different phenomenon to what it would have been during Oscar's time in the *fin de siècle*. Now that we are all on social media, the effect is diluted; it is hard to resist the impulse towards conformity. We are just as likely to adopt group personas as our own, creating bubbles and echo chambers, shaping our tweets to glean likes, mimicking the language of our circle. In the nineteenth century, self-creation could also be an act of resistance. For dandies and *flâneurs* like Péladan and Baudelaire, it was a reaction to the growth of capitalism and mass commerce, people being herded into becoming consumers: kaloprosopia was a way of standing out.

The adoption of a mask might be both protective and illuminating, allowing someone a chance to flout convention and explore aspects of their character that would otherwise remain repressed.

At Oxford, Oscar embarked on the first of many reinventions. He wore his hair long, eschewed manly sports, exchanged his Irish accent for an English one, and became notorious for his wit; after decorating his room in the style of Aestheticism, he quipped, 'I find it harder and harder every day to live up to my blue china.' Oxford was also the place where Oscar had his first sexual experiences with a woman. He was discovered with a student, Fidelia, sitting on his lap; the girl's mother later caught them kissing in a hallway and she briskly told Oscar off: 'Oscar, the thing was neither right, nor manly, nor gentlemanlike in you.'

Julia Constance Fletcher was another of his early crushes. Born in America, she was only eighteen years old when she published her debut novel, *A Nile Novel*, under the pen name George Fleming. She was living in Venice when Oscar took a break from his studies to travel to Italy. When they met in Rome, there was an instant spark. In 1878 Oscar won the Newdigate Prize, which was given to Oxford students for best composition in English verse. His poem, 'Ravenna', was about a young man's journey to the Italian city. Oscar dedicated the poem to Julia. He declared that 'she writes as cleverly as she talks' and he was 'much attracted by her in every way'. His attraction to men was latent at this time; it does not seem to be something he was toying with or repressing. He wrote to his friend William Ward in 1876: 'Last night I strolled into the theatre about ten o'clock and to my surprise saw Todd and young Ward the quire boy in a private box together . . . Myself I believe Todd is extremely moral and only mentally spoons the boy, but I think he is foolish to go about with one, if he is bringing this boy about with him . . . He (Todd) looked awfully nervous and uncomfortable.' There is no jealousy here, no lust; he writes as though he is channelling Victorian unease and disapproval with sincerity.

The first woman he hoped to marry, he lost. Florence Balcombe grew up in Dublin and was renowned for her beauty. On meeting her, Oscar wrote to a friend enthusing, 'She is just seventeen with the most perfectly beautiful face I ever saw and not a sixpence of money.' Six months into their relationship, he gave her a beautiful gold cross with his name engraved on it. But distance came between them: she was in Ireland, he in Oxford, and Oscar had a rival – Bram Stoker, who later wrote *Dracula*. Whereas Oscar was still a student, Stoker was eleven years older than Florence, and it is likely that he was considered a more suitable match by her parents. They became engaged in 1878 and Oscar heard the bad news indirectly. Anguished, Oscar asked Florence to return the cross he had given her, declaring he would carry it at all times in memory of 'two sweet years – the sweetest of all the years of my youth'. Neil McKenna states that Oscar's courtship of Florence was a smokescreen, for Oscar was involved with Frank Miles during this time. But I am unconvinced. Most biographers – such as Richard Ellmann – believe that Oscar's first love affair with a man came later: with Robert Ross in 1886, a few years after he was married.

Frequently in 1879, Oscar could be found walking down Piccadilly holding a white amaryllis as a gift for Lillie Langtry. It was a theatrical gesture: he was simultaneously courting the actress and cultivating his own stardom. Following Oxford, Oscar had moved to London and shared a flat with his friend, Frank Miles. He was keen to mix with the great and the beautiful – indeed, he and Frank held afternoon 'tea and beauty' parties in their cramped apartment. It was at one of these parties that Oscar met Lillie. When she entered society, artists clamoured to paint her; her golden-haired beauty was preserved in portrait by Millais, Burne-Jones and Whistler and later in life, as her fame as an actress swelled across the Atlantic, a town in Texas was named after her by a community of cowboys. 'I would rather have discovered Mrs Langtry than have discovered America,' Oscar declared. For Oscar her exquisite looks were 'a form of genius' – 'Pure Greek' was her face, 'Greek, because the lines which compose it are so definite and so strong', and 'Greek, because its essence and its quality, as is the quality of music and of architecture, is that of beauty based on absolutely mathematical laws'. The author Eleanor Fitzsimons has pointed out that 'it is often assumed that Oscar used the adjective "Greek" to refer to male beauty or homosexual love', when in fact he used it for both sexes. He vowed to pen sonnets to Lillie until she turned ninety years old. She inspired the poem 'To L.L.', which describes a passionate encounter on a bench –

> *And your eyes, they were green and grey*
> *Like an April day,*
> *But lit into amethyst*
> *When I stooped and kissed*

Sadly, Oscar's passion for her was unrequited and she ran from the bench. Though Lillie valued him as a dear friend, she did not find Oscar attractive.

Oscar married Constance Lloyd a year before the Criminal Amendment Act of 1885 was passed and homosexuality crim-inalized in the UK. It is hard, therefore, to argue that Oscar felt forced to marry to conceal his gay leanings. His main motivations, it seems, were love and money. Oscar, with his penchant for a lavish existence, spent his life struggling with debts and straining to earn as much as he spent. His mother, too, encouraged him to consider marriage with a dowry in mind, writing to him when he was on tour in America that 'you must bring home the American bride'. Jane Wilde was struggling financially after the death of her husband; Oscar often sent her money.

Constance Lloyd was twenty-three years old when Oscar met her; he was twenty-six. She was beautiful and shy, intelligent and strong-minded. She was well educated, could speak French, read

Dante in the Italian, and was gifted in the arts, from painting to playing the piano. Born into a wealthy Irish middle-class family in Dublin, she lost her father when she was sixteen years old and suffered a troubled relationship with her mother, Ada, who inflicted physical and emotional abuse on her.

When Oscar and Constance first met during the summer of 1881 at a tea party in Devonshire Terrace, there was an immediate frisson between them. Oscar began to court her; Constance was thrilled. But their courtship was interrupted by Oscar's lecture tour of America, which began in January 1882. Originally Oscar planned to tour for three months, but it was such a success that he was abroad for a year.

*

Oscar's tour made him a celebrity in the US, albeit a controversial one. He broke gender codes and ruffled feathers when he advised an audience to be freed from the restrictive clothing that defined their genders. His unconventional appearance – from his long, flowing locks to his flamboyant dress – was endlessly commented on and analysed. Oscar was sometimes seen as 'effeminate', sometimes androgynous, as bisexuals can be labelled today, floating in that liminal, Tiresian realm. The *Lowell Daily Courier* reported that 'manhood is absent from his composition. He is neither a man nor a woman. He is between the two.' Thomas Wentworth Higginson, a prominent American thinker – who, unsurprisingly, sported an extremely bushy Victorian beard – crossly declared that Oscar's writing was 'Unmanly'.

At the age of twenty-two, a relationship with a man resulted in a crisis within me that mirrored this description of Wilde; for me, however, feeling 'unwomanly' came with a sense of shame.

People said we were a lovely couple, Henry and I. We'd been dating a few months. I remember the moment our relationship shattered. It all changed in the space of one phone call. Henry was overseas and I had emailed him a draft of my work in progress. He said, 'I've been reading your book . . .'

'Yes?' A nervous twist in my gut. A familiar feeling: I was at that time sending the book out to publishers and agents, who responded with polite fuck-offs on cream headed paper.

'My worry is – what are people going to *think*?'

Think? My novel-in-progress was outrageous and provocative, I knew, though I hadn't stopped to worry too much about that; I had worked hard to protect it from the weather of public opinion, and I'd allowed it to grow in its own warped way.

It was all there in the tone of his voice: the dismay, disgust, the disappointment. In retaliation, I put down the phone, like a V-sign at him, though it was more a symptom of my inarticulateness, highly pronounced at this time. I was an introvert; words poured from my pen but piled up in my throat and turned to papier mâché when I tried to express them in speech. I felt sick with churning betrayal. He had spoken as though my book merely represented a wrong turning I'd taken, a bad habit I'd picked up, a hobby I might drop. What the book represented, in its darkness and filth and madness and black humour, didn't fit with the version of Sam that he wanted.

Yet I could understand why he was confused. People often complained about the gap between my persona and my inner self, told me I was not as I seemed. My hair was long and I looked girlish. One man told me I looked as though I'd make a good children's author, as though art was dictated by hair length and smile. I feared that in some way I had fooled Henry, cheated him, with an exterior that was a lie, but the deceit had not been purposeful. I felt frustration boil through me, hot against my skin, as though I willed a Hulk-like transmogrification, to find colours and hairs splitting through which would turn me into some bestial creature of wild locks and warped features that I could show to people as my writing self.

As a child, I believed I would grow up to be a writer and that I would get married to a man. It had never occurred to me that there might be a friction between these two wishes. As a teenager, I had discovered the merit of having a room of one's own as I sat in my little box-room bedroom, scribbling away in the evenings after my homework was done. Attending a girls' high school meant that love and work were two separate dimensions; romance was for weekends, and study was for the weekdays. I had yet to discover the world, yet to read about Colette, whose novels were published under her husband's name; or Anaïs Nin, who was chided by her analyst for trying to surpass men in her work and for the strong 'masculine' element in her writing; or Daphne du Maurier, who wished she had been born a boy and saw her personality as one of two halves: the loving wife and mother that she showed to the world and her inner, hidden world of writing, which was fuelled by a 'male energy'.

Henry's words lingered, spread a slow poison through me.

That friction, between what society tells you you ought to be, and how you feel inside, is a story that repeats ad infinitum, of course. The concept of womanhood is reinvented with every decade, though; like tired Hollywood remakes, the same clichés and tropes are rehashed. In the late 1990s, *Bridget Jones's Diary* was a defining text for many young women. It was a huge hit, its influence lasting over a decade, spawning a thousand imitations that also served to reinforce the cultural mood of what it was to be a woman. Bridget worried about her weight. She counted her calories. She got pissed. She had a tumultuous love life. Bastards treated her badly. She had a gay best friend, Tom, who possessed a witty, rather Wildean flamboyance. She made silly mistakes at work. But that was okay, because Bridget was ditzy but loveable. In one newspaper article I read, Helen Fielding's creation had been so evocative that the columnist had witnessed women arguing drunkenly at parties: 'I'm Bridget' – 'No, I'm Bridget!'

As someone who had grown up being far too influenced by books, devouring them as bibles and handbooks for living, I felt lost in the gap between my life and mainstream art. Earlier in my childhood, there had been identification: I had grown up with two brothers, in a household of men, and found inspiration in Enid Blyton's Famous Five books. The gang of children includes two girls, two boys. Whereas Anne is patronized by her brothers and told to stay behind when danger lurks, Georgina rebels and declares that she wants to be a boy. She insists on being called George, a refrain which I took up for a while in real life (my family took no notice). Had I read de Beauvoir, Germaine Greer and bell hooks instead of *Bridget Jones*, I might have found illumination rather than alienation, but I had developed an inverse snobbery in reaction to my Oxford degree. I was tired of the classics and theory. I wanted to read about the here and now, about characters my age, who might give me insights as to who I might become, how I might grow in life. And so I devoured chick lit, as it was disdainfully called, and *Men Are from Mars, Women Are from Venus*, and magazines such as *Heat* and *Now*, which asserted that achieving happiness as a woman was all about dieting and dating and included pictures of shamed celebrities like Britney and Jordan tripping up or smudging their lipstick or showing an inch of fat flesh, any flaws highlighted by a savage red circle around some part of a woman's anatomy. It seemed to me that men got to live their lives without commentary, whereas for women, every action had a condemnatory footnote. As for Girl Power, it passed me by, though it always seemed to me more like a brand than an ethos, a slogan used to sell products by girl bands, feminism appropriated by the market.

Henry came back to the UK a few weeks after our phone call. I kept hurrying from my house to my local station, waiting for him to step off the train – but each time the crowd dispersed it left a lonely platform. He had been waiting for me at the airport, while I had thought he was coming straight to mine. On meeting, we embraced happily, but within hours we were disintegrating. I had no desire to make love to him, for my heart felt as though it had been slashed and drained of feeling. I knew that we were over, that we had been since that phone call, and instead of being thoughtful and truthful, I opted for 'show, don't tell', letting the relationship slide, an unintentional cruelty. Guilt and doubt also prevented me from definitively breaking it off. Wasn't Henry just the sort of tall, dark, handsome, lovely, clever guy that the heroines of contemporary novels raved about and went to agonizing lengths to find? Wasn't he really a Mr Darcy, whom I was throwing away instead of trying to cajole into a ring and a commitment?

Now I decided that if I was going to be in love, it would be with my books, my pens, my notebooks, my hours spent in cafés writing, and that was enough.

But it didn't last.

I craved more: some sort of intimacy, in a shape or form I couldn't quite define or name. I had a sense that I wasn't going to fit into conventional society, not realizing that the perfect marriage with 2.4 children was the illusion of adverts and that behind all relationships are cracks and secrets and idiosyncrasies. The overriding cultural narrative was that a woman must want a man, not lightly, not loosely, not casually, but in a determined pin-him-down manner, for the fairy-tale conclusion at the end of all these romances – let's not forget that *Bridget Jones* was a kind of updated *Pride and Prejudice* – was marriage. It did not appeal to me. Nor did dieting. I had never suffered from PMT. I did not want babies. I hated to be seen as ditzy, though that epithet was often applied to me.

And therefore, I feared, I was not a proper woman, but an impostor suffering a hermaphroditism of the soul, a male psyche lurking in a female body. For me, the heterosexuality I had grown up with encouraged contrast, reinforced clichés. I knew that I felt freer away from Henry because in his presence I had to be defined against his gender, I was pulled into a role of difference; single, I could be more well rounded, fully expressed.

*

On his 1882 US lecture tour, women attended Oscar's lectures in droves. The police were called to hold back throngs of adoring female fans. Oscar wrote that American women were 'pretty whirlwinds in petticoats' whom 'one gets to love'. Developing a reputation as a womanizer, Oscar ran with it; he spent a night with a female prostitute, Marie Aguétant, at Eden Palace, a music hall, though it was hardly a night of bliss; later he would reflect that sleeping with a female prostitute felt like 'chewing cold mutton'.

Oscar returned to England a celebrity. On meeting Constance again in May 1883, their courtship deepened and love blossomed. As opposites, they complemented each other: Oscar, with his grandiose ego, sharp wit and flamboyance, was frequently surrounded by fans who mimicked his dress and witticisms, nicknamed his 'disciples', whereas Constance was shy and known to be quiet in company, even sullen. He proposed to her with a ring he had designed: a heart of diamonds enclosing two pearls, 'surmounted with another bow of diamonds'. Constance declared that she was 'insanely happy'. Her mother, Ada, saw that they were a good match, writing to Lady Wilde that 'both are . . . charming, gifted and what is to my mind even more essential to the beginning of married life, immensely attracted to each other.'

During their six-month engagement, they exchanged numerous telegrams and letters. 'We are of course desperately in love,' Oscar wrote to his friend Thomas Waldo Story. 'We telegraph each other twice a day, and the telegraph clerks have become quite romantic in consequence.' He confided in Lillie that 'it is horrid being so much away from her'. Oscar bought Constance a pet marmoset to keep her company, which they named Jimmy. Robert Sherard, a close friend of Oscar's, reported that 'he was very much in love and joyous' at this time.

On 29 May 1884, they were married. It was a small wedding at St James's Church in Paddington, and a large crowd of Oscar fans gathered to watch them from the street outside. There is something poignant in these lines from the *Lady's Pictorial* that described them walking down the aisle – 'the bridegroom happy and exultant; the bride with a tender flush on her face, and a happy hopeful light in her soft brown eyes' – which, though sentimentalized for their readership, do appear to capture the innocent joy and love they shared, oblivious of the dark days to come. Oscar's close friend, Ada Leverson, observed that: 'He was quite madly in love, and showed himself an unusually devoted husband.' When they honeymooned in Paris, Oscar was prone to the extravagance which fireworked when he was in love; the moment he left Constance in the hotel room to see his Parisian friends, he would send back bouquets of flowers and return laden with presents for her. Their hotel room was full of 'flowers, youth and laughter', Robert Sherard observed. He was less delighted when Oscar tried to exuberantly divulge all the glorious details of his newfound sex life with his wife. Their relationship was rich in both love and passion, and when they returned home and Oscar returned to lecturing, being away from Constance filled him with a yearning that was both physical and emotional: 'I feel your fingers in my hair, and your cheek brushing mine . . . The air is full of the music of your voice, my soul and body seem no longer mine, but mingled in some exquisite ecstasy with yours. I feel incomplete without you.'

Their first son, Cyril, was born in 1885 and Oscar was a delighted father. He wrote to the actor Norman Forbes-Robertson that his son was 'wonderful' and enthused about the joys of matrimony, encouraging him to marry '*at once!*'

That his marriage turned sour is too often held up as proof that Oscar was really gay, using marriage as a respectable mask so that he might carry on with men behind it. But many marriages fail, often for complex and numerous reasons, and Oscar's was no different. Whilst Oscar's attraction to his wife did fade, this is also nothing particularly new or shocking. Franny Moyle argues that they married (as many Victorians did) without knowing each other well; marriage, the process of discovering each other, brought both intimacy and disillusionment. It is a mistake to assume that Oscar's marriage was a sham and that the second act of his sexuality defines him absolutely, so that his past is rewritten to fit this narrative.

For bisexuals like Oscar Wilde, Anaïs Nin and others, you can trace that moment where awakening begins: you have followed society's relationship conventions, married, settled down, but the result is stagnancy, giving rise to restlessness rather than peace. The pattern of Oscar's sexual shift is not dissimilar to bisexuals today. Lesbians and gays often discover their sexual orientation at a much earlier age, usually in their teenage years. I have met numerous bisexuals who have discovered their sexuality in their twenties because society steers them towards the heteronormative at first and they then find new dimensions to their sexuality.

Following Henry, I found myself floundering, sensing that a conventional romance was not going to suit me, but uncertain as to what shape my love life should take. My next liaison was reactive: an affair with a TV presenter, thirty years my senior. I decided that being a mistress was a more empowered position than a wife. It also meant that romance now belonged to a nice neat compartment that did not overlap with my writing. It was easy to make my lover happy. Our routine was simple: an Italian meal, followed by a hotel room, and post-coital confidences, once a month; and a daily exchange of emails in a secret Hotmail account. He looked at me with affectionate pride when I told him that I'd got a literary agent, for he had no motive to curtail my writing or feel he was in competition with it. However, one day when I was apart from him, I broke off from my writing, looking up sharply when I heard a random child crying outside in the street. I thought unhappily of his family. He had told me that his wife hated him, that when they rowed she beat him, and as a man he could not fight back and felt helpless. I wondered if that was true or his guilt creating a narrative.

On a trip to Brighton, I bought a book in Waterstones. The girl at the till had chestnut hair and an energy about her that felt provocative. She gave me a seductive smile as she peeled my receipt from the till and slipped it into the shiny bag. While watching the waves crash onto the bony pebbles: *I could go back – but what would I say? How do you seduce women? Do I have to be proactive?* At a café, listening but not listening to my friend as we sipped hot chocolate: *I could scribble my number on the receipt and pass it to her. But maybe that's just fucking insane!* On the train home: *if only I'd, if only, if only . . .* And then she was forgotten, one of many maybes that we all carry through life and that form a backdrop of wistfulness.

I had another Italian meal, another session with my older male lover. Something that had once been bright between us was becoming pastel. One afternoon, I found a magazine left strewn on a train, read a piece about a woman who had outraged her lesbian community by announcing that she had fallen for a man. She said she felt that while loving a man was a fiction, loving a woman was a form of poetry.

*

Oscar had been married to Constance for two years when she fell pregnant with their second child. His desire for her waned around the time of this pregnancy. He felt that her exquisite looks, one of the elements that had most attracted him to her, were lost. 'When I married, my wife was a beautiful girl,' Oscar confided in his friend Frank Harris, 'white and slim as a lily . . . In a year or so the flower-like grace had all vanished; she became heavy,

shapeless, deformed . . .' These words need to be taken with a pinch
of salt, for Harris's memoir may have contained exaggerations
and Oscar was also reminiscing when he was in exile, bitter and
saddened. However, Oscar also wrote to another young friend,
Harry Marillier, in 1885, that his marriage had devolved into 'a
curious mixture of ardour and indifference. I myself would sacrifice everything for a new experience, and I know there is no such
thing as a new experience at all.' Oscar was restless. When he and
Constance had been courting, obstacles – her family's doubts about
him, the debts he had to pay off first – had injected a frisson into
their courtship. Now these excitements had passed. Oscar had
won; they lived in a pleasant house on Tite Street in Chelsea, which
W. B. Yeats visited and found 'too perfect in its unity'. He reflected:
'I remember thinking that the perfect harmony of his life there,
with his beautiful wife and his two young children, suggested some
deliberate artistic composition.' Oscar was a loving father; he often
got down on his hands and knees to play with Vyvyan and Cyril
in the nursery, willing to indulge in games for hours, and, 'When
he grew tired of playing he would keep us quiet by telling us fairy
stories, or tales of adventures, of which he had a never-ending
supply', Vyvyan recollected. But going home to the same place
every night was very different from their whirlwind courtship,
where he wrote Constance romantic letters from various hotels on
a lecture tour. Now that he was married, his long locks cut in a
short, respectable style, his clothes more conventional, his star was
waning and he featured less in the press. The domestic had tamed
his life towards tedium.

Even in the midst of his blissful honeymoon, Oscar had been
stirred by temptation. He read *À Rebours* by Joris-Karl Huysmans,
a book that was later obliquely referred to in *The Picture of Dorian
Gray* as a book that Dorian is corrupted by, for it centres on a
wealthy, ailing aesthete who shuts himself away in a villa and pursues a path of decadent hedonism. The book's poison works slowly

on Dorian, as it did on Oscar. During that honeymoon, whilst Oscar was dining with high society and sending his wife flowers, a shadow side was also pulling him. Robert Sherard notes that he also 'enjoyed slumming visits' to the poorest parts of the city, which fascinated and repulsed him.

Because one aspect of Oscar's desire was forbidden, it cleaved his bisexuality into two distinct halves with opposing character-istics: one half respectable, one rebellious; 'one Apollonian, one Dionysian'. Oscar enjoyed love affairs with men in part because they were forbidden, a delicious rebellion against a society he loved and loathed. 'The danger was half the excitement,' he reflected later, in prison, 'I used to feel as a snake-charmer must feel when he lures the cobra to stir from the painted cloth . . . that holds it . . .' And so, male lovers became associated with decadence, marriage with duty, men with the underground, his wife with the acceptable surface.

Oscar's early affairs with men were discreet. His first male love was Robbie Ross, a handsome, articulate young man who went on to study at Cambridge, just seventeen years old when they first met. It was Robbie who seduced Oscar. He had grown up a fan of Oscar, imitating his shoulder-length hair and devouring his poetry. Robbie's mother, Eliza, arranged for him to stay with the Wilde family in 1886, as a paying guest, to gain a foothold in the capital. Robbie and Oscar's physical relationship – which did not last long – soon settled into a warm, platonic tenderness and a loyal friendship that would last a lifetime. Similarly, when Oscar fell for Lord Alfred Douglas, the man he would end up going to prison for, desire blazed early on, but 'Sodomy never took place.' Douglas later explained that 'I never liked this part of the busi-ness . . . After a time [Wilde] tumbled to the fact . . . and he very soon "cut it out" altogether.' As for Constance, the fact that sex waned between them was not necessarily due to a new, exclusive preference. Franny Moyle has pointed out that 'there may have been post-natal medical issues on Constance's side that were also a contributing factor.' Lord Alfred observed in 1892 that Oscar 'adored his wife' and was 'still on great terms of affection' with her. Over time, however, Constance began to feel neglected and lost as Oscar spent more and more time away from home, confiding in a friend that 'I cannot make out whether it is my fault or Wilde's that he is so cold to me and so nice to others.'

Wilde would not have labelled himself as 'bisexual'; the term is apt, but anachronistic. Prior to the late Victorian era, sex was a practice, not a sexual identity. The idea of a bisexual identity did not exist, and it would only develop decades on in the mid-nineteenth century, later than a homosexual one. Before the Victorian era, it was the act of sodomy – whether a man with a man, a man with a woman or a man with an animal – that was made illegal, under the reign of Henry VIII. The Buggery Act of 1533 put the death penalty in place for anyone who engaged in sodomy. The last two men who were hanged in England for gay sex were James Pratt and John Smith in 1835, pleading 'Not Guilty' and weeping before a hissing crowd as ropes were placed around their necks. The penalty was abolished in 1861, though was still punishable by imprisonment. Homosexuality came to be seen not as a sin but as a sickness. Sexuality was no longer the domain of the church, but came to fall within the medical establishment, who then set about classifying and constructing various sexual identities.

The first mention of the terms 'homosexuality' and 'bisexuality' – as a sexuality, rather than a reference to androgyny – occurred in 1869 when Károly Márie Kertbeny, a Hungarian journalist, wrote an open letter to the Prussian minister of justice asking for him to abolish criminal laws against 'unnatural acts'. In 1886, Richard Krafft-Ebing, a well-regarded psychiatrist who helped to establish sexology as a scientific discipline, published *Psychopathia Sexualis*, where he diagnosed homosexuality as a form of degeneracy. Homosexuality, then, was seen as a pathology. Victorian attitudes towards sex were complex and their reputation for prudishness has become a cliché, but they certainly adopted a surface puritanism towards sexuality. Like masturbation, which was also frowned on, homosexuality was a sickness which wasted vital seed.

Bisexuality, too, was classified as a pathology. Krafft-Ebing argued that the mental state of sex criminals should be taken into account when they were on trial; they should not be judged, but receive treatment rather than sentences. Krafft-Ebing called bisexuality *psychosexual hermaphroditism*. He framed bisexuality as the first of four stages of sexual 'inversion' – with homosexuality being the final stage. Bisexuality then, was a milder form of illness and it was not a fixed or static identity but one that had direction; other European sexologists of this era called it 'a light form or precursor of sexual inversion' or 'an incomplete inversion' or a 'periodic' or 'temporary pederasty'. Bisexuality was often seen as the starting point of sexual degeneration, although the Russian sexologist Benjamin Tarnowski compared bisexuality to alcoholism, with sudden bursts of indulgence: 'the patients satisfy their perverse impulse two or three times a year, no more often, and the rest of the time they have normal intercourse with women.'

As Freud would later assert, bisexuality was associated with immaturity, with adolescence. It was something you might indulge in, but would – hopefully – grow out of. In 1906, the Italian physician Cesare Lombroso noted that childhood was 'often accompanied by a temporary type of homosexuality . . . sometimes only a semi-sexuality, a kind of moral hermaphroditism which, according to [the moral philosopher] Marchesini, expresses itself in girls' boarding schools as platonic love and is truly warmhearted.' However, doctors did warn that this stage would need to be suppressed by 'careful education and willpower'. Growing beyond it was about learning to discriminate, for bisexuality showed a certain 'lack of differentiation', as though it was a state of indecision – a prejudice that still lingers to this day, over a hundred years later.

The question of whether or not bisexuality was caused by nature or nurture was up for debate; Marc-André Raffalovich, the French poet and writer on homosexuality, wondered: is it the result of 'circumstances . . . or congenital?'

The Victorians introduced the Offences Against the Person Act in 1861, which removed the death penalty for sodomy, but it did create a new punishment: of ten years to life penal servitude. Then, in 1885, the introduction of the Labouchere Amendment meant that men could now be prosecuted not just on the basis of anal sex, but kissing, cuddling, chatting each other up. The act was named after MP Henry Labouchere, after he added to the Criminal Law Amendment Act. The overall bill was a good one, for it aimed to protect teenage girls and raised the age of consent from thirteen to sixteen. Any boy over the age of thirteen who suffered an assault short of rape also had no legal protection in place, so Labouchere's addition was supposed to be progressive and protective. It was the vagueness of the wording in the act that was the problem: that tricksy phrase 'acts of gross indecency'. It meant that two men could be taken to court simply on the basis of a few love letters, with no witnesses needed; it is no wonder that it became known as the Blackmailer's Charter. *The Strange Case of Dr Jekyll and Mr Hyde* was published in January 1886, the same month that the Criminal Law Amendment Act came into effect – Robert Louis Stevenson captured the mood of a certain number of men when he said he had long been trying to write a story on the 'strong sense of man's double being which must at times come in upon and overwhelm the mind of every thinking creature'.

However, whilst the Victorians toughened their stance on homosexuality, a growing public hostility to 'sexual inversion' was accompanied by a collective curiosity: what were the characteristics of a man who loved men? How did he dress? How did he behave? What were the tell-tale signs? In the UK in 1870, two men, Ernest Boulton and Frederick William Park, were arrested for dressing as women, and a doctor was asked to examine them 'for physical "signs" of homosexuality' – but he admitted that he was not sure what he was looking for. As journalist Eric Berkowitz notes, 'it was an early effort' at defining what characteristics a gay man might have.

When Oscar fell for Robbie Ross, the year following the Labouchere Amendment, his sense of self fundamentally changed, as Richard Ellmann sums up: 'After 1886, he was able to think of himself as a criminal, moving guiltily among the innocent.' If he was discreet with Ross, however, then in his next affair he would take far greater risks.

It is often assumed that Lord Alfred Douglas inspired the character of Dorian in *The Picture of Dorian Gray*. Like Dorian, he was physically beautiful, golden-haired and blue-eyed, and looked younger than his years. However, it was a case of life imitating art; Wilde's character seemed to step forth from the pages. Lord Alfred adored *Dorian Gray*, reading it fourteen times, seduced by the novel in the same way that Dorian is seduced by *À Rebours*: 'It was the strangest book that he had ever read. It seemed to him that in exquisite raiment, and to the delicate sound of flutes, the sins of the world were passing in dumb show before him. Things that he had dimly dreamed of were suddenly made real to him. Things of which he had never dreamed were gradually revealed.' Like Oscar's creation, Lord Alfred was afraid of ageing. On his twenty-first birthday he shut himself in his bedroom, weeping at the thought of his future 'vanished youth'. His youthful looks and character – he had a tendency towards a charming sweetness alternating with tantrums and a short temper – were epitomized in his nickname, Bosie, which had been affectionately bestowed on him by his mother, from the Scottish *boysie* for 'boy'.

It is also frequently claimed that the character of Lord Henry Wotton in *Dorian Gray* – who is charming, witty, clever and possessed of 'wrong, fascinating, poisonous, delightful theories' – is based on Oscar. Quotes by Wotton that condemn marriage are often cited as though they must be Oscar's opinion and therefore reflect on his feelings for Constance. But Oscar himself declared that 'Basil Hallward is what I think I am: Lord Henry what the world thinks me: Dorian what I would like to be.' His verdict on Wotton's theories that disparage marriage was: 'I highly disapprove of them.' Basil is an altogether softer, kinder character in the book.

When Bosie first met Oscar, he wasn't initially attracted to him. He found him 'comic looking'. It was Oscar's melodious voice that wove its magic, his ability to transmute the ordinary things of life and invest them with 'strangeness and glamour'. Their love affair did not begin until the spring of 1892, when Bosie wrote to Oscar pleading for help. He was being blackmailed; a love letter to another man had fallen into the wrong hands. Moved by his predicament, Oscar came to the rescue with money and legal help, settling the matter. United by secrecy and danger, their infatuation began.

On trial, Oscar would be portrayed as the corruptor of Bosie. But early on in their relationship, it could be argued that it was the other way round. It was Lord Alfred, the more experienced of the two, who introduced Oscar to a sexual underground, gritty and thrilling, where they would rent young men for sex. It was Bosie who introduced him to Alfred Taylor, a gatekeeper to the world of male prostitution, who procured the men for them. Soon Oscar was a regular attendee of the all-male tea parties Taylor held in his Westminster flat. Oscar was discreet in the early days of his homosexual affairs, but over time he became bolder, more careless, more carefree. He was seen in public with Bosie; seen at the Empire Music Hall, the pair pressed close together, looking like lovers. Soon rumours spread about them.

It was a tempestuous love affair. Lord Alfred had a nasty temper and his mood could suddenly turn. Oscar, by contrast, was more tender and forgiving. On one occasion, Oscar lovingly nursed Bosie through a bout of flu. Bosie got better only for Oscar to fall ill. Instead of nursing him in return, Bosie stormed off, declaring he was bored. When they holidayed in Florence, staying with Bernard Berenson, Mary Costelloe (his mistress) thought that Bosie was a bad influence, turning Oscar into a 'loathsome beast'. As is often the case with love triangles, Oscar zigzagged back and forth between lover and wife, favouring one, then the other. Marriage might be dull at times, but it could also be a refuge and a relief. In 1893, tired of Bosie's behaviour, he wrote to Lady Queensberry, advising her to send her son abroad on holiday, and turned back to Constance, playing the loving husband and father again, enjoying domesticity.

Robbie Ross had grown up without a father and Bosie had a terrible relationship with his father: Oscar was a paternal figure to them both. Oscar, in turn, declared, 'I am a lover of youth . . . I like to study the young in everything. There is something fascinating in youthfulness.' Oscar never referred to his love affairs as homosexual, a term rarely used then; nor did he use 'inversion', for the Victorians saw same-sex love affairs as a symptom of a female soul being born in a male body, or vice versa. Instead, he favoured 'Uranian', a term coined by Karl Heinrich Ulrichs in the 1860s, derived from a dialogue on Eros in Plato's *Symposium*. Having studied Classics at Oxford, Oscar saw his sexuality in a very specific tradition: pederasty, a practice dating back to Ancient Greece and Rome where an older man would play sexual guide and intellectual mentor to a younger boy. Socrates argued the case for same-sex love as a source of vital creative inspiration: you could marry an attractive wife and birth beautiful children, but to produce a rarefied work of art, then an exquisite young male lover should be your muse. Certainly, Oscar's love affairs with men gave spark to his genius. His early marital years produced little great work, aside from his fairy tales; subsequently, he enjoyed a tremendous artistic flourishing, from essays such as *The Decay of Lying* to his later plays: *Lady Windermere's Fan, A Woman of No Importance, An Ideal Husband* and *The Importance of Being Earnest*.

Bisexuality was not an identity in Greek or Roman times, nor a choice outside a hetero norm; it was an everyday, integrated strand of life, albeit one still controlled by customs and culture. In Greece, for example, the pederastic tradition played a key part in the growth of a young male from boyhood to adulthood. An older male figure would play tutor and lover to him before he was married and adopted a heterosexual lifestyle. In Crete, it was acceptable for an older male teacher to kidnap a boy, take him into the countryside, give him military training and life wisdom and make love to him. In Rome, meanwhile, things were a little different. Male/male sex was accepted, but it didn't play a part in adolescent education. What was important was whether the man making love was receiving or giving. A young Roman man, brought up to dominate the world and expand the Empire, had to be active, not passive. To lose your virginity through a sexually passive role was 'a crime for the free-born', wrote Seneca. Indeed, the Latin term *muliebria patitur* – to be penetrated – translates as 'to have a woman's experience'. Passive sex was for slaves and prostitutes, not men of power and status. Interestingly, this preoccupation lingered into the Victorian era; as gossip about Bosie and Oscar spread, an entry in the Goncourt diaries noted that everyone was speculating as to whether Oscar was *'passif'* or *'actif'*, feeling that it must be *passif*, whereby a man encounters 'pleasure that he does not enjoy with a woman'.

The bisexual way of life faded when Roman society shifted from paganism to Christianity, favouring heterosexuality and deeming homosexuality a crime. Again, the backlash is laced with misogyny, motivated by the primitive ideal that men should be men, active and aggressive, and any trace of effeminacy is a sin. In the late Roman Empire, Constantine's sons, Constans and Constantinus II, ordered a decree attacking those who indulged in sex 'when a man couples as though he were a woman'. In 533 came an explicit law against homosexuality, decreed by the Emperor Justinian, who tortured and killed gay members of the clergy and blamed male sexual acts as a cause of famine, earthquakes and plagues in Constantinople.

Centuries later, British colonialism, twinned with Christianity, found the British exporting their homophobia across the globe, destroying cultures in Africa and Asia that were relaxed about gender identity and sexual orientation. Bugunda (now Uganda) was ruled by an openly gay monarch, King Mwanga II; now, thanks to the long-term influence of colonialism, homosexuality is criminalized in Uganda. In India, the British historian Thomas Babington Macaulay drew up the Indian Penal Code of 1862, including section 377, which was based on the Buggery Act, forbidding anal sex, and was used as a basis for criminal law in many other territories controlled by the British; India would not repeal this act until 2018.

*

It was Lord Alfred's father, the Marquess of Queensberry, who seduced Oscar into his downfall. Queensberry was a pernicious character, prone to fits of bad temper, and when he heard the rumours about Oscar and his son, he became inflamed. Bosie, who had a poor relationship with his father, delighted in provoking him. Oscar was caught in the rising tensions between them; their quarrel was not just about homosexuality; rather, homosexuality became the means through which a son taunted his father and a father tried to savagely bully and rein in his son.

As Queensberry upped his campaign of intimidation against his son and Oscar, he turned up at Oscar's house one day with a friend. In the heated argument that followed, Queensberry declared that Constance was going to divorce him for sodomy. Oscar retorted sharply, 'I'm not a sodomite.' Queensberry came back with, 'You pose as one though.'

Oscar's mask as a happy family man was slipping. Gradually, his reputation as a man with a penchant for the same sex was gaining ground. Oscar and Bosie were satirized in a cartoon strip called *The Decadent Guys* in *Punch*. *The Importance of Being Earnest* was a huge success, but on the first night Oscar had to call the police to prevent Queensberry wrecking the performance with a rotting vegetable bouquet which he planned to throw on stage. On the one hand, his literary success was finally catching up with his celebrity; his fame was soaring with authenticity rather than notoriety; on the other, shadows and threats were becoming more insidious. 'Since Oscar wrote *Dorian Gray* no one will speak to us,' Constance claimed, an exaggeration but one which captured the mood surrounding them. At a performance of *John-o-Dreams* at the Haymarket theatre, Oscar found himself snubbed by various audience members.

And so Queensberry laid a trap for Oscar. On 18 February 1895, he left a card for Oscar at the Albermarle Club on which he had scrawled: *For Oscar Wilde, posing somdomite*. The spelling mistake may have been deliberate, as well as the use of ambiguous language, which would make it easier to win a case if Oscar sued. Nevertheless, it was also about personas and the Victorian need for masks of heterosexual respectability. To simply *look* like a sodomite, in a society that had rigid ideas about gender, was bad enough; Queensberry's words echo the accusations levelled at Oscar during his American tour, where Thomas Wentworth Higginson saw him as 'Unmanly', only now they took on a more serious tone.

In the UK, homosexuals were increasingly seen as predators: devils who preyed on young innocents. That was perhaps best illustrated by the Cleveland Street Scandal of 1889. The story began with a boy called Charles Swinscow, who was caught by a policeman with eighteen shillings in his pocket – twice his usual weekly wage as a telegraph boy at the General Post Office. It emerged that many of the boys working there were also moonlighting as rent boys at Cleveland Street, a brothel frequented by a number of wealthy, powerful and aristocratic men. A scandal erupted, filling the tabloids week after week. Among the men said to patronize the brothel were Lord Somerset and the Earl of Euston. Lord Somerset fled to France, whilst the Earl successfully sued a reporter at the *North London Press*. The public disgust was not directed at the boys, who were seen as innocents; they weren't prosecuted, though some lost their jobs. Instead, the ire was aimed at the older men who procured them. A year later, when Oscar published *The Picture of Dorian Gray*, a book ripe in homoerotic undercurrents, it was slated in the *Scots Observer* as a story which 'would be of interest mainly to "outlawed noblemen and perverted telegraph boys"' – a jibe that referenced Cleveland Street.

And so we can see why Oscar responded as he did when Queensberry's calling card appeared at his club. Queensberry was playing a nasty, calculated game, laying bets on whether he could provoke Oscar into suing, and the card must have exemplified what Oscar saw as a gathering threat to his anxious self. His friends advised him against it, but Bosie cheered him on: Oscar decided to settle the matter in court.

Picture Wilde on 3 April 1895: arriving at the Old Bailey in a stylish overcoat trimmed with velvet and a white flower in his buttonhole, stepping down from his brougham carriage. His friends have seen the danger of his situation, advised him not to prosecute. But Wilde is overconfident. It is in part a matter of class; he doesn't believe that reports by lower- class men will be taken seriously. On the stand, he performs with flair and wit. He lies about his age, claims he is thirty-nine (he is forty). Sir Edward Clarke, his barrister, reads out a letter from Wilde written to Bosie and elegantly argues that Wilde is a poet, and the sentiments therein are 'the expression of poetic feeling'. Wilde defends his writing when the prosecutor reads aloud from the introduction to *Dorian Gray*: 'There is no such thing as an immoral book. Books are well written or badly written.'

It is on the second day that reality punches him. Presents are produced – fine clothing, silver-mounted walking sticks – which Wilde gave to his young companions. He slips when asked if he ever kissed a boy called Walter Grainger; tripping up on his own wit, Wilde retorts flippantly, 'Oh dear no! He was a peculiarly plain boy.' The libel case is withdrawn. But it is too late: Queensberry's solicitor has pulled the snare, forwarded copies of statements from young men to the Director of Public Prosecutions. Now Wilde is the one under arrest, for twenty-five counts of 'gross indecency' and 'conspiracy to commit gross indecency'. The prosecution paints a portrait of him that epitomizes all the caricature qualities of the homosexual villain of the time, making Wilde fit the stereotype. His novel, *Dorian Gray*, is held up as a corrupting, 'sodomitical' book; meanwhile Lord Alfred is portrayed as the young innocent who ended up writing dodgy poetry, 'turned under the domination of Oscar Wilde' to 'the frightful subject of the passion of man for man'. Wilde is the dark corruptor ruining London's golden youth.

He becomes quieter, more furtive, more thoughtful, as the trial closes in on him. He makes a speech that we remember now for its beauty and its dignity:

The 'love that dare not speak its name' in this century is such a great affection of an elder for a younger man as there was between David and Jonathan, such as Plato made the very basis of his philosophy, and such as you find in the sonnets of Michelangelo and Shakespeare. It is that deep spiritual affection that is as pure as it is perfect. It dictates and pervades great works of art, like those of Shakespeare and Michelangelo, and those two letters of mine, such as they are. It is in this century misunderstood, so much misunderstood that it may be described as 'the love that dare not speak its name', and on account of it I am placed where I am now. It is beautiful, it is fine, it is the noblest form of affection. There is nothing unnatural about it.

He could have escaped prison. He could have fled. The magistrate, Sir John Bridge, issued a warrant for Wilde's arrest, but delayed signing it until the last boat to Dover had sailed that day, to give Wilde time to flee. John Betjeman's poem 'The Arrest of Oscar Wilde at the Cadogan Hotel' captures that moment:

> *Is this the end or beginning?*
> *How can I understand?*

'I decided that it was nobler and more beautiful to stay,' he reflected, 'I did not want to be called a coward or a deserter . . .' He did not want to adopt a false identity. His name, enamelled with fame, was precious to him; he was still naive, perhaps, as to how much it had been scratched and sullied; the idea of losing his aura of notoriety was anathema. He was too shielded by a charmed life to be aware of the harsh realities of prison. His letters to Bosie just before he entered jail were full of elation and wild declarations of love; not long after, in his cell, he would be writing with sobriety and bitterness that he wanted all his love letters destroyed. Wilde did not fully realize what he was about to face.

A process of depersonalization, as he entered prison: his clothes stripped from him, and replaced with the standard uniform with arrows on it. He became 'merely the figure and letter of a little cell in a long gallery, one of a thousand lifeless numbers, as of a thousand lifeless lives'. A machine line of misery, men forced onto a treadmill, pacing and pacing like rats on a wheel, six hours a day. His house ransacked due to the debts he owed; precious papers going missing, beautiful signed editions, his sons wondering where their toys were, not realizing they had been sold; the name Oscar Wilde being erased from the playbills outside theatres. He was moved from the treadmill to picking oakum, from Pentonville to Wandsworth, unravelling the twine of old rope in his cell until his fingers bled. His bed a plank to lie on each night, his sleep ruined. His latrine a metal bucket. When he developed diarrhoea the putrid smell of his illness fogged his cell. His mental health became a scream, he lost weight. He developed an ear infection, wrote a letter to the governor pleading that he was terrified of losing his hearing, his eyesight too, due to the poor light in his cold, dark cell. He had resolved to commit suicide when he entered but now he found himself flailing in a kind of purgatory: 'I have the horror of death with the still greater horror of living.' The present was a nightmare, the future hopeless: 'on the day of my release I shall merely be passing from one prison into another'. But he hoped to see his children; Constance visited him in person to disclose the tragic news that his mother – who had not been able to visit him – had passed away.

*

Following Wilde's trial, 600 men, fearing they might suffer similar prosecutions, fled across the Channel. Numerous men in Wilde's life were also forced to run: Lord Alfred went abroad, as did Wilde's former lover and dear friend, Robbie Ross. Ross, mentioned in various newspapers in connection with the trial, found friends spurning him and his membership of various London clubs revoked. He had been hesitant about deserting Wilde, but his mother offered to contribute to Wilde's legal fees if he fled. He did return to the UK intermittently; when Wilde was dragged out of jail and into the bankruptcy court in September 1895, surrounded by jeering crowds, where he 'cried a good deal', Ross waited for hours for him to come out so he could tip his hat at him. It's one of those small but huge gestures that is immensely moving. For Wilde, 'men have gone to heaven for smaller things than that'.

Wilde was released from prison in 1897. He left the UK to go into exile, catching the ferry to Dieppe, where he lived under the name Sebastian Melmoth (chosen after St Sebastian, icon of homoerotic desire). His final years tend to be portrayed as tragic and melancholy, Wilde as a broken man. But, as Nicholas Frankel argues, he was euphoric to be free, writing that he was 'dazed by the wonder of the wonderful world. I feel as if I had been raised from the dead.' There is an echo of *De Profundis* in that playful last line, the secular 'gospel' that Wilde penned in prison: Wilde has been crucified but he has risen again. He had a choice to repent, to redeem himself, to compromise and obey the society that had condemned him by living a meek existence as a 'literary bachelor'. Instead, to the horror of his friends and family, he returned to Lord Alfred Douglas. It was a brave decision: 'I must remake my maimed life on my own lines.' Living in Naples together, they were loving, happy, inspired, even if they were ostracized; in Capri, they were booted out of a hotel when English guests stood up in dismay and walked out at the sight of them in the dining room. When Constance and Bosie's mother threatened the withdrawal of their allowances, they were forced to separate; society would simply not allow them to be together. Back in Paris, Wilde lived hand-to-mouth, drinking too much, staying in cheap hotels and at the homes of friends. His wife passed away in 1898; he never saw his two sons again. His health still scarred from prison, he suffered an ear infection that led to meningitis and died in 1900, in a dingy hotel room.

In his 1906 edition of *Sexual Inversion*, one of the first English medical textbooks about homosexuality, sexologist Havelock Ellis argued that the Wilde trials 'generally contributed to give definiteness and self-consciousness to the manifestations of homosexuality'. Wilde gave flesh and blood to our modern idea of the gay man: he was a dandy, he was effeminate, he was a predator, he was a corruptor, he was associated with the arts. Tom Crewe has also reflected that Wilde's 'scandalous exposure created a set of public assumptions and prejudices that persisted for well over half a century, often twisting how gay people saw themselves' – such as 'the belief that gay men, like Wilde, imposed themselves on the world by their difference: that they dressed differently, talked differently, were "theatrical". That their relationships were . . . crudely sexual, exploitative, mired in inequalities of age and class.' He argues that Wilde's trial obscures the birth of a potential gay rights movement that was taking place in the 1890s, spearheaded by sexologist Havelock Ellis, the writer Edward Carpenter and poet John Addington Symonds. Edward Carpenter, for example, was working on a pamphlet, *Homogenic Love and Its Place in a Free Society*, which was subsequently rejected by his publisher. In 1897, Havelock Ellis published *Sexual Inversion*, which sought to depict homosexuality as 'a common, recurrent part of human sexuality', rejecting Krafft-Ebing's theory of degeneration in favour of 'inversion', as well as the stereotyping of homosexuals, denying that most were 'effeminate'. The book was deemed 'lewd, wicked' and 'scandalous' and Ellis's editor, George Bedborough, was prosecuted for obscenity.

The narrowing of Wilde's sexuality from bisexual to homosexual, then, was the direct result of his trial. He had become the villain and he was made to represent what was then considered a social evil. Bisexuality, a term rarely used then, would not fit the bill; and it would have been too complex for a public determined to simplify Wilde with their hatred and prejudice. However, as academic and writer Jonathan Dollimore reflected in 2000: 'My feeling about Oscar Wilde is that clearly he was bisexual, and there is a sense in which I do deplore that representation of Wilde as living entirely in bad faith in relation to his wife. Ten years ago, one would've wanted to talk about him exclusively as gay. Now, I think, is precisely the time to rethink Wilde's message.'

Robbie Ross helped to restore Wilde's reputation. He became his literary executor, organized translations of his work across Europe, got him back into print. A decade on from Wilde's death and his plays began to be revived, his witticisms remembered. As LGBT rights were advanced later in the twentieth century, Wilde went from gay villain to gay icon, no longer reviled but lauded and celebrated from the 1960s onwards. Susan Sontag's iconic 1964 essay, 'Notes on "Camp"', is dedicated to him, whilst in 1995 he was commemorated with a stained-glass window at Poets' Corner in Westminster Abbey. However, when LGBT groups took Wilde up as the ultimate gay martyr, his sexuality was simplified as he came to represent a warning tale, a tragic story of the dangers of public persecution and cruel prejudice, of a genius stunted, of lives ruined. In 2017 Wilde was one of 50,000 gay men posthumously pardoned under the Turing Law, and even if I believe Wilde's sexuality was a little more ambiguous, it still gladdens my heart as a significant step forward for gay rights.

Oscar Wilde, initially buried in a pauper's grave, was given the dignity of a proper burial in 1909, when his remains were moved to the Père Lachaise cemetery.

In the early months of 2023, I pay the tomb a visit on a trip to Paris. Wilde's grave is graced by a large grey slab and a sculpture of a naked winged figure designed by Jacob Epstein, most likely inspired by Wilde's poem 'The Sphinx'. The tomb is protected. There was a tradition for visitors to don lipstick and kiss it, until the stone was covered in them, like imprints of rose petals, interwoven with hearts and graffiti such as *Je t'aime*, and *I cry for you every day*. So many kisses that the stone became corroded, had to be restored and surrounded with a protective shield. Such love for him, dancing all over the stone – as Stephen Fry has said, if only Oscar could wake up for five minutes to know that he might have died in ignominy but a century on, he inspires such adoration and admiration.

2

Colette and Bessie Smith

In Père Lachaise cemetery in Paris, on the opposite side to Oscar Wilde, is the tomb of the French writer Colette: a large black headstone with urns of flowers on it. Just before her death in 1954, the *New York Times* declared her to be 'the greatest living writer of French fiction'. A national treasure, she was the first woman in France ever to receive a state funeral. The author of around fifty books and twelve hundred articles of journalism, she reported from the front lines in the First World War and was nominated for the Nobel Prize in Literature in 1948. Her first novel, *Claudine at School*, detailed the amorous, bisexual adventures of her eponymous heroine, a ground-breaking book that was the first to give a voice to a female coming of age. The ideal of the New Woman – an independent, sexually liberated female – was taking hold in Europe, and Colette presented 'a new vision of what women's lives, particularly middle-class women's lives, could be in France in this period'. She was one of the first major writers to explore desire and relationships from a female perspective; the first female writer to include abortion and domestic violence in her novels. Colette was avowedly *not* a feminist – she declared that suffragettes deserved 'the whip and the harem'; she was never overtly political, but she did explore the dynamics of power play between the sexes, and was ahead of her time in seeing gender as performative. In Simone de Beauvoir's feminist classic *The Second Sex*, Colette is the most cited author, with twenty-one mentions. Colette remains much loved and treasured by contemporary female authors, who cite her as an inspiration. The writer Vivian Gornick reflects that 'my friends and I read Colette as others read the Bible . . . we read her to learn better who we were, and how, given the constraint of our condition, we were to live.'

There's another reason Colette received a state funeral – the Catholic Church refused to give her a religious service. She once described herself as an 'erotic militant', living a life suffused in scandal. Her daring, colourful, bisexual love life gave her the inspiration for her novels, many of which would now be regarded as autofiction, from her marriage to Henry Gauthier-Villars, to her love affair with Missy de Morny, and there were times when her life also mirrored her art. After writing *Chéri*, which explored an older woman taking on a younger male lover, she seduced Bertrand de Jouvenel, the sixteen-year-old stepson of her husband, Henry de Jouvenel, and they engaged on a five-year love affair.

Sidonie-Gabrielle Colette, born in 1873, grew up in a village in the Burgundy countryside. She read Balzac at the age of seven and insisted on being called by her surname, echoing the trad-ition amongst European men of adopting patronyms to command respect. As a teenager, one of her first crushes was on a friend of her father's: Henry Gauthier-Villars, who was fourteen years her senior. She had known him since she was ten. Drawn to her whiplash braids and alluring catlike eyes, Henry flirted with her, despite the fact that he was living with another woman in Paris, Germaine Servat, who had recently given birth to their son. For Henry was a notorious womanizer and libertine, and when he married Colette in 1893, the union did nothing to change his ways. A successful publisher and critic, he published a stream of books and essays under the name Willy, penned for him by ghostwriters.

Colette was only twenty years old when she first moved to Paris in 1893; Henry was thirty-four. There, he introduced her to the demimonde and intellectual avant-garde circles. On one occasion, she attended the same literary salon as Oscar Wilde. That first year of their marriage was one of the unhappiest of Colette's life. Introduced to an older crowd, drifting in circles and salons whose glittering conversation she could not yet match, she felt isolated and alienated, like a 'nobody'. When she had fallen for Henry, she had been enchanted by the erotic idea of a master who would dominate and control her, someone whom she could also rebel against. The reality fell short of the fantasy. Henry carried on having affairs; Colette discovered he had a mistress, Charlotte, and coped by befriending her. He encouraged his wife to have infidelities too, but only with women, whom he did not regard as serious rivals. And so her early experiences of bisexuality were framed and controlled by him.

Colette was certainly bisexual, for she had numerous love affairs with men and women across her lifetime. However, to call her bisexual is also anachronistic, because bisexuality was not yet an identity. Even the word *bisexual* wasn't commonly used at the time, although it started creeping into the language more around the beginning of the twentieth century. Even then, it was used by doctors and sexologists more than the general public. In France during the 1890s, bisexuals were sometimes referred to as '*indifférént(e)s*'; the French sexologist Saint-Paul started to favour the term '*bisexuels*' in 1910, an umbrella term for '*occasionels*' and '*indifférént(e)s*'. Havelock Ellis used the term in the 1915 preface to his *Sexual Inversion*: 'sexual attraction to both sexes, a condition formerly called psychosexual hermaphroditism, but now more usually bisexuality'. As academic Diederik F. Janssen notes, 'The term with its new sense, in short, can be said to have become English medical jargon between 1907 and 1915.' The word that Colette used to describe her sexuality was 'unisexuality', which she penned in a letter to a friend, which at this time referred to lesbianism. Whilst she rarely labelled her sexuality, she did explore the complexities and contrasts of erotic relationships with each sex: how loving a woman or a man might be coloured by issues of power, freedom and social mores.

Though she adopted the public persona of a liberated woman enjoying an open marriage, in private she was often tortured by jealousy over Willy's misdemeanours; her affairs with women were an opportunity for revenge and solace. Her 'unisexuality', then, sometimes played out like a game from *Les Liaisons Dangereuses*, cynical on the surface, emotions seething beneath.

Colette's illustrious writing career began when she became one of her husband's literary ghosts. The story of who created *Claudine*, of who wrote what, eventually became a literary tussle that ended up in court. Colette wrote down some memories of her schoolgirl years; Willy claimed that his contribution was to advise her to spice them up and make her heroine, Claudine, bisexual. In any case, it was Colette who breathed vitality and life into her and created a trailblazing icon in the process. The public were hungry for a heroine like Claudine: a wild, sexy tomboy, she was the first literary incarnation of the modern teenager, a feisty rejection of the chaste, demure Victorian heroine and a nod to the contemporary rage for the New Woman.

There were four *Claudine* novels in total. Colette turned conventional ideas about gender on their head in her writing. This was an era when very traditional ideas about 'masculine' and 'feminine' traits prevailed; Colette herself struggled with the clash between her girlish exterior and her interior feelings of masculinity, declaring herself to be 'a mental hermaphrodite'. As her biographer Judith Thurman sums up: 'Colette's early work is a fascinating and baroque form of transvestitism. She is a woman writing as a man, who poses as a boyish girl, Claudine, who marries a "feminised" man, the ageing Renard, who pushes her into the arms of a female lover, Rezi, with whom she takes the virile role.' In the *Claudine* novels, men puff and posture, but their manliness is often a pose and underneath they are sensitive; Claudine is often aggressive and described as 'virile' when she pursues another woman. Gender is shown to involve the donning of a mask.

The *Claudine* novels – which ranged from the heroine's adventures as a schoolgirl to her marriage to an older man – became a sensational success. Women mimicked Claudine, dressed like her, walked the streets pretending to be her. A successful play led to Henry launching a range of Claudine merchandise, from soaps to cigarettes. Photography was just coming into fashion, and Colette and Henry became a much-snapped literary celebrity couple. But look at a photo of Colette during this time and you'll see a characteristic fierceness in her eyes, a sense of something simmering. For all the books that she wrote were published under one name: Willy. Colette began to rage with indignation, and yet the financial success of the books created a pressure to keep producing. On one occasion, Willy locked her in a room in their country home, not allowing her to come out until she had produced her words.

The third novel in the *Claudine* series, *Claudine Married*, was based on a love triangle between Colette, Henry and Georgie Raoul-Duval, who was Colette's first serious female lover. Georgie was a beautiful, wealthy American, married to a Frenchman, who moved in rarefied circles. Initially Colette didn't realize that her lover was also seeing her husband; Georgie would organize a rendezvous with Colette, then Henry, in the same room, just an hour apart, so that on one occasion Henry could smell his wife's perfume on her. Colette immortalized the love triangle in fiction, though the book was nearly pulled from publication when Georgie threatened a libel suit. However, the playful farce of the novel ends with Claudine and her husband reuniting, her asking him to dominate him, peace established through a return to heterosexual union and old-fashioned power dynamics, which reflects the mood of the day. Lesbian chic was acceptable in artistic circles but there was still an underlying unease about same-sex relations. Traditional Napoleonic codes from 1804 still governed marriage; Willy, for example, had complete control over Colette's finances. *Le mari doit protection à sa femme, la femme obéissance à son mari* was another: the husband owes protection to his wife, the wife obedience to her husband. Women were also unable to work without their husband's permission, a law not overturned until 1965.

There were no crimes of lesbianism then. In the UK, no law had been put into place as it had for men: there is an apocryphal tale that Queen Victoria saw no need for legislation against same-sex female relations because she did not believe they existed. It was also felt that a law would introduce the dangerous idea into the minds of respectable women, who were assumed to be sexually innocent and unaware of such matters. Looking back to Ancient Rome, we have far fewer records of female bisexuality; unlike male development, it played no part in the shaping of a citizen and so it was not deemed as important.

France had a more liberal attitude towards same-sex relationships than the UK; since the Revolution all victimless crime had been abolished. Indeed, Paris was nicknamed 'Paris Lesbos': the place that lesbians from the Anglo-American world flocked to, from Gertrude Stein to Djuna Barnes to Oscar Wilde's niece Dolly Wilde; the Parisian press thrived on Sapphic scandals. Lesbianism was indulged as something innocent, harmless, eccentric, caused not 'as the result of freedom, but of frustration'; in the eyes of the public, 'the lesbian was not so much preferring women as she was fleeing from man, a different matter altogether.' And female bisexuality was therefore far less threatening than it was in a man, Colette mused: 'The wife of a man who deceives her with another man knows that all is lost . . . She is completely unable to assume the mocking salacious attitude of the man who catches his wife embracing another woman: *"Oh, I'll get you back again".* This was in part because men held all the cards: a woman deserted would find herself in a far more vulnerable situation, financially and socially, than a man cuckolded. Judith Thurman also points out that bisexuality was common for 'respectable married ladies', for taking a female lover had 'distinct advantages': 'there was no danger of pregnancy, almost none of venereal disease, and it was a "safe" way to satisfy their sensual curiosity or take revenge on a brutal or unfaithful husband without risking a scandalous divorce and the loss of their children or social position.'

Sappho had become a popular poet in France in this era. Although the very term 'lesbianism' was derived from her name, since she lived on the island of Lesbos, the fragments we have of her poetry suggest she had both male and female lovers. We can see early prejudice against this bisexuality at the time; Baudelaire's 1857 poetry volume *Les Fleurs du Mal* 'depicted Sappho as an advocate of sapphism, but also as a hypocrite who succumbed to heterosexual love'.

Around 1905, Colette and Willy's marriage slid into stagnancy. Willy fell for a teenager called Meg, a kind of ersatz Colette who braided her hair and mimicked Colette's literary creation; Willy creepily referred to her as his 'daughter' and related how he enjoyed spanking her with a hairbrush. Colette, meanwhile, fell for Missy: Mathilde de Morny, the Marchioness de Belbeuf, in what would be her first serious relationship with a woman.

*

My first serious relationship with a woman began on a trip abroad.

When I first saw Clara, she was performing a cartwheel. It was a fluid movement, but as she righted herself, she became clumsy, nearly slipped, for her pendant had tangled with her hair. We – my mother and I – had been watching in admiration. Now we felt awkward. We carried on walking through the pine forest. She looked up as we passed her. A scatter of vivid impressions: flinty blue eyes. Dark hair that fell to her shoulders in curls, pinned into place by pink clips. The pendant caught the light and reflected crosses onto her cheeks. There was a hostility bristling from her, as though we'd watched her masturbating or read her diary. My lips trembled in an apologetic smile.

In my memory, Rørvig is an island off the coast of Denmark; but looking online I learned that it is a town on a Danish island called Zealand. I was in my late twenties when I made the trip with my mum, sharing a week's holiday, for we were close as sisters. We had to take a short, bumpy ferry ride from the mainland to get there. The island's beauty is intensified by its small size, easy to cover in a day; it is covered in thick green pine forests that break open into fields and serene mountains, and it is fringed with beaches pitted with seaweed. We were staying at the folk school, as it was called – a relaxed, cosy hotel – along with around twenty other people, young and old, from all over the world.

When we got back to our room, I told my mum that I wanted to lie down for a nap. Really, I wanted silence, space to analyse. My body was singing a high octave – and yet what was this low note creeping in? I thought back to Clara's cross. I loved the thick silence in churches and St Francis enchanted me, but strict Christians didn't tend to like me. At university, the hardcore believer in my BA group had found out I meditated (Eastern! Heathen! Satanic!) and made me half-nemesis, half-project, someone in need of correction.

At dinner, Clara sat a table away from me. Her voice sounded surprisingly deep and authoritative, as though a wise old woman dwelled inside her slender frame. A gentle breeze swirled in through the window, carrying flower scents and the joyful zizzing of bees, and lifted up her hair from her shoulders.

Over the next few days, we would pass her from time to time. On the shore or going for a walk in the woods or on a bike as fields of wild flowers waved us on. Her looks became quizzical, analytic; they were always directed at me, and they grew longer, whilst mine shrank, until I hardly dared to look at her at all. I began to regret my mother's presence, feeling inhibited, responsible for keeping her company, as though I was both teenager and old-maid spinster.

My mum and I were attempting to skim stones on the beach when I saw a stone fly out from nowhere and, with the grace of a fish, dance across one, two, three, four, five waves. I turned.

'You have to jerk your wrist like this,' she explained.

'Oh, right.' I picked up a stone and tried to mimic her. It plopped into the shallows.

'No, it's quite simple, just flick your wrist like this.' She frowned. And it struck me that my failure may have been deliberate, a way of playing ditzy to please her. I had been behaving as though she was a man I shouldn't outdo.

I took a pebble and put my will and skill into it.

'Good!' she cried.

'I'm Sam.'

She smiled. Her teeth criss-crossed at the front, a beautiful mess. 'I'm Clara.'

Then I jumped as I saw her introduce herself to my mother. I had forgotten she was even there.

'We're from England,' I said.

'I'm from Sweden,' she said, which surprised me, for her accent was so neutral; there was just the slightest inflection. 'My mother is English. I live in London.'

We walked and we talked and we exchanged tentative titbits of information. She was in her early thirties, five years older than me. She worked for a magazine but really she wanted to be an artist; drawing portraits was her passion. When I told her that I was a writer, her eyes lit up. I felt a wild happiness, then; Henry a vague comparison that soon faded, forgotten.

After we parted, my mum commented that she was so glad I'd found a nice friend.

*

It was cold outside. The moon was a half. It was around two in the morning. I'd felt restless, had slipped out of the bedroom, tiptoeing past my mother's bed, padding down the wooden staircase. The next day we were heading home and, despite the fact that the retreat had soothed me in so many ways, there was a scratch in my heart at the thought of never seeing Clara again.

The island was a party of animal nightlife; but suddenly there were human sounds, the crunch of gravel, rustle of clothing, and she was by my side. Had she woken and watched me and found me? Immediately, the present became taut and loud, the volume turned up on the here and now. My heart whispered, *something's going to happen.*

'So, are you looking forward to going home?' she asked.

'Yes and no.' I gazed at her: she was wearing a jumper over her pyjamas and the crucifix at her throat glinted in the moonlight.

I said that my meditations had been deep and nourishing and she told me about the Desert Fathers, ancient custodians of Christianity, who had meditated. We talked and talked as we both grew visibly chilly, and I tried to still the chatter in my teeth because I wanted the moment to go on and on. Eventually, a silence fell between us and she took a step closer. I tensed. For the past few days, I had been wondering, watching, seeking invisible signs. I knew that clothes could whisper sexuality, that during the 1980s a piercing in a man's right ear signalled he was gay, just as, back in Wilde's age, a green carnation in a buttonhole could signal the same. But this was the mid-noughties and there didn't seem to be a collective sartorial wink that said, *I might be bi.* As she leaned in I panicked, and quickly spread open my arms for a hug. The feel of her breasts against mine was a warm thrill. Her hair against my cheek. She pulled back and said, 'Shall we exchange emails?'

Pens were found inside, in the kitchen; clumsy rips of paper were exchanged.

Back home: our emails started off breezy, friendly – describing our journeys home from Rørvig, sharing our despondency at being back in grey, rainy London after the island's beauty. Then questions began to beget longer and longer answers. I was grateful for the medium of email, knowing that I was more articulate than if we'd been chatting in a bar. She asked what I did for a living besides being an author and I said my writing was full-time and I was impoverished as a result. She said she was bored, being back in her office, that she believed I was in a more rewarding profession.

Was our interaction a seduction or a growing friendship? I knew I ought to let it unfold rather than pinning a label on it, but curiosity and impatience coalesced; at the same time, uncertainty was an aphrodisiac. Analysing our emails felt like plucking the petals off a daisy: she likes me, she likes me not, she likes me, she likes me not, why is today's email late, it's 16.05 and I keep refreshing and there's still no sign of it? We were establishing a pattern: in the mornings I emailed, in the afternoons came her reply. Until the day she broke our routine. Evening came. I was heartbroken. My despair seemed Prufrockian. How ridiculous, how pathetic of me to keep playing refresh, refresh, refresh with my Hotmail. I thought of the cross that hung around her neck again, and realized, *I've been so stupid*. How could she be *that* way? I had seen the news stories; I knew there were still countries around the world where gays were hanged, stoned to death. Surely if you were inclined in that direction, you would not openly sport a contradiction?

At 20.23 her email arrived. There was a mention of Gerard Manley Hopkins in the middle; how much she loved his poems and those lines:

> *I caught this morning morning's minion, king-*
> *   dom of daylight's dauphin, dapple-dawn-drawn Falcon,*
> *   in his riding*

Of the rolling level underneath him steady air, and striding
High there

'The Windhover' was a poem I loved too, and made my heart blaze a little more for her. And was it a sign? Hopkins was a gay Catholic priest who found himself aroused by images of Christ on the cross and who used to scourge himself after suffering erotic dreams; the frenzied lines of his verse suggested a pent-up passion. But: even better then, there, in the middle of the email, was the line, *You have such gorgeous hair – what shampoo do you use?* I read it, reread it, blew it up in my mind from 12-point font to 35 to 3,500. She likes me, she likes me not – she likes me.

Euphoria soon faded, smoked out by panic. How did it work, dating a woman? If we were going to date? How did women flirt? Seduce each other? Go to bed with each other? I was now in my late twenties and I had developed some sort of knowledge about men, a papier mâché formed from diary entries, guides, women's mags, friends. Women were a mystery. How did sex work with a woman? I could picture Act One (kissing) and Act Two (second base) but Act Three was the mystery that daunted me. With men, Act Three revolved around their climax, their pleasure, and occasionally, if I was lucky, mine. I dreaded vibrators. Suddenly they snagged my imagination and I got hung up on them. They were the staple of women's mag pieces and TV programmes like *Sex and the City*, and they instilled a feeling in me akin to looking at a dentist's drill, only involving an even more vulnerable orifice.

Our date/non-date was set for a Saturday afternoon. I turned up at the indie bookshop fifteen minutes early. A cult fiction display blazed across one wall, bricked with the bright spines of William Burroughs and Hunter S. Thompson and Paul Auster and Will Self. All men. The very term avant-garde is a military one, derived from the French for 'vanguard', suggesting masculine power marching forward to smash conventional fictional boundaries, mapping out new territory. It was a display that seemed to cry: let men get out there and fight with their prose, whilst women stay at home and stick to domestic subjects.

Clara entered, early too, breathless, hair scattered by the wind. We circled, chatted awkwardly across tables of books, conscious of browsing customers listening in. It wasn't a great setting for intimacy.

I picked out a Martin Amis to buy. My tastes were shifting back towards the literary and the pantheon seemed made up of male gods: John Updike, Saul Bellow, Martin Amis, Will Self, Salman Rushdie. I thought she'd be impressed, but her raised eyebrow was disdainful.

The coffee shop, a few roads down, was much more private. We sat at a rickety table, sipping tea, spilt sugar between us, chatting about Jean Rhys (I hadn't heard of her); the weather; the novel I was working on. It felt as though the conversation was a hovering bird that circled and circled but never chose its prey. A frustration began to jiggle inside me. As a teenager, I remember a friend's mother listening in on our conversation about boys we wanted, interjecting firm advice: 'You should never chase men, you should let them chase you, and then you must run, but not too fast, just at the right pace so they can catch you.' I had taken this to heart, and with success. At the nightclubs I'd been to with friends, I'd succeeded in pulling by playing the part of a passive siren: signalling that I was interested but waiting for their approach. If, if, if this was a date and we were flirting, was I supposed to be reeling her in, or she me? Who was the hunter, who the hunted?

And then she started to complain:

'My ex is such a pain. She won't accept it's over between us, she keeps wanting to meet and talk. I want to be friends, but I want her to move on.'

The *she* made my blood pulse.

'When did you break up?' I asked.

'Three months ago. I dumped her.'

'My last ex was a pain.' I echoed her.

'Did she—'

'He—'

'Oh.' She looked disappointed.

'I've never been with a woman,' I blurted out and her eyes narrowed in response. She nodded, as though she sensed then just who I was, and I was as she had expected, then laced her hand into mine.

Her flat was on the top floor of a house in north London owned by an elderly couple. We were greeted by their old, shaggy, blonde-coloured dog. Clara showed me her lovely roof garden. Her kitchen was tiny, her sitting room and bedroom decorated with chic flair and a number of her portraits and paintings.

We ended up lying on her pink duvet together. As she started to caress me, I was immediately conscious of *oh, this is different from being with a man*. She was skilful; her touch was delicate. Male caresses usually lacked the art of teasing, used fingers crudely; pleasure was something they hammered out with force, rather than coaxing out with subtlety. Of course, I thought, it makes sense; she'd know what women like. When I climaxed, I felt starry and drunk, and then there was an immediate sobering, a dilution of intimacy, of sitting up and looking around the room, taking in the surroundings; mirror, make-up, books, discarded clothes, an awareness of the traffic moving outside, of the sun fading, of the world outside and what it might think of us. I told her I needed the toilet when I didn't. I looked at the mirror as though I expected it to behave like Dorian Gray's painting, to record fresh cracks, a greying of skin. But my eyes looked bright, my skin flushed. I appeared young and happy. Suddenly I smiled and returned to the bedroom with fresh confidence.

I was surprised at how natural it felt to caress her. I had anticipated a sense of – *sin* would be too strong a word – but I had feared it would feel alien and off-kilter. Instead, it was fluent and easy. Her cries of pleasure made me feel pleased and proud, until a thought snagged my mind, some memory of an article in a women's mag, about how many women fake their orgasms. Men didn't – they were honest in their selfishness; they would grab our hand and put it on their cock; the full stop on the end of a sex act was their climax. But we, as women, were more generous, and more inclined to mimic Meg Ryan's infamous faked orgasm in *When Harry Met Sally*, not necessarily out of duplicity but a desire to avoid hurt. I realized that I was gazing at her, and she muttered, *why did you stop?* This time, when I continued, I lost my anxiety, my intellect stopped twitching and I began to feel her pleasure building not only in her but me, as though our consciousnesses overlapped. It swelled through me in waves and as she broke, its echo shuddered in me.

We lay still for a while. Clara pulled up the duvet, yawning, and pulled me in close. Her hair tickled my nostril.

'So?' she asked. 'How did it feel, losing your virginity?'

I laughed, for I hadn't thought about it in those terms.

'I liked it,' I said in a small voice. Being bi did involve losing your virginity twice: it had gone to a man when I was twenty-one; now, aged twenty-eight, to a woman.

I asked Clara when she knew that she was bisexual and she immediately corrected me: *I'm not bi.*

'But when did you know you . . . ?'

'When I was about twelve or thirteen,' she replied. Only schoolfriends, schoolfrenemies, picked up on it. (I found myself wondering how – a lingering look, a caress?) They teased her and called her a dyke. So, aged fifteen, she came out, but with a lie: she told friends she was bisexual, knowing this would be more socially acceptable. She had briefly dated a hot boy to maintain the lie. In truth, she found men physically repulsive: crude and apish.

'What do you see in them?' she asked.

'I've grown up with men,' I said. 'With two brothers, with a house full of men.'

'So? I'm surprised it hasn't put you off even more.'

Men have been responsible for so much of the suffering in the world, she added. The Christian Church was founded by men and women but gradually men shut women out.

'The crap thing is, we all still go to church on Sundays – my family, me, we all go. You could join us. For me, it's just lip service, keeping my dad happy – but if you came, you'd have a chance to meet him.'

We had slept together once and now I was going to be introduced to her family? I hesitated. Was she going to conform to female clichés, I thought, disloyal to my sex, and quickly try to pin me down? I thought about Henry, wondered how Clara might respond if she were to read my book.

'Don't look so freaked out,' she teased me. 'It's just a trip to church. Anyway, they don't know I'm gay, so . . .'

'Oh. So, how will you introduce me?'

'As a friend?' She looked anxious. 'Is that OK?'

I felt uncertain, surprised that she had to lie to her family. But in an attempt to lighten the situation I told her I found the secrecy sexy, that it added a frisson.

Mathilde de Morny, the Marchioness de Belbeuf, was ten years older than Colette, a lesbian transvestite who had cropped hair, a mastectomy, and liked to dress in three-piece suits with a monocle. As French women had become more liberated from the late nineteenth century onwards, they enjoyed bicycling and tennis, and the growing trend for *culottes* (trousers for women) had caused a stir. Since 1799, it had been illegal for women to wear trousers unless she had special permission, though the law was amended in 1892 to allow women to wear them if they were cycling or riding a horse – otherwise, trousers were illegal. Missy got round this by having detachable skirts made for her that could be torn off to reveal menswear underneath. When Colette began dating her, she adopted more masculine clothing, embracing a newfound freedom in this identity.

Michèle Sarde, one of Colette's biographers, considered that 'Colette's Lesbos is more a comforting womb or a mid-eighteenth century convent than it is a debauched Gomorrah.' Colette's marriage had verged on the abusive; Missy gave her strength and the space to be independent. There was an underlying emotional nourishment, a stability, particularly compared to how capricious Willy had been in his affections: 'Two women absorbed in each other don't fear or even imagine separation any more than they would tolerate it.' Colette felt that passion was less of a factor, for 'Passion is not what creates fidelity between two women but rather, a kind of kinship.' However, as I discovered with Clara: 'A woman enjoys the certainty in caressing a body whose secrets she knows and whose preferences are suggested by her own.'

Although Missy superficially played the parental role for Colette, supporting her financially, at heart she was seeking a mother figure. Missy's father had died when she was young; her mother had been horrifically abusive. Her nickname for her daughter was 'tapir', which referred to her long nose. Missy had a 'profound yearning for maternal tenderness' and so she impersonated her lost father and sought a maternal lover. Ultimately, she and Colette mothered each other. In Colette's novel *The Tendrils of the Vine*, a work of autofiction based on their relationship, she wrote: 'I know that then you will hold me close in your arms, and that if being rocked in your arms is not enough to calm me, your kiss will become more profound, your hands more loving... You will give me pleasure, and you will gaze at me with your eyes filled with maternal concern, seeking in your passionate lover the child you never had.'

My relationship with Clara followed a similar pattern. In the early days of our courtship, I had fretted over who was supposed to be active or passive, who was chasing who; in the early days of our relationship, I felt lost as to who was supposed to be wearing the trousers. I had a stereotypical idea that one of us ought to be the 'man' and wondered if we'd both end up wrestling for that position of power. This is echoed in *The Pure and the Impure*, a fascinating work by Colette where she interviews a range of characters about their thoughts on gender, sex and relationships. Amalia, a provincial actress, says that 'A couple of women can live together a long time and be happy.' But there will be trouble 'if one of the two women lets herself behave in the slightest like what I call a pseudo-man'. By this, Amalia is referring to the tendency of men at the time to behave badly, citing the example of a woman who mimicked men in adopting 'all the mean ways of love'. Women, she suggests, can offer something better, something beyond domination and cruelty.

For me and Clara, it was a relief to gradually realize that neither of us needed to be men, and this was, in fact, the joy of our relationship. Neither of us needed to control the other; not when we could nurture each other. Clara didn't need a male substitute, I came to see, but she craved maternal affection. After we had made love, nothing made her happier than lying in my arms and the feel of me stroking her hair.

In Paris at the turn of the century, however, a certain hostility towards same-sex female relations still simmered beneath the surface. Colette and Missy, protected to a degree by Missy's aristocratic status, were able to live together and thrive in their relationship. But, as for Oscar and Bosie, when it crossed a line and became too public, it sparked outrage.

*

Imagine being there on 3 January 1907. You arrive at the Moulin Rouge that evening, eyeing the poster for *Rêve d'Égypte*. A coat of arms is displayed across the door. It belongs to the aristocratic de Morny family: you know Missy will be performing tonight, even if she's hiding behind the stage name Yssim. You find a seat near the front; it's a packed auditorium and there's an energy in the air: crackling, fervid, dangerous. The show begins. Missy plays an archaeologist in his study, surrounded by old books and arte-facts. She's dressed as a man, in a trouser suit, which provokes jeers, whistles, catcalls; apples and oranges fly, roll onto the stage. To their credit, the actresses keep going. The archaeologist is suddenly struck by a vision; the Egyptian mummy in the study seems to come to life, rising out of its sarcophagus and dancing seductively. Slowly, teasingly, (s)he unwraps its bandages – to reveal Colette, in a dazzling costume and jewelled bra. Missy kisses her. The audi-ence erupts. Yelling, screams, the crowd frothing onto the stage. The performers flee. Meg and Willy, who have been watching in the audience, are subject to cries of 'Cuckold!' As the mob turns violent, only the police save the performers.

The next day's headlines gossip about the controversy: lesbianism was all very well in private, but such a flagrant public display was an outrage. In part, Colette and Missy's kiss caused such trouble because it was real rather than performative, acted out for male titil-lation. Sapphic pornography was wildly popular at the turn of the century; and there were more arrests over gay porn than there were for homosexual acts. Much that was written about lesbianism in the nineteenth century was, ironically, penned by men; male poets such as Baudelaire and Swinburne popularized the term Sapphism and explored female love in their poems. When he was taken to court for obscenity, he defended them by reassuring the court that, 'This book was not written for my wives, my daughters or my sisters . . .' Lesbianism in the arts, then, was more acceptable if it was for the purposes of male voyeurism; for female readers, it would be corrupting.

*

A week after my first date with Clara, we were sitting in a pub, drinking, when a guy walked up. He was big, burly, his eyes shot red with drink.

'Okay, ladies?' he asked.

Clara's eyes narrowed.

A friend shadowed him, and another, and another.

'Can we join you?'

Clara reached across the table and entwined her fingers with mine, giving the man a pointed look. He looked shocked, momentarily.

I said to him, 'I'm bi,' at the same time that Clara asserted, 'We're lesbians.'

'Can't make your minds up – typical women,' he sneered, and Clara and I sharply told him where to go. She turned back to me, frowning, and I sensed her thoughts: *men – why bother?*

He had burst our bubble, spoilt the mood. I felt slightly odd, having announced I was bisexual, in public, to a stranger: a first. Weirdly, the label had felt more comfortable when it had been theory; now that I was a practising bi, it felt more final, restrictive somehow. Or perhaps Clara's disapproval was slowly tainting the term for me. I was starting to lie to her, white lies about how I was losing interest in men, but in truth I did still like them; and when we'd had sex before the pub there had been times when I'd felt both straight and queer all at once, for as I had tasted her, the prickle of her pubic hair had felt like the same sweet tickle of a man's bearded stubble.

'You'll go off men soon enough,' she said, in a tone of parental authority.

I felt irked.

And then I saw the fear flashing in her eyes, the vulnerability, and understood her worry: I could betray her with anyone and everyone. I put my hand on hers, and she smiled. I was falling for her, I wanted to say, falling for her hair and its beautiful sheen, and for her wit, and her rants, and her love of literature, and the fact she'd read my book and praised it as 'bold and brilliant' (though she had added, *you seem to want to write like a man*). Generally, being with her was smoother than being with a man; less tone-deafness around emotions; though when she was tired, Clara could suddenly lash out and wound me with a cutting remark—

I caught myself: I needed to stop constantly comparing her, analysing men versus women, turning individual experiences into sweeping generalizations. There was just this uncertainty which kept rushing back, of what to do and how to act and what to say.

We carried on chatting as the twilight smoked the sky, and the pub became cosy, and Clara related a strange film she had recently watched when channel-surfing in the early hours, an old black-and-white silent movie about a woman who receives a magical seed in the post. She swallows it, and at the ball she attends that evening, she has no interest in dancing with her fiancé; young men now catch her eye. As Clara spoke, bringing the film to life, the light glinting in her pupils, it felt as though we were back in our magic bubble again, but an unexpected sense of sorrow came over me, as though I was already in the future, apart from her and gazing back on this night with painful nostalgia.

*

In the aftermath of the performance, Willy filed for a legal separation from Colette. She, in turn, found it harder to live with her female lover. The divorce left her penniless, so she continued with her career performing mime and dance in music halls. When Willy retained copyright to the books *she* had written, Colette, ever brave and determined, battled for her name to appear on them and continued to write and perform. In *The Vagabond*, as with so many of her novels, she turned her life into art, using her make-up case as a desk to write on during her tour across music halls in thirty-two cities. *The Vagabond* is a work of autofiction which explores what it is to be a woman seeking autonomy in a male-dominated world, conflicted by the needs of security and freedom. The heroine is tempted to marry a man but decides to embrace independence instead.

This was the predicament of being bisexual at the time: society would always weigh in favour of the heterosexual in terms of social attitudes, laws and conventions, which meant men usually stood for marriage, women for affairs. Colette would go on to have more female lovers, for, as she wrote so elegantly, 'we can never bring enough twilight, silence and gravity to surround the embrace of two women.' But her marriages were to men. She would walk up the aisle twice more, to Henry de Jouvenel (the marriage ended when she had an affair with her stepson) and, more happily, to Maurice Goudeket. Her literary career flourished with classics such as *Cheri*, *The Ripening Seed* and *Gigi*, and she was awarded four ranks of the *Légion d'honneur*, becoming the first female president of the Académie Goncourt. She wrote beautifully about the female experience, about the pleasures and pains of love, about sex and sensuality. 'Men are terrible!' she once wrote. 'Women too!'

*

A month after I had started dating Clara, I caught the Tube to her family home in north-west London. It was late morning on a Sunday, and I had been invited to lunch. My fingers were nervous in my lap. I was conscious of a change in my perspective, in my sexual antennae: women were now sharp and clear and men had faded to a background fuzz. Her influence. Although I defiantly asserted that I would never become a full lesbian despite her efforts – it had become romantic banter between us – I was closer to conversion than I wanted to admit.

I walked down the road of elegant, three-storey houses, trees shedding late spring blossom. Clara's front garden was dominated by a large evergreen, which cast a shadow over her porch. As I pressed the bell, a grey cat leapt down and sidled against my legs.

'Sam! Hi! I see you've met Olivia!' Clara's skirt made me double take; I had grown used to her in trousers. She gave me a stiff hug, and a warning look: *remember, we're just friends.* It irritated me: she had no need to remind me that we needed to perform.

Over the previous weeks, I had been steeling myself for meeting her father. Given his prejudices, I'd researched a subject I was once indifferent to. I had been shocked to discover that the Vatican had recently decreed that gay men could not become priests, for they were 'objectively disordered' and practising 'grave sins', thinking: *really? In this day and age?* It read like a news bulletin from a medieval era. All my anger and frustration had sculpted him into some sort of thick-necked, posh, sneering, Bible-bashing idiot. When I entered their large, airy kitchen and came face to face with him, I was stunned by his charisma. He was tall, grey hair curving back from his face in a patrician sweep; wore a white shirt, trousers, and a bright-red cardigan. His handshake was vigorous, his smile warm, his faded blue eyes merry. His partner had blonde-grey curls, a tense face, a slightly brittle smile.

Clara introduced them as 'Dad and Shelley', which made me wonder why she referred to her mother by her first name.

We sat down to eat lunch: quiche, salads, spicy couscous.

'Clara tells me you're a writer,' her dad said. Often people addressed this question to me with a patronizing intonation. But his tone was one of enthusiasm, generosity. He had the rare skill of a true charmer: an ability to look into people and pick up on what makes them feel special.

'I've had some exciting news on that front,' I said. 'I sent an opening chapter to Faber – and they wrote back that same day, saying they like it and want to see more.'

'That's marvellous news!'

'Sam, that's great!' Clara grinned.

Shelley nodded and said, 'Great,' in a put-out voice.

'The only trouble is,' I confessed, 'I haven't got a book to send them. Now I've got to write it and hope they'll still be interested when I finish.'

'You'll do it,' her father assured me.

He raised his glass and made a toast to my future success, and I grinned. I had thought the meal would be something I'd have to endure, not enjoy. I had been brought up in a house on benefits, in poverty; I still found this sort of lunch – where the salad was served with fancy silver tongs and Radio 4 had been switched off shortly before eating – intimidating. Middle-class people scared me; thanks to Oxford, I had learned to mimic their way of speaking but their etiquette remained mysterious. Even if I was donning a mask, pretending to belong to their background, and, for once, pulling it off, I was still aware of another deceit. Her father gazed at me with such warmth; what would he say if he had seen us yesterday, kissing with abandon on her bed? If he found out that she had sketched me naked? He started reciting 'The Windhover' and I realized Clara had inherited her love of Hopkins from him. He made Hopkins sound different; in his crisp English accent, Hopkins became a lover of nature, a devoted priest, a decent sort of chap, not the sort to ever write homoerotic poetry about the 'bellbright bodies' of boys bathing.

Clara was different: I was also conscious of that. It was hard to pinpoint exactly why, because her outward manner was perhaps even more vivacious and friendly than usual. It was in her eyes, I realized. Previously, there had always been a flame in them – a hard, gemlike flame – of desire; now there was not even a simmer. Even though I accepted that she was putting on an act for her parents, for one sad, scary moment I felt as though our love affair was nothing but an illusion.

I excused myself for the toilet. As Clara rose to remove our plates, I heard Shelley address her tersely: 'Careful, you'll drop them', and in that tone was an echo of Clara warning me, 'You'll go off men.' Perhaps Shelley had given Clara her mean streak.

The toilet had a stained-glass window; a religious scene that made me smile. I lingered in the hallway, examining the framed portraits and pictures on the wall, all Clara's artwork. There was one of a woman who looked as though she might be her older sister. Then I looked closer and saw *Ingrid, 1954–1992*. Her mother, I realized. Her mother was – *dead*. Shelley must be her stepmother. Clara would still have been a teenager when she lost her.

I went downstairs feeling as though I wanted to hug and kiss her in consolation. Why hadn't she told me about losing her mother? I felt the strain of having to smile, sit down and enthuse over the blueberry cheesecake dessert Shelley had made.

After lunch, as the meal broke up, Clara went to the piano and tinkled a casual tune. Her father strode over and joined her. Their fingers flirted a duet on the keys. She looked up at him; he at her; love sparkled between them.

That's why she can't tell him, I understood: it would break his heart.

'My dad likes you!' Clara relayed to me the next day. We glowed, and then felt uneasy, for I had gained his approval, but under false pretences. I was touched when I was soon invited back for another Sunday lunch. Her dad was like the paternal figure I'd always longed for; my own father had schizophrenia and our relationship was distant. One night I had a terrible nightmare that Clara had pinned a portrait of me to the wall in her family home and her father had examined it, detected our passion in it, and torn it off, torn it up, yelling. I woke up in a state of shock. My fear intensified: the more I came to visit, the more he might suspect, but Clara kept reassuring me, 'His idea of a lesbian is of an old-fashioned butch skinhead. You look far too feminine for him to ever suspect.'

Feminine: she made it sound like a compliment. I knew this was the paradox of my appearance: in my dysmorphia, I tended to make myself look *more* girlish to compensate, growing my hair long, wearing short skirts, as though trying to convince myself. Perhaps Clara was helping me to feel happier in my body, though recently, when I had caught a taxi and told the driver that I was a writer, he had frowned and said, 'You don't *look* like one. A real writer – he ought to have a beard, and look serious.' Comebacks had simmered in my mind all week: Austen, Eliot and Woolf had hair on their cunts rather than their chins, but it hadn't stymied their genius. You can see the same sentiments being expressed in the Victorian era: Robert Sherard, writing his reflections and memories of Wilde in 1905, mused that he couldn't understand why people thought Oscar was an invert. He couldn't see 'the effeminacy in him', he said. 'He always impressed me as a man, a man of masculine bent of mind. To begin with, I always considered him a genius, and genius is never associated with what is feminine.' Colette, too, fretted that she suffered from a 'mental hermaphroditism', fearing that a male friend had 'detected the masculine streak in my character'. When she chats about this with Missy (who is given the pen name Marguerite Moreno in *The Pure and the Impure*), they link together being bi or lesbian with being smart and funny:

'There's no reason to be so upset . . . Why don't you just accept the fact that for certain men some women represent a risk of homosexuality?'

'You and I may comfort ourselves with that thought, Marguerite, at any rate. But if what you say is true, who will realise that we are women?'

'Other women. Women aren't deluded or offended by our masculine wit. Think it over . . .'

*

And what if we travel across the continents, to the USA – what of bisexuality over there? For the first two decades of the twentieth century, 'inverts' – as gays/bis were called – were frowned upon, though how freely you might express and explore your bisexuality was also a matter of race, class and geography. For women in the Black community in New York, for example, same-sex female relations were more acceptable compared to white women. The 1920s – a time of prosperity, a flourishing of fashion and music, the Jazz Age – is often celebrated as an era of lesbian/bisexual chic. Journalist Lisa Hix has argued that Blues music contributed to the overt sexuality of the time and its flouting of feminine conventions. A decade before flappers became popular, Blues music explored and rejected the idea that women belonged in the domestic sphere.

Bessie Smith, one of the most popular Blues singers in the 1920s, was a favourite among flappers, a bold woman who dared to sing about her bisexuality. She was celebrated as the 'Empress of the Blues'.

Just listen to her singing 'Down Hearted Blues'. It was released in 1923 as Bessie's debut single and was a huge success, selling 780,000 copies in its first six months. The critic Carl Van Vechten once described a live performance by Bessie as like 'a woman cutting her heart open with a knife until it was exposed for us all to see'. Defiance and vulnerability, toughness and tenderness: she captured contradictions in her tone as she crooned about love's complexities. The writer Langston Hughes reflected that, 'The blues always impressed me as being very sad, sadder even than the Spirituals, because their sadness is not softened with tears, but hardened with laughter.' Danny Barker, a jazz musician of the era, heard in Bessie's depth and range a similarity with 'preachers and evangelists' of the Deep South: 'she could bring about mass hypnotism'.

Her childhood was tough. She was born in Chattanooga, Tennessee, around 1894 (the exact date is not known). Her father, William Smith, was a labourer and part-time Baptist preacher; he died too young for her to remember him. By the age of nine, she had lost her mother and a brother too. She and her five siblings were raised by an older sister, Viola, on a shoestring, taking in laundry for money. Struggling under the weight of so much responsibility, Viola was often harsh to Bessie. 'I was raised in a shit-house', Bessie would say later in life, for Viola would punish her by locking her in the out-house for the night. Even at that young age, Bessie's extraordinary voice attracted attention. She earned money for her family by performing on the sidewalk, singing and dancing whilst her brother played the guitar. She longed to escape their poor, narrow existence by following in the footsteps of her older brother, Clarence, who had joined a travelling troupe, The Moses Stoke Company.

Bessie begged him to organize an audition for her and she was hired as a dancer. This was 1912, and Bessie was around eighteen years old. On tour with the troupe, she was to meet the woman who would change her life. Ma Rainey was their lead singer and she became known as Mother of the Blues, for she was one of the first women to popularize the Blues style. On stage, she would transfix audiences with her raw performances, sporting ebullient horse-hair wigs, carrying an ostrich plume, her teeth flashing gold as she belted out her numbers. The Blues songs that she and Bessie sang told stories of the everyday lives of Black people: of love lost and love unrequited, of lying and cheating men, of poverty and politics, of gambling and alcohol, of all the highs and lows of life. Ma took Bessie under her wing, becoming her mentor and her lover, introducing Bessie to bisexuality. Ma herself was married to a fellow performer called William 'Pa' Rainey, but like many Blues singers of the time, she had numerous female lovers.

Bessie stayed with the troupe for three years. She and Ma sang in tent shows, bars, small-town theatres, touring across the Deep South, covering Alabama, Tennessee, Memphis. Bessie's voice was so raw, bold and beautiful that she frequently disdained the use of a microphone, able to project without it. In 1920 she settled down in Philadelphia, and there her talent was spotted by Clarence

Williams, who signed her up with Columbia Records. 'Race' records, as they were known, had become a new buzzword in the music industry in the early 1920s, records by Black artists aimed at Black listeners.

As America roared into the Twenties, flappers became all the rage. Once a term that referred to a prostitute, 'flapper' took on the meaning of a liberated woman who sported an androgynous bob, discarded corsets for daring sleeveless dresses, smoked, partied, worked and dated casually. In Harlem, there had been a huge migration of Blacks from the Deep South to the north, which became the nation's largest Black neighbourhood. The city experienced such a creative explosion of music, writing, art and ideas that this period became known as the Harlem Renaissance. Gay bars and speakeasies sprang up alongside drag balls, which Langston Hughes called 'Spectacles in Colour'. The most glamorous costumes were awarded a prize, creating a 'scene whose celestial flavor and cerulean coloring no angelic painter or nectarish poet has ever conceived'.

Bessie Smith met Jack Gee in 1923, when he was employed as a security guard at a nightclub where she performed. To call their first date 'dramatic' is an understatement: after going out to dinner, they witnessed a street robbery. When Jack chased the villain down the road he was shot and wounded. Over the next five weeks Bessie would visit him on a daily basis and their courtship played out in hospital. By the time he was discharged, they were in love. In those days, their romance was sweet; Jack pawned his watch and uniform to buy Bessie a dress for her first recording. They were married on 7 June 1923, the same year that 'Down Hearted Blues' blazed and launched her career. Soon Bessie hit the big time, becoming the highest-paid Black performer in the country.

'The thing about Bessie is that she was always herself. Some of us were always trying to be little stars, but not Bessie,' Alberta

Hunter declared. On stage, Bessie would favour ostentatious, glamorous outfits; as her wealth grew, she wore diamonds and ermine coats. But even if she was often known as outspoken and boisterous, rude and wild, she remained rooted, down-to-earth, generously spreading her wealth around by moving her family to Philadelphia. Jack was different. Money and fame went to his head. He wore fancy suits and developed airs and graces, not to mention a gambling problem. Leaving his job, he decided to take on the role of Bessie's manager, painting 'Jack Gee presents' across her promotional sign and travelling road train. As she went on tour, her gruelling schedule put a severe strain on their relationship.

Night after night, Bessie would shimmer on stage, alternating between crooning Blues to break your heart, and wisecracks and witticisms to make you laugh. Her troupe, Harlem Frolics, included seven young female chorus girls, some of whom started to catch her eye. In the *Inter-state Tatler*, a column gossiped about her liaison with fellow performer Gladys Bentley; Jack, who was illiterate, didn't spot it.

Bisexuality and gays were tolerated more in the Black Harlem community: there was a sense of unity between two groups ostracized by the white mainstream. 'Bulldiker' couples, as they were known pejoratively, were able to marry, if the 'male' lesbian of the couple adopted a man's name for their marriage licence. That said, there was also disapproval in more conservative circles, as when the popular Black newspaper *The Age* complained that female entertainers were 'extremely careless about their attitudes and actions in dancing'.

White men and women, who had to be more clandestine about their sexuality, sought out Harlem: hence the popularity of the expression 'slumming it in Harlem'. Middle- and upper-class whites would visit Harlem's bars, cabarets and clubs, seeking liberation and a sexual freedom that was compromised in their everyday lives. It's hard to look at this without acknowledging the idea that these privileged whites were seeking out the 'exotic' – it was, as Lillian Faderman terms it, a form of 'sexual colonialism'. The Cotton Club became a place where all-Black performers entertained an all-white audience. Bessie Smith and her troupe performed regularly at another popular haunt, the Lafayette Theatre. Same-sex relations occurred regularly between her dancers. The freewheeling lyrics of the Blues were one of the few places where same-sex passion could be explored. Ma Rainey, arrested for taking part in an orgy with multiple women, had to be bailed out of jail by Bessie. She ended up singing about the controversy in 'Prove It On Me Blues'. The record cover features Ma wearing a man's hat and being eyed up by a cop from a distance, with the eager caption beneath: *What's all this? Scandal?*

The lyrics included the defiant lines: 'Went out last night with a crowd of my friends/They must've been women, 'cause I don't like no men.' In 'Sissy Blues', she sang about a woman whose male lover was stolen by a 'sissy' man. And Bessie Smith's 'The Boy In the Boat' (1930) included, 'When you see two women walking hand in hand/Just look 'em over and try to understand/They'll go to those parties – have the lights down low/Only those parties where women can go.' These lyrics were daring for their time – and a provocative contrast to mainstream white music, which celebrated heterosexual love in an idealized, saccharine way. Bessie poured her own free-living ways into her songs, 'encouraging women of her class to drink, party and have sex as a means of alleviating the burden of everyday life'.

In 1926, Bessie heard from one of her dancers that Jack was being unfaithful. Bessie, who was prone to binge drinking, with a love of moonshine, got crazy on alcohol; she beat the woman up, threw her out and then went after Jack, shooting at him with his own gun. Bessie then sought revenge – or solace – in the arms of a young dancer called Lillian Simpson who had recently joined her troupe. Lillian was struggling with her newfound sexuality and one night she refused Bessie, which caused a fight, Bessie yelling, 'I got twelve women on this show and I can have one every night if I want it.' Lillian attempted suicide and was taken to hospital; as she recovered, she and Bessie took up their affair again. But it was short-lived, for Lillian was terrified that Jack would find out, putting her life in danger.

She left the troupe in 1927, and Bessie went off the rails. She had been sober during her affair with Lillian, but she did tend to seek out debauchery when her marriage was at a low ebb. Bessie took a group of dancers over to a buffet flat, an orgiastic party with a 'cafeteria' for sexualities of all hues. Later that night, she took another dancer, Marie, to bed with her: Jack burst in on them and came face to face – for the first time – with his wife's bisexuality. Their marriage spiralled into ever-more-violent jealousy and abuse. Whilst Bessie managed to hide from him that night, he turned up in her dressing room at her next show and knocked her to the ground with a punch, crying that after the show he'd be back for more: 'You ain't a man but you better be like one because we're gonna have it out.' The bitterness in those words – *you ain't a man* – is unmissable, so too the anger at her betraying him with a woman, acting the role he sees as his prerogative. Later that year, Bessie would record 'Foolish Man Blues', where she sings lyrics that sound close to home: 'Men sure deceitful, they getting worse every day', as well as the ironic lines, 'There's two things got me puzzled, there's two things I can't understand/That's a mannish actin' woman and a skippin', twisting, woman actin' man.' Their marriage ended when Bessie found out that Jack was using her money to fund a show by his mistress, Gertrude Saunders.

The Harlem Renaissance fell into decline as the Great Depression took hold. Black Americans were the first to lose their jobs, suffering two to three times more unemployment than Whites did. Now the arts were seen as an expensive indulgence that many couldn't afford, and the Blues were no longer in fashion; jazz and swing danced in to take their place. Bessie's 1929 song 'Nobody Knows You when You're Down and Out' seemed prophetic: as her record sales slipped, she stopped working with Columbia in 1931, though she carried on performing and making music. She found a steadier, more stable romantic partner in old friend Richard Morgan, an ex-bootlegger and Chicago club owner.

In September 1937, Richard was driving Bessie in Clarksdale, Mississippi, when they smashed into the back of a truck. She was thrown from the car, lost a huge amount of blood, her arm severed from the elbow; she was rushed to hospital and pronounced dead, only forty-three years old. Her funeral was a testament to her legend: a grand affair of 5,000 mourners, Bessie dressed in her coffin like an empress in a long silk gown and slippers.

Bessie's impact on music can be felt across the century, and we can trace it through the decades, from Elvis in the 1950s, to Billie Holiday in the 1960s, Janis Joplin the 1970s, and more recently, the soulful ache of Amy Winehouse lamenting a lost love in 'Back To Black', and Beyoncé's exploration of her partner's infidelity in her album *Lemonade*. As for the flourishing of Black bisexuality and queerness in the 1920s, it went back into the closet as America became more conservative in the 1930s and beyond. Campaigners for Black rights felt they had to hide their sexuality, fearing it would undermine the civil rights movement.

*

I wonder if the term ghosting refers to the person who ignores or the person who is left lost. Surely it's the latter, for you end up feeling ephemeral, unsubstantial, as if your lover has blown out a flame. Your messages could once carve emotions; now they are junk mail. A long week had passed and Clara had not replied to my emails, my texts. We had been dating for four months; this was an abrupt change in the rhythm and tone of our relationship. I buried myself in my writing, in imagined selves. I felt a perverse sympathy for my ex, Henry, on whom I had inflicted a similar suffering.

Finally, I went to her flat. I rang the bell and expected to be turned away. Her landlady informed me that she was in. There was a long wait whilst I stared at the rectangle of hallway; the length of stairs that she finally descended. Her 'Hi!' was breezy, as though nothing was wrong. But, instead of inviting me in, she suggested we go to the local café, as though I was no longer welcome in her private space.

It was almost as though nothing had happened, so relaxed was our chat on the way there, except that she wouldn't look me in the eye. Every time I glanced at her all I saw was profile.

As we sat down, I felt a cold fury. It was over: I could tell. Our tea was served. Clara sat still. I sighed and poured the Earl Grey into cups, bergamot lacing the air.

When I looked up, I was shocked to see tears streaming down her cheeks. Immediately, I felt them well up in my throat too, and all that was hard in me softened.

'I'm so sorry,' she swallowed. 'I just . . . can't . . .'

I was nodding, in sympathy despite my pain, until she began mumbling about someone else, about meeting a 'man' – *a man?*

'But,' I said in confusion. 'You're a lesbian.'

She had been a lesbian for the past four months with me.

'Bi – I think I'm bi, actually,' she asserted, with too much conviction, and for a moment, my tears turned to laughter at the irony of the situation, the reversal from our courtship. Now I was the one who felt as though I could never be with a man again.

'My dad likes Mark,' she faltered.

The cross hanging on her neck, still against her skin.

'Oh God,' I said. 'Your dad . . . did he find out about us?'

'No,' she protested, but I could tell she was holding back.

Eventually, she revealed it: her father had hinted that he felt something was wrong. She had never brought a boyfriend home, and he wondered why. Then he had complained bitterly about a friend's daughter, who 'went off with a woman', and what a selfish, crazed, immoral 'Sodom and Gomorrah' act that was. There had been a subtext to his words: don't turn out that way. Don't let me down. And Clara, given a choice between romance and her family, love and duty, had chosen to keep the peace, even if it meant lying to herself and everyone.

3

Marlene Dietrich

A few months after I broke up with Clara I was sitting in a café writing in a notebook when I heard David Bowie's 'Hallo Spaceboy' come on. It was one of those moments where you feel, with perfect, sympathetic synchronicity, that your thoughts have been translated into lyrics.

'Do you like girls or boys?/It's confusing these days . . .'

It was confusing, these days. The guy in the coffee shop who had served me my Earl Grey had attempted to flirt with me. I'd given him a polite smile but failed to engage. He was attractive – tall, with dark, curly hair – but I'd felt nothing for him. I wondered if I was misattributing the natural numbness that follows a break-up, if the death of my attraction to men was simply part of my grief. And yet: I was not without desire. Women were still catching my eye. I would see a swirl of dark hair, blue eyes, and feel a leap inside; though perhaps I was merely seeking Clara's double. Had I become a lesbian? Discovered my true nature? If so, then my past needed to be rewritten, but the narrative wouldn't hold: there was pleasure with men that I hadn't faked, happiness that had been true. Perhaps it was simply the case that Clara had converted me. I laughed at the thought of what her father would make of that.

A few more months on, I was watching a young man in a park, walking his dog, and became aware that I was admiring the curve of his skull, the muscles in his body that rippled as he tossed a ball.

Fantasies clouded my mind for the rest of the day. I did like boys and I did like girls and it was confusing.

I was reverting to my natural state; I attempted to make sense of what had happened. I considered the obsessive, passionate streak in my personality. When I was absorbed in writing a book, I fell in love with it, woke in the night with ideas fireworking my mind, adored the torture of polishing prose and editing. I considered Will Self's experience of writing *Dorian*, a modern reworking of Wilde's classic novel; he'd been so influenced and inspired that he'd felt gay throughout the process. I had been so fascinated by newfound feelings for women that they had consumed me. Sexuality reflects personality; and I didn't do anything by halves.

Years later, I saw Clara one last time. She was crossing the road, her arm linked through a man's, and surprise came over her face as she spotted me. I gave her a smile; she replied with one that was faint at first, and then full, before passing on. I stood on the pavement and watched her go, disappearing into the swirl of crowds.

It's confusing these days: Bowie had been my consolation during that period of heartbreak. His pose on the cover of *Hunky Dory* – palms cradling his long-haired, androgynous pulchritude – was inspired by a Marlene Dietrich photo-book he took with him to the shoot; as the Thin White Duke, his silhouette echoed Dietrich's famous pose.

Marlene Dietrich was one of the most successful film stars of the 1930s and 1940s, celebrated for her acting, music and style. Images of Dietrich light up my laptop. Most of the photos are black-and-white, capturing her elegant, sultry beauty, the languor of her heavy-lidded eyes and rosebud mouth. Her face is veiled by black lace; haloed by fair locks; framed by a series of hats, from luxury fur to a sailor's cap to a beret. Dietrich vetted every picture released of her. Her beauty was both natural and contrived. She learnt exactly how camera lighting would accentuate every hollow and curve and bone in her face. Film crews observed that she would stand under a light, lick her finger, hold it up and know from its heat if it was the requisite distance away, so that the light and shadows would fall in the correct chiaroscuro pattern to capture her exquisiteness. At one point she had her molars removed so that her cheeks would sink in further.

By the end of 1930, Dietrich was one of the most famous movie stars in the world. She would sometimes refer to herself in the third person, regarding her persona as a lifelong portrait that she added layer upon layer to year after year. She cultivated mystery as part of her allure; it wreaths her pictures like cigarette smoke from an elegant holder. 'Each man or woman should be able to find in the actress the thing he or she most desires and still be left with the promise that they will find something new and exciting every time they see her again . . .' she declared.

Yet this devotion to shaping her image meant that she was the ultimate unreliable narrator, willing to fictionalize parts of her life if it would enhance her legend. It makes her an elusive figure. Her daughter, Maria Riva, published a lengthy biography that portrayed her as a monster. Cocteau said that Dietrich was 'the most exciting and terrifying woman I have ever known'. Hemingway declared that 'she knew more about love than anyone'. Fritz Lang complained that 'her whole life is built on a grand illusion.' Erich Maria Remarque captured her contradictions when he said that she was a 'steel orchid'.

One of her most iconic onscreen moments is that scene in *Morocco* (1930), where she performed one of the first ever female-to-female kisses shown on a Hollywood screen. When I saw it, a year after things ended with Clara – no longer seeing Clara everywhere but experiencing the occasional jolt of reminder – something in her elegance and bravado seemed to catch my ex's quiddity. Dietrich plays Amy Jolly, a wandering cabaret singer with a shady past who ends up on the shores of North Africa. She first meets her main love interest, légionnaire Tom Brown, when she performs at a nightclub. And what a performance it is: iconic, daring, career-defining, gender-bending. Dietrich saunters on stage in a black tuxedo with a spotless white shirt and bow-tie. She looks the epitome of both masculinity and femininity: her face so beautiful it looks like a sculpture, her lips a perfect rosebud, her hair falling from her top hat in blonde waves; yet her tough, cool swagger assuming the power and confidence associated with men in this era. She croons 'Quand l'amour meurt' – a song traditionally sung by a man. Her charisma is dazzling, her voice sultry and she performs with the classic Dietrich verve that became her trademark; an insolent detachment, a cool carefreeness.

Her audience is hot, restless, sneery. At first their reaction is hostile. But then Amy approaches a group at a table, steals a gardenia flower from one of the women, sniffs it provocatively and plants a kiss on her lips. The audience is won over: there are cheers and applause. The woman blushes, ducks her head behind her fluttering fan. We see a close-up of Tom Brown, played by Gary Cooper; he looks aroused and amused. Amy strolls over and gives him the flower in playful courtship. The scene apparently concludes on a heterosexual note, the female kiss a flirtation on the path to the two lovers discovering each other.

How did the kiss get past the Hollywood censors? The film came out pre Hays Code – a set of censorship rules that came into play during the early 1930s, which laid down guidelines for movie producers, ensuring that film plots were shaped by moral ideals and represented more conversative values. However, *Morocco* was still daring by the standards of the era, and it may have slipped through due to its metafictional context. Dietrich was playing a character playing a role; the theatre gave the kiss several layers of remove. Some LGBT viewers today find the scene offensive, feeling that Dietrich's ground-breaking 'lesbian' kiss is undermined because it is performative, a display to titillate a man. But I'd say the kiss is not lesbian, but bisexual, and the scene is more complex than a mere act of performative bisexuality. It is daring on so many levels because it subverts the gender norms of the time. The flower that Amy gives Tom ends up tucked behind his ear, self-consciously subverting traditional male/female roles. Amy not only seizes the active role, the man's, she forces her male love interest to play the passive, female role. It's a scene where Amy has all the power.

The kiss was Dietrich's idea. Her daughter claimed she did it to shock puritanical America; Dietrich once observed that, 'In America, sex is an obsession, in other parts of the world it's a fact.' Her director, Josef von Sternberg, based her costume on the tuxedos he had seen her wear in Germany, back in their Berlin days in the 1920s, when Dietrich had often frequented drag balls and cabarets in male dress. The plot of *Morocco*, like many of von Sternberg's films, explores an uneven love affair: a beloved and a lover. Amy is the lover in this case, ensnared in a love triangle, chasing after the womanizing Tom in passionate devotion. The film builds to a finale in the desert where she kicks off her heels and follows after him. And yet this ending is undermined by the earlier scene in the nightclub. It is such a strong moment that it lingers in the mind, its ambiguity suggesting undercurrents of possibility, as though Amy's devotion to him could easily be diffused, should an intriguing woman catch her eye . . .

*

Dietrich lived a daring life as a passionate bisexual woman. Like the writer Anaïs Nin, she enjoyed love affairs with women during the 1930s, but Dietrich had to deal with greater challenges given that she was perpetually in the limelight. Her female lovers included Edith Piaf, Mercedes de Acosta; her male ones John Wayne, Maurice Chevalier, James Stewart, Cary Grant, Gary Cooper, Frank Sinatra. As Chris Hunt, who made a documentary about her, observed: 'It seems she didn't two-time people. She ten-timed them.' She referred to her female Hollywood lovers as her 'sewing circle', whilst the men were her 'Alumni Association'. She was daring enough to favour male dress when she was out on the town or at business meetings, declaring, 'I am at heart a gentleman.' On one occasion in 1933, she caused a scandal in Paris by wearing a trouser suit at a time when it was illegal for women to wear trousers.

Josef von Sternberg – who she made seven films with – argued that her bisexuality was a crucial part of her appeal as an actress. But whilst Dietrich was a trailblazer who provided inspiration to many in her cross-dressing and her unashamed bisexuality, she was never able overtly to declare her sexuality, playing the Hollywood game whilst pushing boundaries as far as she could. In her desire to maintain a carefully crafted image, she later denied some of her affairs with men and women, or that she was even bi, which means that many of the stories about her love life are told – and therefore shaped – by others rather than Dietrich herself. On the one hand, she behaved as a feminist, carving out a successful career in a male-dominated industry, metaphorically – and literally – wearing the trousers that were frowned on for women; on the other, she reflected the chauvinistic era she was brought up in, declaring that men had superior intellects and wishing she had been born a man.

A 2000 piece in the *Irish Times* declared that Dietrich seemed never to have experienced 'a grand passion or to have sought a relationship of permanence with any of her very many lovers, and consequently, though she was often openly homosexual she did not have to go through the disguises and repressions suffered by so many gay people in Hollywood'. I disagree with the phrase 'openly homosexual' – Dietrich was clearly bisexual, and therefore casting judgement on her for escaping 'disguises and repressions' is odd: the subtext seems to be that her bisexuality was a frivolous get-out clause, as opposed to her being a serious, suffering lesbian. That assertion, that she had never experienced a grand passion, lingered as I dug into my research, wondering if this was true: did her love affairs have depth or were they superficial? A dance from woman to man and back again, as she played a careful balancing act of maintaining her stardom in the press whilst also protecting her reputation? Was this true of her affairs with both men and women: were there any differences between them, and how did this play out in power relations?

She was born in 1901, in Schöneberg, Berlin, the same district where David Bowie and Iggy Pop would later reside when Bowie's *Low* album was being conceived. Her birth name was Maria Magdalene; her family called her Leni. Around the age of eleven she changed her name, compressing its duet into Marlene, practising her new signature in her schoolbooks. The name was purely her invention: nobody was called this at the time.

Marlene's mother, Wilhelmina Elisabeth Josefine Felsing, was from a family of wealthy clockmakers who disapproved of Josefine's marriage to Louis Erich Otto Dietrich, a Prussian police officer. He died when Marlene was very young. She had an older sister, Elisabeth; both were subjected to a controlled, rigid upbringing. Their mother, obsessed with discipline and punctuality, was nicknamed 'the good General'. Josefine remarried, this time into a more illustrious family: Eduard von Losch was a high-ranking army officer. He died soon after their marriage, killed in the First World War.

It's sometimes argued that the First World War led to a flourishing of lesbianism/bisexuality in the 1920s because so many men were killed. It's true to say that women outnumbered men as a result, but the implication of this theory is that women were desperate and explored same-sex relationships as some sort of compensatory second-best. The aftermath of war meant Marlene grew up in an environment surrounded by women; the only men she knew in childhood were 'old or ill, not real men'. However, I doubt Marlene's bisexuality was rooted in this. (I grew up in a household of men, with two brothers and their friends filling the house, but this did not mean I was attracted solely to men.) Rather, the war gave people who had previously been isolated a chance to connect as they worked together as volunteers, nurses and so on, releasing women from the confines of the domestic sphere – and releasing urges that might otherwise have been repressed.

The war led Marlene to reflect on the power imbalance of the sexes. She observed that German women 'did not seem to suffer in a world without men. Our life among women had become such a pleasant habit that the prospect that men might return . . . disturbed us – men who would again take the scepter in their hands and again become lords of their households.' Later in life, Marlene told one of her lovers that as a child, her mother sometimes called her by a boy's name, Paulus. It was an affectionate game between them, but Marlene also reflected that, 'I wanted to take the father's place —against my mother's will.' From an early age, she had a strong 'masculine' side, a desire for autonomy, freedom and control, appreciating the 'structure' that her mother's rule gave her whilst also kicking against it. Of course, these ideas of masculinity and femininity sound much like painful stereotypes today, but they were alive in Marlene's day and governed the way she thought about gender and her sense of self, just as they influenced Colette and Anaïs Nin.

Marlene became conscious of the power of her beauty as her adolescence blossomed; her schoolfriends referred to her seductive 'bedroom eyes', which she tested out on her teachers, causing one male teacher to be dismissed when he responded with enthusiasm. Her diary was filled with crushes, passionately felt and discarded with all the volatility of a teenager. At the age of sixteen, she wrote entry after entry detailing her adoration for Countess Gersdorf, a (married) friend of the family: 'I am dying of love for her, she is beautiful like an angel . . . it's really passion, deep deep love.' Marlene kissed her hand and flirted with her; the countess clearly enjoyed the flattery. Once again, Marlene's developing sexuality was entwined with a desire to occupy a male role – 'if she weren't married, I would do anything to win her heart and get her before her Count Gersdorf. Even now, I'd like to be him.' Perhaps the wish came from her awareness of love's subjugation, for she felt she wanted to 'obey' the countess like a dog; to be her husband would put her into a role of power and authority over her loved one. Trying to understand the nature of her new feelings, she reflected, 'Love suffers, tolerates, hopes' and without naming it as such, she recognizes her bisexual nature: 'It is the kind of love I could feel for a man.' Very quickly, however, her crush faded. Marlene fell for the female movie star Henny Porten, keeping her picture in her locket, leaving the countess a little dismayed.

Teachers also stirred desire in her. Marguerite Breguand, her French teacher, inspired Marlene to imitate her hair and dress. Her mother, nervous of Marlene's flirtatious nature, sent her to a boarding school in Weimar, where Marlene had violin lessons with Professor Reitz and wore sheer chiffon to her classes. Although Marlene's liaison with him has meant she is sometimes portrayed as a young femme fatale in biographies, the diary entries she penned at this time illustrate how desperately lonely she was. Sent away from her family, missing her sister, she felt that 'all those I loved so much have forgotten me . . . I am so unhappy because I don't have anybody who loves me. I am so used to being loved.' Eventually she lost her virginity to her teacher after the Christmas holiday in 1920. It was an anticlimactic event: 'He groaned, heaved, panted. Didn't even take his trousers off. I just lay there on that old settee, the red plush scratching my behind, my skirts over my head. The whole thing, *very* uncomfortable.'

Her mother brought her back to Berlin, where postwar life had left a capital fractured and dangerous, with beggars and maimed soldiers wandering the streets, inflation insane and prostitution rife. Marlene's promising career as a violinist was cut short when she suffered a wrist injury; there are conflicting accounts as to whether the injury was fictitious or genuine, faked by Marlene to wriggle out of the career her mother had chosen for her or a tragic loss of potential. Either way, it paved the way for the career Marlene really wanted to pursue: acting.

The historian Robert Beachy has noted that we tend to associate the birth of LGBT liberation with New York and London, with the Mattachine Society – often cited as the first American gay rights organization, which was set up in Los Angeles in 1950 – and the Stonewall riots of 1969, where six days of clashes between the police and LGBT protestors led to a seminal shift in consciousness about queer rights.

In fact, it all began in Germany, back in the middle of the nineteenth century, with a brave gay man called Karl Heinrich Ulrichs. In 1867 he became the first gay man to make a public speech championing gay rights, standing before the Congress of German Jurists in Munich, calling on them to repeal the penal code that punished and persecuted homosexuals. His bravery is to be applauded, for he carried on asserting that it was unfair to persecute 'a class of persons' in whom 'nature has planted a sexual nature that is the opposite of that which is usual', before jeers and shouts of 'Stop!' and 'Crucify!' forced him off stage. As we know from Wilde's trial, the common word used to describe homosexuals at this time was 'sodomite'; Ulrichs coined the terms *urning* for a gay man, *urinden* for lesbians, *dionings* for heterosexuals and therefore *urano-dionings* for bisexuals. He drew them from Plato's *Symposium*, where Pausanias makes a speech about the origins of same-sex/opposite attraction; *urnings* and *dionings* are named after two origin myths for Aphrodite; *urnings* from the myth that Cronus castrated Uranus, throwing his testicles into the sea, from which Aphrodite Urania was born; *dionings* from Aphrodite Dionea, daughter of Zeus and Dione, emblematic of earthly love.

By arguing that same-sex attraction was innate, and designating gay people as a distinct group, Ulrichs was a big influence on the German physician and sexologist Magnus Hirschfeld, another key champion of gay rights. Hirschfeld opened his Institute for Sexual Science in Berlin in 1919, which offered sex education, health clinics, and research on gender and sexuality. As a medical student, he had been appalled to witness a gay man paraded naked before the class, verbally abused as a degenerate. Sympathetic to homosexuals, gays, bisexuals and trans, Hirschfeld declared that 'Love is as varied as people are.' Weimar Berlin became the gay capital of the world as the 1920s unfolded, notorious as a city of 'divine decadence', as Sally Bowles in *Cabaret* famously described it. It was a city of the glorious and the nefarious, gangsters and artists, of high inflation and high creativity, of huge gains in arts and science and a thriving film industry in the form of the government-sponsored UFA, which resulted in cinematic classics such as *The Cabinet of Dr Caligari*, *Metropolis* and *Nosferatu*. Berlin is 'the most lurid Underworld of all cities, where the German . . . enjoys obscenity in a form which even the Parisian would not tolerate', said the English gentleman crook Netley Lucas. Thus, queerness and bisexuality came to be associated with decadence and dissolution; rights were not so far advanced that gay couples could marry and build lives together, but they could certainly visit the 400-odd bars and cabarets listed in tourist notebooks according to sexuality. One famous bar which Dietrich liked to frequent was called the Eldorado. There starred acts such as Anita Berber, who would perform in nothing but a fur coat and heels, a pet monkey at her neck and her cocaine in a locket. Androgyny was celebrated; one performer, upon being asked what her gender was, replied: 'Whatever you want it to be.' Our perception of Berlin's golden era, however, is poignant, foreshadowed by the horrors that would come in the next decade under Nazi rule. Soon the lesbian and gay clubs would be closed down. Soon the Eldorado would become the SA (*Sturmabteilung*) headquarters.

It was against this backdrop of liberation and dissolution that Marlene spent a decade developing as an actress and performer and exploring her bisexuality. She took a wide range of jobs: a showgirl in a chorus line, a legs model, bit parts in theatre that gradually became bigger parts. She starred in nearly twenty silent films (which she later denied and disowned), looking very different from the glamorous blonde icon we know today, appearing with dark hair, a little chubby, unpolished. In one theatre show, *It's In the Air*, she performed alongside Margo Lion, a French chanteuse who was openly bisexual. They sang 'When My Best Girlfriend' in a flirty duet, playing young married women shopping for lingerie. Marlene had the idea of pinning violets to their costumes (a flower associated with Sapphic love) to make the act even more provocative.

Marlene liked to frequent gay bars and drag balls, often sporting a tux and a monocle that had once belonged to her father. One of her early lovers was a feminist intellectual called Gerda Huber, whom she lived with for a time. One friend at the time remarked that Marlene told him she was 'much more interested – although not exclusively – in women', and when she desired a man she 'showered him with sweetness – but any direct offer would have to come from her', suggesting that with men, she was already turning the tables and putting herself in a position of power.

Rudi Sieber was a blond, handsome assistant casting director Marlene met when she was auditioning for the film *Tragedy of Love*. They were married in 1923 and the following year she gave birth to a daughter, Maria (there is speculation as to whether Rudi was her father or not). Marlene, who observed at the time 'it had been instilled in me . . . that a woman's role is to complete the home with children', was a loving mother to her baby, though, later on, their relationship would fray. But she was not the conventional wife Rudi was expecting. Although she loved him with a passion, she was not willing to compromise her nature. She remained wilful, carefree, selfish and a rebel. Only two weeks after their marriage, she fell for a woman she met when auditioning for a Bjørnstjerne Bjørnson play, *When the Young Vine Blooms*. Rudi did not react well; he took to accompanying Marlene to her theatre performances, waiting for her backstage to chaperone her home. Before long, however, Marlene had her way. The relationship became an open one, sustained by the fact that Rudi loved her so deeply, caring about her happiness above his own. Marlene showed him letters from her other lovers and confided in him about her affairs, whilst Rudi also took a mistress, a woman called Tamara Matul whom he ended up living with. Tamara was publicly referred to as his secretary or Maria's nanny at various times.

This unconventional union has helped to feed into the myth of Marlene being rather shallow and careless in her love affairs. In part, I wonder if this is monogamous judgement being cast on a polyamorous couple, along the lines of 'If they had affairs, their relationship can't have had depth.' In fact, it did have depth and soul as well as shadows and compromises and tragedies. Marlene reflected on how passionately she adored Rudi, to whom she remained married for the next five decades and whom she called 'the perfect husband'. As Otto Preminger, a theatre director she worked with, observed, she was a 'free spirit'. That said, Marlene would also use her marriage as a foil against lovers wanting to pin her down, which is not the same as wanting to keep lovers at a distance. She enjoyed intimacy and intensity, but it was not in her nature to commit solely to one person.

*

In 1929, Marlene went for an audition that would change her life. Josef von Sternberg, a well-respected Austrian-born director, was searching for a female star for his forthcoming film *The Blue Angel* – Germany's first feature-length 'talking' film. He attended the theatre to see the play *Two Neckties*. When he saw Marlene on stage, he was struck by her beauty and cool disdain for the farce she was appearing in, her not-giving-a-damn allure that concealed an icy passion.

Marlene auditioned for von Sternberg, UFA producer Erich Pommer and Emil Jannings, already attached to the film as a male star. She was asked to remove her hat and pace the room ('like some horse!' Marlene later complained to her husband). She moved, von Sternberg recalled, with 'bovine listlessness'. Pommer and Jannings were not impressed. Pommer had already objected to her casting, saying, 'Not that whore!' (It is ambiguous as to whether he was referring to her private life or her films.) But von Sternberg was convinced that she was his star. Following a successful screen test, Marlene got the part. She would play Lola Lola, the showgirl who performs cabaret at the sleazy club the Blue Angel. One day the prim and proper Professor sees her act and falls in love with her, eventually marrying her, but Lola Lola treats him with nonchalant cruelty, leading to his downfall, the loss of his career, and eventually his total destruction. The Wall Street Crash had just occurred and the film captures the erratic, nervy mood of a country terrified of hyperinflation. It is also a critique on the excesses of Weimar's debauchery, the consequences of human relationships and commitments frayed in favour of hedonism, capturing both its allure and its dissolution.

From the moment she got the part, Marlene reflected, 'Von Sternberg had only one idea in his head: to take me away from the stage and to make a movie actress out of me, to "Pygmalionize" me.' However, whilst Pygmalion breathed life into the female statue he created, in some respects von Sternberg performed the reverse on Marlene, helping to shape her as the star whose beauty, staged and carefully lit to perfection, was almost statuesque. Declaring that his actors were 'marionettes, pieces of colour [on] my canvas', he would give Marlene precise instructions as to where she should stand, walk, talk, pause. She had to work in total submission to him.

But Marlene was not just a doll, manipulated for his fantasies.

Their relationship was collaborative. Each was a muse to the other, challenging, flinging down 'artist's gauntlets like duellists'. Von Sternberg would go on to make seven films with Dietrich and each of the characters he created was directly inspired by his infatuation with her, a melding and blending of fact and fiction, her character and his imaginative fantasy.

As filming on *The Blue Angel* unfolded, it became clear that Marlene was stealing the show with her charisma, becoming the star over Jannings. A key aspect of her allure was her bisexuality. Von Sternberg felt that when actresses had lesbian affairs, they 'exerted a powerful androgynous magnetism through the camera's lens, attracting the unwitting desires of both men and women in the audience as they watched through the dim, smoky air of a movie house'. In 1932 Ruth Biery, writing in *Photoplay*, observed that Hollywood 'had created a new woman, a different type of heroine – mysterious, glamorous, possessed of a subtle combination of both feminine and masculine characteristics'. It was a sentiment that came to be echoed later in the century, when androgyny and bisexuality became fashionable once again, epitomized in artists such as David Bowie and Lady Gaga. Theatre critic Kenneth Tynan observed that Marlene Dietrich 'has sex, but no particular gender. She has the bearing of a man; the characters she plays love power and wear trousers. Her masculinity appeals to women and her sexuality to men.' And: 'Marlene lives in a sexual no man's land – and no woman's either.'

The 'no man's land' is an interesting image. Androgyny can sometimes be seen as that liminal place where masculinity and femininity are melded into a compromise, not quite one nor the other. With Marlene, both aspects of her gender were turned up to full volume, both richly colourful. She would appear in films in both stereotypical extremes, sporting the most voluptuously seductive feminine outfits, lace and frills and feathers, alternating with tuxedos and top hats. Later in life, following her Hollywood career,

Marlene toured as a successful cabaret performer. She would appear in a sheer dress during the first half of her act and sport a tuxedo during the second half, for 'There are just certain songs that a woman can't sing as a woman, so by dressing in tails I can sing songs written for men.' Her daughter recalled that: 'In her glitter dress, she sang to men; in her tails, to women.'

The Blue Angel premiered in Berlin on 31 March 1930: an instant roaring success. Paramount had already offered Dietrich a deal before the film's release, inspired by the buzz around her and seeking their equivalent to Greta Garbo. Immediately after the premier, Dietrich boarded the SS *Bremen* and left for New York for the start of a new chapter in her life, leaving her daughter and husband behind. On the boat over, she attempted to seduce Bianca Stroock, who was married to the owner of an American theatrical costume company. Dietrich had a fresh bunch of violets delivered to her each morning; sending flowers was becoming a common flirtation technique for her. She invited Bianca into her cabin and showed her an illustrated book about lesbian lovemaking. 'In Europe it doesn't matter if you're a man or a woman,' Dietrich told her, in a failed seduction attempt. 'We make love with anyone we find attractive.'

Arriving in the US, she missed her family deeply. She phoned them every day, writing passionate letters to Rudi, making recordings on 'thin celluloid records' for him and her daughter that were full of yearning: 'I walk around this beautiful house and you are nowhere to be found.' Dietrich found America a puritanical place, and she wasn't averse to pushing boundaries there and shaking things up. Americans, she discovered, were conservative about female clothing. 'The feeling is that no man looks at a woman in trousers,' she wrote to Rudi. Dietrich soon set about changing this. She attended a party wearing a navy blouse, white flannel trousers and a yachting cap. Von Sternberg took a photograph and

Paramount printed pictures with the slogan *The Woman Even Women Can Adore*. By 1936 she was the highest-paid actress in the world.

But Dietrich's adventurous love life also threatened her celebrity image at times. She found herself in trouble when von Sternberg's wife launched a legal case against her, blaming Dietrich for their divorce. Dietrich was shaken. There was a 'morality' clause in her Paramount contract, which was typical for Hollywood in this era, a way of controlling actors and making sure they weren't too wild in their private lives. Dietrich publicly denied the allegations – although the truth was that she was von Sternberg's lover. Rudi and Maria came over to the US to help establish Dietrich's image as a loving wife, a loving mother.

Initially Paramount had been keen to market and promote her as a mysterious character; they hadn't wanted her to reveal she had a child, 'a completely new concept for a Hollywood glamour star', which incensed Dietrich. Dietrich had her way, pushing boundaries once again by marketing herself as both a femme fatale onscreen and a madonna-style figure offscreen. It was a public persona that allowed her to be seen as a complex woman, just as, later on, she would resist the ageism surrounding female actresses in Hollywood and play sexy roles in her later forties, before eventually marketing herself as 'The World's Most Glamorous Grandmother' when her daughter gave birth. By crafting an image of herself as a married woman, she managed to deflect press attention, maintaining a certain purity whilst also attracting the gossip columnists by going out on the town with her new love interests, such as Gary Cooper and Maurice Chevalier. (Paramount would claim they were business meetings.) In 1933 she rarely bothered with traditional female clothing, opting to dress stylishly in trousers and sport slouch hats.

Maurice Chevalier objected to her clothes. He felt it was all too much: as a married man, he was already risking his reputation by having a mistress. He gave Dietrich an ultimatum. She refused, choosing her freedom and her own dress choices, a pattern that repeated again and again throughout her life as she refused to let lovers pin down or control her.

Marlene had many love affairs with women. In his memoir, Klaus Kinski recalled how Marlene seduced his girlfriend, Edith Edwards, with lurid detail: 'Marlene tore down Edith's panties backstage in a Berlin theatre and, using just her mouth, brought Edith to orgasm.' One of her other famous affairs was with the Hollywood screenwriter and poet Mercedes de Acosta. They met at a dance concert hosted by Harald Kreutzberg. Mercedes was a tall, striking Spanish woman with very pale skin and dark hair, whom the actress Tallulah Bankhead nicknamed Countess Dracula. When they were introduced, Marlene was captivated. She visited Mercedes the next day, taking a huge bouquet of white roses, playing with the petals in an echo of her role as Amy Jolly in *Morocco*. Marlene, who liked to nurture her lovers, observed that, 'You seem so thin and your face [is] so white', saying that she wanted to cook for her so that 'she got well and strong'. And, in words that remind me of her teenage diary entry about Professor Reitz, where she recorded her loneliness, she said to Mercedes: 'I felt you were very sad . . . I am sad, too. I am sad and lonely.' In a letter to her husband, Marlene reflected that, 'For me, she was a relief from this narrow Hollywood mentality.' It captures Marlene's feelings of alienation in a country where she was both revered and a stranger, struggling with a culture that was very different from her homeland's.

They exchanged love letters. They wrote to each other in green ink, sharing love poetry. Mercedes wrote a poem for Marlene – 'You are the essence of the stars/and moon and the mystery of the night' – and Marlene translated 'Portrait' by Rainer Maria Rilke, her favourite poet. Marlene sent Mercedes so many bouquets that she recorded that 'the house became a sort of madhouse of flowers' and had to gently ask her to stop. Soon they were spending part of the week together, hiking in the Pacific Palisades, driving to Santa Barbara beach for lunch. Marlene tidied her house, baked for her and they hosted small dinner parties together. It was a relationship of tenderness and passion.

Many of Marlene's friends observed that she seemed to favour women over men. Bernard Hall, her secretary, said that, 'She always admitted to me that she preferred women to men. She said, "When you go to bed with a woman, it is less important. Men are a hassle."' And Marlene's daughter made the observation that she weaponized sex with men – 'it was a way of controlling and manipulating them', whilst her affairs with women were more warm and tender: 'She actually enjoyed the sex and the relationships were much more satisfying to her.' The American biographer Donald Spoto suggested that it was easier at this time for two female lovers in Hollywood to live together. As we've seen, laws at the time revolved around homosexuality, not lesbianism. Two women could name their relationship a 'Boston marriage' and pretend it was a simple friendship. For men it was harder. Spoto cites the example of Cary Grant and Randolph Scott, who shared a beach house at the weekends for years but were eventually given an ultimatum by RKO – one of the big studios at the time - who demanded Grant choose either his career or his love life. But I'm not sure that it was much easier for women to live together in the long term. Marlene once said, 'You can't *live* with a woman', a statement with two meanings – that women were harder to date, and also that society would never have approved. Could Marlene and Mercedes have lived together for decades and maintained the pretence; could Marlene have maintained her star appeal? It seems less likely. Marlene managed to get away with her bisexual affairs in part because they did not usually last a long time. She declared, 'I haven't a strong sense of possession towards a man. Perhaps because I am not particularly feminine in my reactions. I never have been.'

If we fast-forward several years to 1940, and consider how things progressed for Marlene and Mercedes, then we see how Hollywood steered women towards heterosexuality. Mercedes, aged forty-six, found herself floundering, for 'a woman of only moderate talent . . . needed a husband, lavender [gay] or otherwise, or a male lover in high places to push and protect her.' For Marlene, too, men had been vital in shaping her career; early on in her relationship with Rudi, he had helped her to get parts and publicity. Marlene was a woman who was deeply ambitious and passionate about her career; she would not have wanted to wreck it. She was certainly prepared to push boundaries, to take risks, but she was also very conscious of playing the Hollywood game, and that meant that marriage to a man was a vital cover.

The Hays Code, introduced in 1930, dictated that 'no picture shall be produced which will lower the moral standards of those who see it'. This was the brainchild of Will H. Hays, a Republican politician who became President of the Motion Picture Producers and Distributors of America. Public concern about the messages that films were giving out, the way they were impacting the morals of the population, was gaining momentum, particularly amongst religious and Catholic groups. Written by a Catholic layman, Martin Quigley, and a Jesuit priest, Father Daniel A. Lord, the code was a list of rules about sex and violence – sexual 'perversions' such as homosexuality were banned, as was lustful kissing. Adultery should not be justified or presented attractively, childbirth was banned, and morals should be present, like a watermark, in plotlines that should promote wholesome American values – i.e. the family, the heterosexual white couple, though even then they were not allowed to be seen sleeping in the same bed.

Until 1934, it wasn't strictly enforced. And so films like Dietrich's *Morocco* slipped through, as did *Mädchen in Uniform*, a 1931 movie by one of the first female directors, Leontine Sagan, which tenderly explored a lesbian love affair; while in 1933's *Queen Christina*, Greta Garbo plays a bisexual ruler who likes wearing men's clothes, being called King, and has three romantic interests, including one with a countess whom she kisses onscreen.

In 1934 came the clampdown. Joseph Breen, a staunch Catholic, became head of the PAC, the Production Administration Code, which dispensed a certificate of approval to all films before their release. Their office vetted scripts before the films were made, making suggestions to sanitize and simplify them, often with disastrous artistic effect. As a result, actresses like Anna May Wong were unable to get parts as the main love interest opposite a male lead, due to the ban on interracial relations. Complex female characters were simplified or punished for their transgressions – as critic David Denby sums up: 'For years few adulterous women managed to escape such calamities as prostitution or losing a child or driving off a cliff.' It meant that feisty Mae West, a box-office queen who often played bad girls, was soon replaced by demure and innocent Shirley Temple. Queer and bi characters could not be shown as sympathetic and so they appeared as drag queens, child molesters, villains or cowards. Consider the Lion in *The Wizard of Oz*, who is a 'sissy' (the implication being that he is gay) and who is also a coward. Some critics argue this trend later influenced films such as *Basic Instinct*, featuring Sharon Stone as a bisexual sociopath, or the trans villain in *The Silence of the Lambs*. The flipside of this was that bisexuality might also be whitewashed out of films: *Alexander the Great*, the 1956 epic starring Richard Burton, portrays him as straight.

For Dietrich's career, the code was fatal. She had built her career as a seductive, mysterious, transgressive star with androgynous appeal. Von Sternberg had cast her time and time again as a dangerous femme fatale. Now her films – and von Sternberg's artistic vision – were terribly compromised. One film that the code succeeded in wrecking was *The Devil Is a Woman* (1935), where Marlene played Concha Pérez, a seductress in a story of erotic bedazzlement. The themes and complexities that von Sternberg and Dietrich had explored in their earlier films were no longer permissible. The censors, upon reading the script, wanted to punish Dietrich's sexy character, suggesting she become a 'scrawny, impoverished hag' by the end of the film, and that her love interest could choke her to death in its finale. The film was cut from ninety-three to seventy-six minutes and was a terrible critical and commercial flop. Decades later it was reassessed by critics and received late recognition as a strange, complex and superb film.

Following the film's flop, her collaboration with von Sternberg came to an end. She was labelled 'box office poison' in a now-infamous advertisement by Henry Brandt, who named and shamed various Hollywood stars who had lost their bankability. Her career seemed to be over. Then she enjoyed one of the greatest comebacks in cinema history with the 1939 western *Destry Rides Again*, starring opposite James Stewart. She mocked her previous incarnation as an impervious, icily beautiful goddess, playing a role that was much more likeable, accessible and down-to-earth. So were many of her roles in the 1940s, but she never quite recaptured the complexity of her female heroines from the decade before.

*

Whilst she was a star in the US, Dietrich was no longer loved in her homeland. The Nazis banned a number of her films, condemning *The Blue Angel* and *Dishonoured*. Her work was included in the Nazis' *Entartete Musik* exhibition, a public display of what the regime saw as 'Degenerate Music', held in Düsseldorf in 1938. It followed on – like some dreadful sequel – from their exhibition of Degenerate Art in 1937 in Munich. Marlene Dietrich's rendition of 'Falling In Love Again', written by Friedrich Hollaender, came to be one of the most iconic songs of her career. The Nazis had it playing out over the speakers in condemnation because it was written by a Jew. The poster for the exhibition featured a racist caricature of a Black jazz musician playing a saxophone with a star of David emblem on his lapel: a symbol of the rabid prejudice driving the exhibition and their hatred of 'non-Aryan' music.

During the 1930s, many Germans had fled the country as the Nazis gained prestige and power; many German intellectuals and artists ended up in Los Angeles, which the philosopher Theodor Adorno called 'Weimar under palm trees'. Dietrich was vilified in the German press for working abroad and supporting the American film industry. With the release of *Song of Songs*, she was accused of taking 'prostitute roles' in the US. The Berlin newspaper *Der Stürmer* declared that she had 'spent so many years among the film Jews of Hollywood' that her character had become 'wholly un-German'.

Behind closed doors, however, the Nazis admired her success and made repeated offers to lure her back to the Fatherland, to become queen of the UFA and make propaganda films for them. Hitler enjoyed watching her films in his private retreat and it is alleged that he proposed Dietrich become his mistress. In April 1936, Goebbels watched Dietrich in the film *Desire* and reflected in his diary that she was 'a very great actor'. He regretted that 'unfortunately we no longer have her in Germany'. They approached her on several occasions with offers of money. But Dietrich expressed strong disapproval of Nazi ideology, from their book burnings to their dismissal of prominent intellectuals. Not only did she refuse their attempts – including one offer of £50,000 to return to Germany for a month to make a film – she applied for American citizenship, which she was granted in 1939. Later, as the Second World War raged, Dietrich made her feelings clear: she called Hitler an 'idiot' and Goebbels a 'grotesque dwarf'.

In 1937 – the same year that Nazis tried and failed to lure Dietrich back to her homeland – Himmler gave a speech about homosexuals to high-ranking SS officers in Bad Tölz. He declared that they

were 'pathological liars', 'enemies of the state' and cowardly characters failing in their duty to produce children for the Fatherland. He
compared his crusade against homosexuals to digging up weeds in
a garden. Hitler also believed that Ancient Greece collapsed due to
the 'infectious activity' of homosexuality.

In 1929, the German parliament had been planning to abolish
paragraph 175 of the German criminal code. Paragraph 175 punished what was considered 'unnatural fornication', whether between
persons of the male sex or of humans with animals. With the Nazis
in power, the law was toughened. In 1935 it was changed so that it
no longer referred to 'unnatural acts' – now the phrase 'sexual acts'
was vague enough that it was up to a Nazi court to decide what
qualified. Another amendment to the law for the 'prevention of off-
spring with hereditary diseases' enabled a judge to order castration
if a man was found guilty of homosexuality. Those suffering from
'chronic homosexuality' were sent to concentration camps.

The physician and sexologist Magnus Hirschfeld came under
condemnation as a gay Jewish man. Initially he had believed
homosexuals formed a third sex, being neither purely feminine
nor purely masculine, but a distinct sex that lay between male and
female. Anticipating the sexologist Alfred Kinsey, he saw sexuality as being on a spectrum and also coined the term transvestite.
He was not entirely sympathetic to homosexuals, given that he
compared inheriting a biological tendency for same-sex attraction to inheriting a hare lip. However, he felt that once the public
understood that homosexuality was innate, there would be more
sympathy and understanding towards gay men. The Nazis rejected
his theories. In 1933 he watched his life's work being destroyed in
a Parisian newsreel: his institute trashed, his papers and archives
thrown onto a huge bonfire of 'un-German' literature.

During this era in Germany, theories on same-sex attraction had
gradually separated into two main opposing camps. Adolf Brand,
once a colleague of Hirschfeld's, broke away from him in 1903 with

Benedict Friedlaender, forming a group called *Gemeinschaft der Eigenen*, the Society of Self-Owners, and publishing the first homosexual magazine, *Der Eigene* ('The Unique'). This group became known as the 'masculinists'. They rejected Hirschfeld's equation of homosexuality with hermaphroditism, finding it emasculating, and preferring to see it as an aspect of virile manliness. They also disliked his medicalization of homosexuality, which 'took away all beauty from eroticism', favouring the arts rather than science as a better vehicle for exploring such ideas. They wanted to revive the tradition of *Freundesliebe*, the homoerotic friend-love that existed between men in Ancient Greece, and which Wilde cited in his trial. Brand and supporters such as the physician Edwin Bab did not believe that homosexuality was an inclination affecting a minority of men; most men were bisexual, and therefore a man could marry and have children whilst having homosexual affairs. The masculinists tended towards misogyny, rejecting leading roles for women in society and regarding male-male love as superior to male-female love. They were also horribly anti-Semitic; in one issue of *Der Eigene*, Brand vilified Hirschfeld. But Brand, like Hirschfeld, was persecuted by the Nazis, who raided his house several times, taking his books, photographs and copies of his journal, which he was forced to shut down. Academic Lauren Stokes has argued that the lingering idea of the 'disloyal bisexual' – 'more allied with the patriarchal status quo than with the emancipatory project of the queer community' – has its roots in this masculinist tradition.

The Nazis also rejected the idea of homosexuality as innate. They saw it as a virus that could be easily spread; Hitler declared that even 'the best and most masculine natures' could be afflicted by it. Much like the Victorians who prosecuted Wilde, the Nazis indulged the stereotype of the dirty older man who seduces young men and corrupts them. When men were charged with homosexuality in Nazi Germany, a key question was whether they were seducers or the seduced; in the case of the latter, punishments were not quite as harsh, since it was thought that they could be 'cured'. Treatments were offered at the Göring Institute, which declared by 1938 that it had cured 341 of 510 patients.

Around 100,000 men were arrested in Germany and Austria on suspicion of homosexuality between 1933 and 1945; 50,000 put in prison, and between 5,000 and 15,000 sent to concentration camps, where their uniform would display a pink triangle to indicate their homosexuality. Even when the war ended, homosexuals did not receive reparations; many were released from camps only to find themselves put into prison in a continuation of their sentences. The 1935 law that the Nazis had introduced remained in place until 1969, meaning that many homosexuals did not speak out about the experiences they had suffered during the Holocaust.

Dietrich fought against the Nazis with a passion. She contributed to the European Film Fund, giving aid and money to exiles fleeing Germany. She sold war bonds, along with stars such as Judy Garland. Dietrich was successful in selling the most; it is estimated that she raised over a million dollars. The Hollywood Victory Committee was formed by the movie industry in order to help support the war effort and entertain troops. She worked with the OSS, the US Office of Strategic Services, recording a series of American songs in German which aimed to weaken the morale of Nazi troops. A survey found that the programmes 'were just as devastating to German morale as an air raid'. She was prepared to roll up her sleeves too and do the nitty-gritty, helping out at the Hollywood canteen, washing dishes, and making coffee and scrambled eggs for the GIs.

In 1944 she packed up all her belongings and auctioned them off. She was going on tour with the United Services Operation, who sponsored tours to entertain troops, and as breadwinner she needed funds to keep her family going whilst she was away. Performers for the shows were given military titles. Marlene became Major Dietrich. She would appear on stage in army uniform, and then perform a flirtatious costume change behind a screen, emerging in a nude sequinned dress, crooning songs such as 'See What The Boys in the Back Room Will Have'. She went on two gruelling tours across 1944–5, in North Africa and Italy, and then in France, Belgium and Holland, putting on over 500 performances, suffering frostbite, pneumonia, influenza and a severe infection in her jaw, sometimes working in sub-zero temperatures, her teeth chattering as she sang in her barely-there dress. At one point she risked her life by entering Germany to perform, right at the end of the war, knowing that if she was caught they would react by punishing her – 'They'll shave off my hair, stone me and have horses drag me through the streets,' she said.

Dietrich was scared for her mother and her sister. She hadn't heard from them in seven years. They had ignored her pleas to flee the country before the war and she was terrified that her work for the Allies might have resulted in their punishment. She discovered that several actors whom she had worked with on *The Blue Angel* back in 1930, including Kurt Gerron and Karl Huszar-Puffy, had ended up in concentration camps; Gerron died in Auschwitz.

Assisted by an army contact who helped to track them down, Dietrich was shocked to discover that her sister Elisabeth and her husband Georg Will were involved in a support group for the concentration camp at Belsen, where they were helping to run the Wehrmacht canteen and cinema. Later in life, Dietrich would deny that she ever had a sister.

Dietrich received the *Légion d'honneur* from the French government for her wartime work. In 1947 she became the fourth woman to be awarded the Medal of Freedom, the highest award that can be bestowed on an American citizen. Dietrich said that her war efforts were 'the only important thing I've ever done'.

In 1960 she visited Germany, where she was performing on a European tour. She was greeted with both love and fury, with standing ovations and Germans waving placards that said *Marlene*

Go Home. 'The Germans and I no longer speak the same language,' Dietrich said, shocked and stung, and she never returned to her birth-country. She did, however, choose to be buried in her native Berlin. This story has a shocking coda: her grave has frequently been vandalized and in 2002, when she was posthumously made an honorary citizen of Berlin, there were protests.

During the 1950s, Dietrich featured in *Confidential*, a tabloid scandal sheet that gossiped about the sex lives of Hollywood stars. One front cover of 1955 depicted her with a headline in red: *The Untold Story of Marlene Dietrich*. *Polari* magazine reports that she was outed as a 'lesbian', when in fact she was outed as a bisexual. It touched on her relationship with 'blonde Amazon' Claire Waldoff, whilst her lover Mercedes de Acosta was described as 'a writer who favoured clothes that seemed to be tailored by Brooks Brothers'. *Confidential* magazine concluded: 'In the game of *amour*, she's not only played both sides of the street, but done it on more than one occasion.' Dietrich was at this point reinventing herself, leaving Hollywood behind to become a successful cabaret star, touring the world with her show. The 1950s was a dangerous, difficult time for bis and gays, particularly in the US, where cities formed vice squads to root out 'deviants'. Alongside the Red Scare, which targeted communists, was a Lavender Scare against homosexuals working in government. But Dietrich survived the scandal, perhaps because she did not comment on it; and perhaps because there was so much goodwill towards her given all that she had done to battle the Nazis.

Still, Dietrich's final comments on her sexuality are sad to read. In 1984 she was interviewed for a documentary called *Marlene*, lending her voice but refusing to appear in person. She complained to her friend Eryk Hanut that her gay fans had turned her into 'an androgynous Madonna' – her verdict on this was 'Rubbish!' She ranted against masculinized women. Against women's lib. And in her 'approved' biography with David Bret she declared that lesbianism was a 'perversion' she had never indulged in, denying her affair with Mercedes, undermining many of the principles for which she was admired, remaining a complex, contradictory character, both inspiring and frustrating.

In the *Marlene* documentary, Dietrich claims that she was not ambitious, suggesting that her career simply happened to her, whereas throughout her life everyone who knew her attested to her fierce determination to become a star. It was this obsession with maintaining her myth that caused her to spend the last decade and a half of her life shut away in her Paris apartment, refusing to go out in public, chatting to her friends on the phone, so that her wrinkles and blackened teeth could not destroy the collective memory of her iconic beauty. I believe that she denied her bisexuality as a continuation of her determination to be an icon. She had grown up in an era that was not accepting of queers and bisexuals, and so she knew that she could never publicly promote this part of herself. And, like some other figures I explore in this book, she was not interested in championing her sexuality as a political cause.

The gap between her words and her actions yawns. I think of that scene in Paris in 1933. I picture Dietrich arriving at Gare St Lazare. She has been given an official warning from the *Préfecture de police* that her outfit made her liable for arrest. She is wearing a man's polo coat, a grey man's suit, and a beret – it is illegal for women to wear trousers. She meets the policeman at the station, tucks his arm into hers, and elegantly leads him away.

4

Anaïs Nin

Anaïs Nin, according to her official online blog, was not bisexual. This is listed as Nin 'Myth no. 1':

While there are rare accounts in the unpublished diary (some-times graphic) of her relations with women, and while she could be erotically aroused by women, she found actual sex with them uncomfortable and strained. She once said, for example, 'I never liked kissing a woman's sex.' In the famous case of June Miller, Nin was brought to the pinnacle of eroti-cism, but it was a peak she didn't traverse physically. So, the conclusion is that while Anaïs Nin found some women erotic and actually wound up in bed with a few of them, in the strictest sense of the words 'lesbian' and 'bisexual', she was neither.

I was fooled by this for a while – until I dived into Nin's diaries, letters and stories. There I read passionate accounts of her affairs with women. And what does the blogger mean by 'strictest sense'? Presumably that she ought to have enjoyed the physicality of sex with women as much as men, loved cunts as much as cocks. This is absurdly narrow and prescriptive, especially given that she grew up in an era when attitudes towards lesbianism were not as liberal as they are today.

Anaïs Nin was a woman ahead of her time. Her biographer Deirdre Bair says that she deserves to be remembered as a major minor writer for being a pioneer who explored three key concepts of the twentieth century – sex, the self and psychoanalysis. She was a prolific writer from a young age. Her work encompasses short stories, erotica, surrealist novels and essays, as well as non-fiction, beginning with a study of D. H. Lawrence that she penned in her twenties. She also kept a diary, which chronicled six decades of her life. After many years where she felt frustrated by a lack of recognition in the literary world, she achieved international renown in 1966 when the first volume of her diaries was published – albeit a heavily censored one, omitting the rich detail of her love affairs, for fear of hurting her husband, friends and family.

Born in France in 1903, she was the daughter of a Spanish-Cuban father, a composer and pianist, and a French-Danish mother, a singer. Her womanizing father abused Anaïs as a child, and abandoned the family for a young piano student when Anaïs was ten years old. At the age of eleven, on a boat from Europe to New York, Anaïs started to write a letter to her absent father, which eventually evolved into her diary. Anaïs was also one of the first women to give us erotica from a female viewpoint, with the collections *Delta of Venus* and *Little Birds* which have recently been rediscovered and celebrated, adapted for television. She wrote about sex with subtlety, tenderness, elegance and beauty. And she lived a life soaked in sex: she would have been labelled polyamorous in today's society.

In 1923, when she was twenty years old, she married the financier Hugh Guiler and they moved to Paris. Following the financial miseries of the Great Depression, they moved into a country house in the quiet Parisian suburb of Louveciennes in the early 1930s. It was there that she met Henry Miller, a writer who would become her lover. She was twenty-eight, he was forty. She was restless in her bourgeois life, keen to write, to take risks, to embrace adventure, to break her marriage vows. Henry was short, bald, crude, with a raucous Brooklyn accent, a promising writer devoted to his craft who survived by begging meals from friends or sleeping where he could, once on a park bench. 'I was always living on the edge of disaster,' was Miller's summary of his life at that time. Anaïs was a crucial support in the early days of his writing career, paying for the first print run of *Tropic of Cancer*, now considered a classic of American letters. She also fell for his wife, June; the three of them created one of the most controversial love triangles in literary history.

Anaïs Nin deserves a rethink. The only official biography of her, by Deirdre Bair, is something of a hatchet job. Many of the criticisms levelled at her might not have been so barbed were the biography written today, against the backdrop of a fourth wave of feminism. Bair begins by wondering how to pin down the life of a woman who was an unreliable narrator – in contemporary times, her diary would have been regarded as autofiction, belonging to that blurry realm between subjective memory and fact. Anaïs reflected that 'the topsoil of our personalities is nothing', and that within her diary she could dig deeper, explore 'the inner life, the uncensored dream, the free unconscious'. Her daily habit became an obsession, Anaïs often taking her diary to bed with her to scribble down the day's events in 'a white heat' before sleep. By the time she died in 1977 it ran to a quarter of a million pages. It was published late in her life, when she was sixty-three. Anaïs was always worried about hurting people she loved, so it came out heavily censored. After a lifetime of failure, of rejections, poor reviews and having to resort to self-publishing, Anaïs Nin was suddenly a feminist icon, celebrated for her accounts of thriving in the male-dominated literary world. When she died, her erotica was published – along with franker versions of her diaries. These were still heavily edited, but they revealed that Nin had love affairs with a range of men and women, from Gore Vidal to Henry Miller to June Miller to Edmund

Wilson to her own father. At the end of her life she was a bigamist, married to two men who lived in different states, maintaining her 'trapeze' existence between Hugh Guiler and Rupert Pole. She was no saint: she was neurotic, manipulative and sometimes callous. By today's standards, she might be celebrated as a difficult woman, an outrageous experimenter exploring her sexuality – 'I am, against my will, a vagabond, a wanderer, a complex troublemaker,' she declared. But in Bair's book she is slut-shamed. Bair's biography lays out how difficult Nin's childhood was, and how hard she found it to develop herself as an artist in an era where she had to grapple with the prevailing traditional ideas of male and female roles, but Bair fails to join the dots with any sort of imaginative empathy or compassion.

When Henry Miller comes to Paris in the spring of 1930, Anaïs has been married to Hugh for seven years. They are in a state of both crisis and stasis: she is hungry for new experiences, but nervous too, afraid of losing her husband. Influenced by Freud and interested in psychoanalysis, they share their dreams: Hugh of going to a hotel to fuck a prostitute; Anaïs of a 'monstrous' woman seducing her, suggesting that her bisexuality is already seeded, waiting to flower. Anaïs is hungry for adventure, something which she justifies as part of her art, her need to feed her writing: 'I really believe that if I were not a writer, not a creator, not an experimenter, I might have been a very faithful wife.' Having married at a young age, it's as though Anaïs grows out of love as she grows up, and leaves her husband behind, finding his banking job tedious, wishing that he was more intellectual. She's already had one flirtatious affair, shared a kiss with an American professor. She and Hugh have discussed the possibility of livening up their relationship with parties and orgies, whilst also being afraid of the risk, of how far they might go and where they might end up – 'Abnormal pleasures kill the taste for normal ones.'

Reading between the lines of her diaries and letters, it seems that Hugh is happier in the marriage than she, that the rows that spark between them – which are resolved by passionate love-making – are motivated by a stronger restlessness on Anaïs's part. Middle-class women are trapped in narrow roles. Anaïs hates being known simply as 'the daughter of Nin' or 'Hugh's wife', finds it tedious to socialize with the other bankers' wives. Hugh's income falls after the Great Depression, and Anaïs suggests she might earn her own money by teaching dancing, or finding a job, but this is out of the question. Hugh refuses: it wouldn't be acceptable for a wife of her class to work.

Anaïs and Henry first meet in December 1931. Anais has just finished a book about D. H. Lawrence, an author she admires, particularly for his subtle explorations of sexuality. It is a risky, daring project for the era, given that Lawrence's *Lady Chatterley's Lover*, recently published in Italy and Paris, has been banned in the UK and the US. Anaïs has also read and enjoyed extracts from Henry's work-in-progress, *Tropic of Cancer*, which their mutual friend Richard Osborn has shown her. She admires the violence and the primitivism in his writing; she looks forward to meeting him, to an encounter between 'delicacy and violence'. When Henry comes to lunch, she finds him 'flamboyant, virile, animal, magnificent'. He is the lover she has been yearning for; having been abandoned by her father at a tender age, she has craved 'a man stronger than me, a lover who will lead me in love' and longed to put herself 'under the protection, the nobility, the grandeur of a man' who is a 'great writer'. Despite the frisson between them, Anaïs tells Henry that they cannot have a sexual relationship, that she will be the one woman he'll never have, they'll just 'write and talk' – a line which doesn't sound very convincing given the energy between them. Hugh also senses danger – 'You fall in love with people's minds,' he warns his wife. He is scared he will lose her to Henry.

And then, just as we sense they will begin an affair, her narrative swerves in an unexpected direction. Suddenly her interest in Henry fades, for Anaïs has a new obsession: his wife.

*

Let's go back to that moment when they first met: Anaïs and June Miller. It's a winter night in 1931. June and Henry are coming to Nin's house for dinner. Nin watches June walk towards the house, emerging from the darkness into the light of the doorway. She has pale skin, burning eyes. Anaïs is instantly overwhelmed: 'her beauty drowned me'. Anaïs sits in front of her and feels she would do anything for her, she is so dazzled: 'she was colour, brilliance, strangeness.'

Anaïs often struggles with being a woman in the 1930s: she refers to her gender time and time again in her diaries. What does it mean, she wonders, to live as a woman, to write as a woman? How she should conduct relationships? What should she do with her 'masculine' side, that element in her which she defines as domineering and independent, and feels nervous of? She is often attracted to men who are like her absent father, brutal and womanizing. Drawn to their power, she is happy to flatten herself into the secondary role of muse. For she notes that, aside from sex, men need to be 'soothed, lulled, understood, helped, encouraged' in a tender manner. She gives Henry a stipend, lavishes him with gifts, enables him to concentrate on his writing – though, paradoxically, this also represents an inherent desire for power, by playing benefactor in an era when men were the breadwinners and controlled all finances.

When she first falls for June, however, she feels masculine: 'By the end of the evening, I was like a man, terribly in love with her face and body, which promised so much.'

June represents a part of Anaïs which exists in chrysalis form. She is wild, bold, superficial, outspoken, irresponsible, reckless. 'I will always be the virgin prostitute,' Anaïs writes in her diary before meeting her, 'the perverse angel, the two-faced sinister and saintly woman'. June represents the perverse, the sinister, the unfettered. Hugh thinks her 'mannish' and hates her.

Despite raving about June's beauty over and over, Anaïs is cautious, nervous about their relationship. She is, at this point in her life, hungry for experience because she's had so little. Confusion amazes her. She writes that June doesn't reach the same sexual centre of being that a man reaches, but a sentence later muses that 'I have wanted to possess her as if I were a man, but I have also wanted her to love me with the eyes, the hands, the senses that only women have. It is a soft and subtle penetration.' Nor does her cousin Eduardo, who plays analyst, help with much insight; Anaïs goes to him, it seems, to get permission to allow June to become her lover, to talk through her fears and doubts, only to be told that she can't be a lesbian because she doesn't hate men. She feels reassured that she dreams erotically of Eduardo; but then June creeps into her dreamscape too: 'I was at the top of a skyscraper and expected to walk down the façade of it on a very narrow fire ladder. I was terrified. I could not do it.'

What were social attitudes towards bi- and homosexuality in this time? In Paris, there had been a flourishing of bisexuality in the 1920s, with a vibrantly gay community akin to Berlin's or the Harlem Renaissance in New York. The famous Monocle club had opened in the 1920s, where the women – guests and staff – would adopt a cool outfit: a tuxedo with a white carnation in the lapel, slicked-back hair and a monocle in one eye. The Great Depression changed attitudes, facilitated a lurch towards the right, and lesbianism became frowned upon. The wrecked economy meant that women found it harder to support themselves without a husband, and women were discouraged from working and stealing jobs that were supposedly meant for men. When women began to fight for their rights at the start of the century, there was a perceived link between feminism and lesbianism; men, puzzled by women's desire to work, often saw such an impulse as 'masculine' and linked to old-fashioned ideas of inversion – a male psyche in a woman's body. Over in the US, where the economic crash was blamed by many on the 'cultural experimentation' of the 1920s, new laws and regulations were introduced that prohibited restaurants and bars from hiring gay employees or even serving gay patrons. The growing prejudice against the LGBT community reached a zenith with the Nazi occupation. Between 1940 and 1944 the Vichy regime, collaborating with the Germans, amended article 334 of the penal code. Now anyone who satisfied 'his own passions, commits one or several shameless or unnatural acts with a minor of his own sex under the age of twenty-one' would receive a prison term of six months to three years. Just as a virulent homophobia swept Germany, closing the gay clubs in Berlin, the Monocle club in Paris closed during the 1940s. It was some decades before the queer community rebuilt itself.

It's January 1932. Anaïs and June are sitting side by side in a café together. June is dressed shabbily, sporting a dress with a hole in it, whilst Anaïs's clothing is pristine: a dress and an elegant velvet jacket. They have just dined together. June mostly smoked and drank, whilst Anaïs felt too nervous to eat, channelling her energies into maintaining a calm façade.

June reaches out and presses her hand against Anaïs's. Anaïs says that she wants to give her a going-away present, for June is soon to return to New York. 'Give me the perfume I smelled in your house,' June replies. 'Walking up the hill to your house, in the dark, I was in ecstasy.'

Their courtship is fragile, tender, nervous. They flirt cautiously, on the brink of delirious passion, pulling back from it again and again. When they next meet, they go up to Anaïs's bedroom so that June can try on a pair of her sandals – but they are too small. Anaïs has a gorgeous black cape which she lets June try on, overwhelmed by 'the beauty of her body, its fullness and heaviness'. Downstairs, Anaïs notices that the opening of June's dress kisses the tops of her breasts – 'and I wanted to kiss her there'.

Clothing becomes a theme in their courtship: a way of connecting. They swap jewellery. This might sound cute, adolescent, but their exchanges are loaded with pain and possession. Anaïs gives June her coral earrings and a turquoise ring, a gift from her husband which it 'hurts' her to part with. June gives her a silver bracelet with a cat's-eye stone. Anaïs wears it and tells her that the bracelet clutches her wrist like 'your fingers, holding me in barbaric slavery'.

They go to buy sandals. Anaïs commandeers the shop, scolding an unhelpful shopkeeper, declaring in her diary: 'I was the man.' I consider how it would have been if she'd gone shoe-shopping with Hugh, where, if she'd taken control, it would have looked like a public undermining of his authority. But though June can make her feel masculine and empowered, freeing her from playing a submissive role, Anaïs feels lost and anxious when it comes to making a move on her. When Henry and June lived in New York, a young poet called Jean Kronski moved in with them. Anaïs broaches the subject with June: 'Are you a lesbian? Have you faced your impulses in your own mind?' The word 'faced' is telling, as though lesbianism is a sickness one has to come to terms with. June says that Jean was too masculine – thereby complimenting Anaïs, who is outwardly very feminine – and asserts boldly: 'I have faced my feelings, I am fully aware of them, but I have never found anyone I wanted to live them out with, so far.' Then she changes the subject to the dress Anaïs is wearing – they are back to a discussion about clothes weighted with subtext. Their inhibition continues; they do little beyond holding hands.

Anaïs has, in effect, created a double love triangle: Anaïs-June-Hugh and Anaïs-June-Henry, which puts her in a position of power, desired in triplicate. Their husbands are wild with jealousy.

Hugh tells his wife he hates June. When Anaïs bumps into Henry at the bank, she is startled to realize that he hates her, and recalls that June told her, 'he is more jealous of women than men.'

But what does June want? Even Anaïs, whilst drugged with attraction, recognizes that June is prone to lies and fabulous stories that contain 'discrepancies', observing, 'She is like a man who is drunk and gives himself away.' Anaïs showers June with gifts and money in the same way that she did Henry, but June blows it quickly, carelessly. She lacks sufficient funds to buy her ticket back to New York, and when they visit some steamship agencies, June starts bartering and beguiling a male clerk selling tickets, agreeing to meet him for cocktails the next evening, hoping it will lead to a low-price fare. Anaïs feels angry, returns home and tells Hugh she has come back to him. But the next day love's illusions creep back in. She reassesses the situation more gently, feeling that she is the one who is 'too scrupulous and proud' about money matters. She concludes that June may be immoral but she is also unfettered – and she admires this so much, she doesn't want to change her.

They meet one last time – and how frustrating it is! They have champagne and caviar in a Russian tearoom. It is not until their goodbyes that June says with regret and wistfulness, 'I had wanted to hold you and caress you.' Anaïs tells her she wants to kiss her and June offers 'her mouth, which I kiss for a long time'.

After June has gone, Anaïs and Hugh visit a high-quality brothel together. There, Anaïs picks out two women and she and her husband play at voyeurs, watch them having sex together. Anaïs learns for the first time what a clitoris is, the pleasure it can bring. It's as though she is watching what she wanted to enact with June, but felt too inhibited, and there is a note of unease in her admission that by the end of the night she felt, 'I am no longer woman; I am man.'

*

The critic Tony Tanner argues that the *Iliad* marks the beginning of Western literature. It details how the Trojan War was triggered by the adultery between Helen and Paris, for 'it is the unstable triangularity of adultery, rather than the static symmetry of marriage, that is the generative form of Western literature as we have it'. The books and films that I devoured as an adolescent presented the love triangle as fascinatingly seductive. The protagonist was usually female, tugged between two men, one more kind and sensible, the other more wild and wicked; in romantic comedies, she would learn her lesson and choose Mr Nice; in sweeping, serious love stories, choosing adultery over marriage, danger over safety, usually led to tragedy and death (see *Dangerous Liaisons*, *The English Patient*). It was the latter genre that appealed to me more. I found comedies too trite and preferred the gothic melancholy of the doomed romance, re-reading *Wuthering Heights* more times than is healthy. But there's a difference between a heterosexual amorous triangle and a bisexual one, a *ménage à trois*. The heterosexual stories that I have cited are simpler. They work well as a narrative device because they are propelled by conflict driving inexorably towards resolution. The triangle cannot be sustained; it must collapse; a choice must be made; the ending will reduce three to two once more, as though three represents an unstable, uneven, unbalanced friction.

But what of the bisexual love triangle? If all three parties are in love or lust with each other, it offers less opportunity for resolution; its kaleidoscope patterning of power and desire can be recast endlessly in fresh colours.

With June gone, Anaïs and Henry resume their friendship. They write long letters to each other (although Anaïs is also writing daily to June, who doesn't reply). Their subject matter is always June, June, June. Anaïs is secretly triumphant that she has shared an experience with Henry's wife that he can't quite conceive of; addressing June in her diary, she writes, 'He senses uneasily that there is a certain side of you he has not grasped.' Henry is determined to know what went on between them. Anaïs gradually reveals more and more, so that her stories of June become part of a new courtship. Even when Anaïs begins a love affair with Henry, initially it feels more like a substitute for what she failed to enjoy with his wife. When Anaïs and Henry first make love in his room, Anaïs notices the photograph of June on his mantelpiece, which she finds hard to bear. Everything they experience is played off against her psychic presence.

Over time, Anaïs and Henry's affair becomes more solid, vehement; June fades into the background. Anaïs supports him financially, siphoning off half of the housekeeping money that her husband gives her. Their writing fuels their lovemaking; their lovemaking fuels their writing. Henry immortalized June as the character of Mona in *Tropic of Cancer*; now he refers to Anaïs as 'Mona Païva', after the Russian ballerina, illustrating how both mistress and wife have mingled in his imagination. They reach a point of intensity where Henry fantasizes that Anaïs will become his wife and he will let June go. June, hearing of their affair, re-enters the story, revisits Paris. The love triangle becomes vivid again.

Henry and June, the first part of Anaïs's diaries, captures the complications of their entwinings. They are, in part, fighting over whose narrative is true, over whose stories she should believe; June fears that Anaïs will believe 'Henry's version of her', which is of her as a hysteric. Henry and June sometimes treat her as a therapist, giving her competing versions of themselves and each other (just as Anaïs is also relating their experiences to her therapist, relaying every titillating detail of sex between her and Henry). Anaïs has both weakened and strengthened their relationship. Having 'mellowed' Henry, she observes that, 'They can talk together. I have changed him . . . and he understands her better.' Has she just been an 'other', then, a way of resolving their relationship? Yet Anaïs realizes she is important to Henry because she is his muse, the nurturer of his writing. She and June are playing angel and demon in this department, for Anaïs wants Henry to enjoy literary success and she feels June is destructive towards his talents, creating a paradox of intimacy and paranoia. When Anaïs and June embrace in a taxi, she muses: 'This scene in the taxi – knees touching, hands locked, cheek against cheek – is going on while we are aware of our fundamental enmity.' In the final pages of *Henry and June*, Anaïs sums up the ever-thickening fog of their ménage: 'But what a superb game the three of us are playing. Who is the demon? Who the liar? Who the human being? Who the cleverest? Who the strongest? Who loves the most? Are we three immense egos fighting for domination or for love, or are these things mixed?'

*

Anaïs, like Colette, observed that there was a difference between loving a man and loving a woman. In words that remind me of Colette's observations, Anaïs tells Henry: 'The love between women is a refuge and an escape into harmony. In the love between man and woman there is resistance and conflict. Two women do not judge each other, brutalize each other, or find anything to ridicule. They surrender to sentimentality, mutual understanding, romanticism. Such love is death, I'll admit.'

Death – a surprising word, one she uses frequently when discussing their love. And that death is often described as a dissolution of self. Just after June first leaves Paris, Anaïs wears a dress with a hole in it – 'I felt like June.' She listens with fascination to Henry's description of what life with June was like in their Brooklyn apartment, the filth and the chaos: 'Sinks stopped up from too much garbage. Washing dishes in bathtub, which was greasy and black-rimmed . . . Breaking up furniture to throw into fire.' Anaïs calls herself a chameleon several times in her diary. Though June liberates her, she also fears herself mimicking the colours of June's nature – which would represent the death of her feminine side, for 'I have discovered the joy of a masculine direction of my life by my courting of June. Also I have discovered the terrible joy of dying, of disintegrating.' To live like June, to let go, to be wild and free, would also represent the collapse of her bourgeois life, her neat apartment, her comfortable income. Henry, meanwhile, represents 'life', for he dominates her, shaping Anaïs into a submissive through contrast, giving her a role that chimes with the one society decrees she ought to be playing.

Anaïs's love affair with Henry works because that's all it is – an affair. It has comfortable limits, safety valves. Henry represents the liberated, exciting artist next to her boring banker husband. But Henry is also volatile, passionate, selfish, destructive. Anaïs and Henry sparkle as lovers but I doubt they would have thrived as husband and wife. When Henry and June visit their home, they relate their quarrels, dramatizing their marital warfare. Anaïs feels angry because Hugh tries to 'laugh off the jagged edges, to smooth out the discord, the ugly, the fearful, to lighten their confidences'. Yet what she finds dull in Hugh is simultaneously nurturing. The foundation of their steady marriage enables her to play, knowing that she can always come home to someone safe. In the midst of her affair with June, at peak obsession, Anaïs witnesses June's dubious seduction of the clerk in the steamship agency and feels repelled; returning home, she tells Hugh, *I've come back to you.*

Anaïs oscillates between wanting to be safe in domesticity and traditional marriage and wanting to risk it all and smash it apart. Bair's biography details all of this in a tone of 'poor Hugh – having to put up with such a faithless, vicious wife'. But she doesn't consider enough that Anaïs Nin was a brilliant woman out of synch with the time she lived in, one that expected women to play a submissive, secondary, supportive role. Anaïs can play the role and enjoy it, to an extent. But it is never enough. In 1927, four years into her marriage, she observes that, 'I have known three cases of "steady" home women going to pieces, for no apparent reason. It isn't moodiness, temperament, or anything like that. I can only explain it by a sudden sense of emptiness in their lives, or of suffocation. A regular life, such as they lead, housekeeping, canning fruit, sewing, gardening, nursing children, would drive me into an insane asylum.' She tastes the fear of anticipation, of a life she might end up living. Rather than slipping into stagnancy, she rebels. Her desire for adventure is a determination to fight against such a fate. To remain in a safe domestic space was to remain innocent, infantilized, even: 'I cannot stay home,' she wrote in 1928. 'I have a desperate desire to know life, and to live in order to reach maturity.' While I do feel sorry for Hugh, I can also see the cruelty that monogamy at that time entailed due to stagnant gender roles; that to be promiscuous was a way to breathe.

The bisexual love triangle between her and the Millers isn't resolved at the end of *Henry and June*. If the two lovers represent two elements of her fragmented self, then she needs them both in order to feel whole. The diary ends with a situation that feels more complex and more involved than it did at the start. If heterosexual love triangles end with resolution, the traditional marriage, the full stop, then bisexual ones end with ellipses . . .

*

Nin's tendency to see her sexual conflict in terms of masculine/feminine traits shows the influence of Freud on her thinking. (She spent much of her life in analysis and trained to become an analyst herself.) Freud's theories on bisexuality are not positive but are worth exploring, given how hugely influential they have been on twentieth-century thinking. Freud used the term 'bisexual' in three ways. He used it in the Victorian, biological sense; Darwinian evolutionary theory posited that an embryo had no sex for the first three months, which meant it was 'bisexual' and hermaphroditic; Freud then expanded this into a psychological equivalent, male and female traits, the 'polymorphous perversity' that we are born with before our identity develops definitively into male/female, so that bisexuality was associated with 'very early, primordial stages of psychic development'. Finally, he also used it to describe sexual attraction to men and women.

In a 1905 essay on sexual 'aberrations', Freud classified bisexuals as 'amphigenic inverts' (as opposed to 'absolute inverts', homosexuals). He rejected the prevailing idea that inversion was caused by degeneracy, arguing for an 'originally bisexual disposition'. Heterosexuality is a state of maturity, albeit one that is achieved with struggle and conflict; homosexuality, however, is a development mid point between immature narcissism and mature heterosexuality. For Freud, homosexuals were 'perverts' rather than 'neurotics', but he did not believe in conversion therapy. 'It is not for psychoanalysis to solve the problem of homosexuality,' he said, which might be reassuring were it not for the fact that he sees them as a 'problem'.

His views on female 'inverts' are particularly cruel. He saw male attraction as a shade of bisexuality, referring back to the Greek tradition of pederasty. The Ancient Greeks made love to boys, he argues, who physically resembled women in their beauty, 'as well as . . . feminine psychical traits, such as shyness, modesty and the need for instruction and assistance'. Therefore, 'the sexual object is not someone of the same sex, but someone who combines the characteristics of both sexes.' Women experiencing same-sex attraction, however, 'frequently and peculiarly exhibit somatic and psychical characteristics of men', he declared. Freud defined masculinity as proactive, feeling that men had more developed superegos than women, whereas femininity represented passivity. However, Freud noted that 'all human individuals, as a result of their bisexual disposition and of cross-inheritance, combine in themselves both masculine and feminine characteristics, so that pure masculinity and femininity remain theoretical constructions of uncertain content'.

Nin suffered a certain guilt and unrest at exploring her

'masculine' traits, even though they seem, to a contemporary readership, perfectly normal and healthy aspects of any psyche. Her analysis at this time did her more harm than good, I believe, leading to a greater fragmentation of her selves, tying her sexuality and creativity into sharply defined modes of male and female. Jenny Diski, writing in the *London Review of Books*, observes that, 'Most of those who knew her believed the diaries themselves prevented her from becoming what she most wanted to be – a creative writer.' But consider the challenges of being a female writer in this period when you are so wedded to Freudian theory and to traditional ideas of gender. Nin was keen to write like a woman, to find a voice; though, when Henry Miller read and praised her book on D. H. Lawrence, he complimented her on writing like a man, 'with tremendous clearness and conciseness', words which made her sing. Struggling to write fiction, she went away on holiday in 1932, had a creative breakthrough, and wrote forty pages of detailed notes about June. Finally, she felt, she had found a female literary voice. When Nin showed them to Henry on her return, he was impressed by the subtle, nuanced portrait. 'Would you mind if I borrowed these?' he asked, incorporating the material into *Tropic of Capricorn*. Miller did give Nin vital writerly encouragement, praising her diaries and editing her work, but the borrowing might have thwarted a potentially good novel.

Meanwhile, the analyst she was seeing at the time, René Allendy, chided Nin for trying to surpass men in their work and, on reading her notes on her dreams, was concerned about the strong 'masculine' quality in her writing, which he feared was a flaw. It can't have been easy to be a female writer trying to find confidence and a literary voice in the 1930s and 1940s. Nin's experiences bring to mind those of Zelda Fitzgerald, who, in 1930, was institutionalized in a clinic in Switzerland, doctors assuring her husband, Scott, that her affairs with women, her desire to have a career and succeed as a writer, were all symptoms of 'schizophrenia', which she would soon be cured of. (Their treatment did not heal her; she went on to write *Save Me the Last Waltz*.) Many female writers of this time who did achieve greater success still suffered this sort of gender anxiety around their creativity. Daphne du Maurier felt that her masterpieces, which included *Rebecca*, *My Cousin Rachel* and *Don't Look Now*, were propelled by an inner 'male' energy which was the kernel of her creativity. From a young age, she felt that she was a woman 'with a boy's mind and a boy's heart', calling her male alter-ego Eric. She saw her personality as one cleaved into two: her masculine creative side, and her performative female side, the loving wife and mother she played in public. When she fell in love with Ellen Doubleday, the wife of her US publisher, she wrote her love letters that declared she was not loved by a woman but 'Eric', her other half. Her biographer, Margaret Forster, saw du Maurier's struggle with her bisexuality as motivated by a 'homophobic fear'.

Many writers, however, have not seen their craft in terms of masculine or feminine traits, but a mingling of the two as a positive for their creativity. The terms 'nonbinary' and 'gender fluidity' would not have been used then, but this is certainly what they mean when they discuss androgyny as their ideal. The word comes from the Greek, from *andrós* meaning male, and *gyné*, meaning female. In the Renaissance era, androgyny was seen as an ideal, a harmonious union of opposites. Virginia Woolf said that Coleridge thought a 'great mind is androgynous'. She concluded that 'Coleridge . . . meant, perhaps, that the androgynous mind is resonant and porous; that it transmits emotion without impediment; that it is naturally creative, incandescent and undivided.' Woolf came to the playful conclusion that 'Shakespeare was androgynous; and so were Keats and Sterne and Cowper and Lamb and Coleridge. Shelley perhaps was sexless. Milton and Ben Jonson had a dash too much of the male in them. So had Wordsworth and Tolstoy. In our time Proust was wholly androgynous, if not perhaps a little too much of a woman.'

In 1989 Milan Kundera described how writing transcended gender: 'It's the sex of the novels and not that of their authors that interest us. All great novels, all true novels are bisexual. This is to say that they express both a feminine and masculine vision of the world. The sex of the authors as physical people is a private affair.' Once again, bisexuality here is being used in the archaic sense, echoing its Victorian meaning as hermaphroditic, rather than the more modern meaning of attraction to more than one sex.

*

Shifting from a lesbian relationship to a heterosexual one can make you feel like a character in Ovid's *Metamorphoses*. And you definitely come with baggage; the relationship you're entering may have been regarded as a sacrilege by your ex. You can feel flustered, as though you only had a quick break for a hasty costume change and you look down and find you're still wearing those shoes that your female lover fetishized and your male lover thinks you should exchange for high heels. As Hera Lindsay Bird writes in her poem 'Bisexual':

> *It's like climbing out of a burning building into too much*
> *water*
> *Or climbing out of a burning building.......*
> *into a second identical burning building*
> Why does everything have to be so on fire? *you ask yourself*
> But when you look down, your fretwork is smoking

Which sums up how I felt when I met Z.

'Look, there's Z! Would you like to meet him?'

'I'm . . .' *not sure*, I thought, as my friend Michael beckoned me. I took care not to spill my drink as I wove through the crowds, elbowing a Booker winner here, stumbling over a Nobel Peace recipient there. The party was being held in a green square, elegantly lined with trees; the sunset was a serene backdrop. Two weeks ago, I had signed my first publishing contract. This was the first time I'd been to a literary party and the first thing I learnt was that in the hierarchy of people worth talking to, I was classed as the lowest of the low. I had written a 'YA' novel and even though I'd been inspired by *Lord of the Flies* and *I'm the King of the Castle* rather than *Twilight* and *Divergent*, it didn't matter. Nor did it help that my baby face made me look far younger than my age, twenty-nine.

Michael was different. He had published a literary novel, but he seemed keen to be friends; or, I feared, more than friends.

And here was Z, clearly at the top of the hierarchy, an aristocrat in his castle of prestige; whilst people asked for my name and quickly forgot it, despite its sole syllable, with Z there was no need to request it: he was a Name. Michael introduced us. I managed about three sentences, stammery and foolish, my eyes fixed on the torso-creases of his shirt. He was at least fifteen years older than me, maybe twenty. His confidence had a worldly aura, a masculine grandeur that was almost old-fashioned, anachronistic. He looked as though he would have thrived in earlier literary eras. I could imagine him going fishing with Hemingway or downing martinis with Fitzgerald. Indeed, when I look back at that party, the majority of the 'Names' there were male. This was the mid-noughties, and the playing field was far from level. At one point, I was introduced to a male editor who seemed entirely indifferent to my presence, but one of his writers assured me: 'Don't worry, he's just not particularly interested in female writers.'

It was both a relief and a disappointment when my conversation with Z was brought to a halt by an agent spilling his glass of red wine all over Michael's jacket. In the midst of profuse apologies and the offer to exchange jackets, Z was commandeered by someone else, the air a-flurry with mimed kisses.

The party followed the usual narrative: small talk and polite greetings at first, then ties being loosened and jackets creased, cigarette smoke thickening, hands lingering on arms and shoulders, conversation becoming more blurry, language less precise. Michael popped up again, asking me to feel his jacket and attest that it was still damp. A drunk poet climbed a tree and began to quote verse. A memory was triggered: of Clara. My last lover. She had once climbed a tree and bent forward over a branch, catcalling me playfully, her long hair hanging down. It had been three months since we'd broken up and I no longer opened her copy of Don Paterson's *Landing Light* and pulled out the sketch of me tucked into the back. After losing her I would check it every hour, seeking enlightenment in her pencil strokes, in that which she'd superimposed onto my features. At least a fortnight had passed since I'd last looked at it. I no longer found stray dark curly hairs folded into my sheets, and her scent on a left-behind jumper had faded into the smell of my own living habits, infused with incense, the faint aura of my shampoo. I wondered if she would ever get in touch to get the copy of Paterson back, or indeed if I would ever hear from her again. As I watched the poet nearly fall from the tree, the collective laughter lifted my spirits, prompted a smile from me, and evoked a sense of longing, of hope for a new experience to layer over my memories of Clara and turn them sepia. Something that would ease this tension in my stomach that I was a failure at this party, a nobody; something that I could savour the next day as transgressive, adventurous.

As everyone surged towards the nearby pub for the after-party, I found myself bumping into someone.

Z turned to face me. He looked down at me and smiled.

'You're rather lovely.'

I blushed and let him guide me into the overflowing pub. His attention was like a bright spotlight on me, a fusion of his personal charisma and the power he represented. His attempts to chat me up were constantly being thwarted. People kept coming up and trying to give him their number, or behave as though he was their best friend: 'Z! Long time no see! How about lunch? How about lunch next week? Let's put the date in the diary now.' Z was very charming but he looked a little exasperated. He turned his back to them and tucked my hair behind my ear, then asked to kiss my cheek; I liked the cheeky ludicrousness of his excuse: 'I think someone put lipstick on me and I need to check it's come off.'

Another interruption, in the form of Michael, his jacket now dry. He looked at Z, and he looked at me, and he looked cross. I resisted the guilt pinching my stomach, reminded myself that we were just friends. Michael put his arm firmly around me. Z raised an eyebrow and I found myself wailing inside as he slipped away gracefully.

Hours had passed since I'd gone to bed around 1 a.m. There was the hint of sunrise behind my curtains.

Z: I would never see him again. 'You should come and visit me in France,' he'd said in the pub, 'to my second home.' Holding my eyes with his. Pupils like black moons. It all kept repeating: *you're rather lovely*, the lipstick on the cheek, my hair being tucked behind my ear. No matter which position I lay in, my body hummed with longing. Finally, around 6 a.m., I rose with a conviction. There were times in life when I'd let opportunities slip away and times when I had grabbed them. Desire became resolve, a fierce, hot determination.

I emailed the agent I had met the previous evening, the one who had flung red wine over Michael, asking for a couple of email addresses for people I'd met at the party. I was convinced I'd receive a bodyguard's reply.

By the time his response came – cheerful and chatty, freely offering the emails – I was in a state of madness. A moment of sobriety, where I recalled how life does not repeat but it does rhyme, how once I had been crazy over Clara, had catastrophized over emails from her when they had arrived an unbearable hour later than expected, and before Clara, there had been Mr F, and a few years before him, Henry, and before him, Paul. But none of those fevers had ever been quite like this – a new strain, virulent, poisonous, with a higher temperature and headier symptoms. With Clara, there had been no lightning strike on our first meeting. Our affection had been slow and gradual, built over a dozen dates, like the spring creeping in, sunshine growing warmer.

My email to Z began with, 'I hope you don't mind me emailing you . . .' and then went through numerous drafts.

SEND.

My fingers were still trembling.

A hazy tiredness came over me; I slumped back into bed.

There was no way he would reply. He represented everything I wanted to be as a writer; I felt I could offer nothing in return, except the invocation of his lust, and that was probably because he had been drunk. I felt sad and went to bed early, grateful for sleep.

In the morning, I opened my inbox:

Hey,
Not drunk enough to forget you. Shame we couldn't chase the drinks into a mutual kind of amnesia. Perhaps we'll get another shot at it soon.

Darkness. I was lying in bed, somewhere between sleep and waking consciousness. I rolled over, pressed my phone. 2.35 a.m. There was a burn of tiredness behind my eyes that had been building for some days. It was the result of a new routine: going to bed at 10 p.m. and waking four hours later and reaching for my laptop to see his name in bold at the top of my inbox and that little envelope waiting to be clicked and opened. I told myself that I ought to be sensible, return to bed, wait for morning. If Z was a night owl I was someone who needed to wake from a deep and restful sleep in order to set down good prose. Yet, despite my internal arguments, as I opened my laptop and light flooded my face, I realized how much I was enjoying this. There was something thrilling about his emails arriving at night, carrying that energy of romance and moonlight and danger with them, rather than reading them in the brisk light of morning, when the sun was sharp and the country was in the rhythm of work and sensible activities. A new reply. Happiness a somersault inside me: we were going to meet. I loved the fact that he was taking the planning of it seriously, musing through plot possibilities:

Won't probably kick off till 9 or later – a) because darkness becomes it, and b) because I'll possibly only fly in that night.

Have to throw dice as to what or where. End up in a Paris gutter the Wednesday after.

The beginning of any such decision is usually:

Upscale (cocktails, decadence, take piss out of plummy types and Americans)

Or

Dives (dubiously licensed foreign basements on the edge of Soho)

Or start at the top and work down.

He was currently abroad, in New York to see his publisher and sign a new contract, but he would be back in the UK soon. The date of our date wasn't specified. It was clear, I thought, that I had to fit in with his busy and glamorous schedule. Back in the dark, I was too fizzed to sleep. *Ms Mills*, he had called me. Once I had been a *Mr Mills*, to Clara.

Now that I was falling for Z, I felt as though I had taken off the dark suit I'd worn in my relationship with Clara; as if it was being packed into my wardrobe and a dust cover pulled over it. Relishing the preparations for my date with Z, I found myself uncharacteristically enjoying shopping. Normally clothes bored me, but now they were an aphrodisiac; I tried on dresses long and short, played with shades of lipstick in plum and cerise, asked a friend for help on how foundation worked. 'What do you like about men? What do you like about Z?' I could hear Clara asking, offended but curious. And if she'd been here, I would have replied, 'Well, he's funny and clever, he's rich and successful, he loves books and writing like me, and he has such panache, a kind of wild energy. I feel like our date won't be like the average. It won't just be dinner and drinks. It's going to be an *event*. An adventure. With him, I feel as though anything might happen...' The thought thrilled me. And then saddened me, because I realized that I was silently narrating my experiences to Clara as they unfolded, seeking her wisdom and opinion, creating a psychic *ménage à trois* that reminded me of Anaïs Nin in the early days of her affair with Henry Miller, both of them haunted by the presence of June.

Our grand adventure: was it on or was it off? Was it about to end before it had even begun? I was perched in the bar of a hotel in Bloomsbury, dressed eccentrically in a short gold skirt and a Dougal-from-the-Magic-Roundabout T-shirt, shredding a napkin. He was late. I knew that he was flying over – but where was his text of apology, reassurance, reschedule? I sipped my Coca-Cola. The hotel was grand: marble steps, fancy columns, the bar softly lit and spidery with plants. Another half hour went by and hurt was goose-prickling my skin when suddenly he was there in front of me, apologetic, flustered, charming, confident and shy all at once.

He wore a smart black jacket over his jeans, tall and handsome, rough and ragged around the edges. He thrust a present into my hands, which he'd picked up at the airport: a small sculpture of a black cat, which was supposed to bring luck. (Fifteen years on and I still have this cat in a box, together with a few other mementos from the night – a glass jar, once filled with jelly beans, a sketch of his face, scrawled in biro on hotel headed paper.) I admired the cat whilst he went to check in and dump his luggage. Joy plumed in my chest: he was here. It was one of those rare times where reality is sharpened into moments of slow-burn euphoria.

We were giggling in the back of a rickshaw as neon lights blurred past. The driver got lost and Z had to direct him and teased him that he should be paying us. We hit a nightclub which was barely a club: more like a random room with a speaker and flashing lights; I loved its amateur teen-disco vibe. In the queue outside we got chatting to a few young Italians; Z, in an act of generosity, paid for them to get in too. Always, everywhere we went, people were drawn to him, and he charmed them, like a movie star bestowing favours or benign royalty. We were dancing, lights butterflying over us, when we shared our first kiss.

'You kiss all the time. You can't stop,' the Italian girl observed half an hour later, when we took a cigarette break outside. I was smoking too – the first time in fifteen years.

'You must be so much in love,' she teased us.

Smoke curled from our cigarettes, wreathing our frozen expressions.

'Ah, but I am married,' Z broke the moment, adopting an accent, turning embarrassment into comedy, 'and I play golf with her husband.'

He didn't wear a wedding ring. Had he removed it or was that a joke? Still: he was making it clear this was going to be a last tango in Bloomsbury.

Z passed me my earring, which had fallen off when we were dancing. He'd found it in the dark. 'Just in case you think I don't notice the details,' he said.

His hotel room was lush but the minibar had been stripped bare. Apparently he had a black mark by his name. The last time he'd stayed there, he'd enjoyed a small party in his room and things had been broken, a chair dismembered. He ordered champagne and as I sipped it, I managed to knock over a glass and break it. We both giggled: no doubt he'd be banned for life now. We lay and listened to 'Lay Lady Lay'. We played cards, gambled away fortunes. He kissed me and we smiled at each other, dreamy, and then became passionate, and made love over and over as the night moved through its blacks and blues.

When we met again, six weeks later, for another night at a hotel in Manchester, he played a kidnapper and I was a girl he had trapped and was not allowed to leave the bed, or there would be trouble. This was my fantasy: being a control freak in real life, I enjoyed someone else being in control of me, inflicting their power and strength.

Around 4 a.m. we pulled up the covers, sleepy together, and he said, 'This kind of passion can't last – it's too intense. It'll burn out one day . . . and then we'll be friends, and it'll be a beautiful friendship.'

Sleep eluded me; my days felt blurry and vague from insomnia and overexcitement. I saw an acupuncturist the following week, despite my fear of needles. 'Are you lovesick?' she asked, seeing how skittish and fragile I looked. If it was a sickness, it had burrowed deep into my psyche, hollowing me out; the world was spinning off-kilter, axis lost, an eclipse where the moon never broke free from shadow. I was desperate for a break from the scarlet madness of it all; I wanted to be my old self again, sober, out of love, rational, able to sleep. I told Z that I was going away to a retreat, would be offline. His reply was cool, casual: *catch you down the track when some anecdotes have collected.* It was another fortnight before I resumed replying, my pleasure edged with dread. I realized I had made a mistake, lost a part of him, burst the bubble. His replies were offhand, hurt; then became warmer; then remote. He was going away, he said, and it would also be hard for him to email. His replies stopped for a day, a week, a fortnight, a month, and I was left broken.

But perhaps this was what I had been seeking all along. I had materialized into life what the art I loved had taught me to desire. I was more of a romantic than I was ever willing to reveal to a lover. The seeds that films and books had planted had blossomed. I had come to romanticize doomed love, or feel that a love affair that was illicit and secret was of greater value than an affair where you cooked a meal together, sat down in front of the TV together, cuddled under a blanket. These love affairs, however, arched across a lifetime, whilst ours had been a matter of months. So: was it grand, was it last tango, brief encounter, or was it merely trivial, fleeting, empty? Had I imbued it with a depth when it was light, a gravitas when it was farce?

There followed a painful, angsty period where our relationship hovered in a liminal space. We shared our news, daily, via email, with the ease and warmth of friends; but there was an underlying tension, a desire easily aroused by flirtation, a jealousy that frequently sparked. I once mentioned to him that I was thinking of going to Rørvig to see my ex, Clara (a lie; though it sounded more exotic than saying I was going to look her up in London). It was the first time I had intimated that I was bi. He replied: *Be Free.* A few days later, he mentioned a story of how he had once come close to sleeping with female twins, which made me roll my eyes.

Like Colette's husband, Henry, Z didn't feel threatened by the idea of me with a woman; but if I mentioned any men who might be interested in me, something primal stirred in him and he would become territorial.

If Nin saw relationships with women as a kind of death, for me it was the reverse. Clara had been a nurturing influence; someone to whom I could show a draft of a chapter and know that I would receive sharp insights softened with praise. With Z, I would read all of his books, which he would sign for me; though he offered advice and encouragement, he never read mine. With Z, I wanted to be him; with Clara, I became more myself, a better version of me. I missed her, sometimes, during that fraught autumn, as the leaves browned and I found myself fretting daily over Z: *what is this, between us?* I wondered if I would be better off with a woman, but rationality was hopeless for now: I was too addicted to Z.

*

I am reminded of Z when I read Nin telling her analyst that 'Henry's great need of woman was due to his being such a man, a hundred-percent man; glory be to the pagan gods that there was no femininity in him.' She tended to see relationships between men and women in terms of traditional masculine/feminine power structures, writing with elation in her diary about 'the joy when a woman finds a man she can submit to'. But this joy came early in her life, in her affair with Henry Miller. Later in life, she came to question it.

'I cannot reach a mature control of my own life. Will I ever be free?' Nin asks herself, angrily and painfully, at the age of fifty. By then she had had numerous love affairs, mostly with men, including her own father, with whom she reunited at the age of thirty after a twenty-year separation. They had a brief affair, which left her 'tortured by a complexity of feelings'; when she ended the liaison, he continued to send her amorous letters. Nin ended up with two husbands. She was still with Hugh Guiler, her 'East Coast' husband, who lived in New York; and there was Rupert Pole, her 'West Coast' husband, who lived in San Francisco. She met Rupert Pole in an elevator in a Manhattan apartment building – a handsome, dark-haired man wearing a full-length white leather jacket – and they discovered they were both heading for the same cocktail party. He was twenty-eight, she was forty-four. As their affair started, he assumed she was divorced, and she didn't correct him. She told Hugh that she needed a writing cabin; there she spent six weeks at a time with Rupert, writing Hugh letters each day about how lonely writing was; when she spent her next six weeks with Hugh, she told Rupert that she had meetings with New York editors and journalism work, writing him letters about how hard she was working. Each man gave her something unique, for Hugh offered financial and emotional stability, whilst Rupert satisfied her sexually. But neither knew of each other, not until she was old and weak and dying of cancer and had to confess. Nin made a 'lie box' in which she kept details of her double life. Maintaining this subterfuge made for a tightrope existence. Reading her diary from this period is a heart-trembling experience, in which Nin lives like a spy, suffering close shave after close shave.

Though she is fulfilled to an extent by both men, she also realizes how frustrated she is. Her heterosexual relationships have resulted in her feeling 'tired of the entire relationship to men . . . I give the man the reins and then feel trapped in his patterns.' Much of this, she realizes, is tied to money and the independence it brings. Hugh still gave her an allowance, and in repetition of her early days with Henry, she takes a proportion of that and gives it to Rupert – who then gives some back to her for housekeeping. Nin concluded that, 'the status of a wife is worth nothing. If I had worked, I would be free and not afraid to stand alone.' Back to her lament, 'I cannot reach a mature control of my own life. Will I ever be free?' It suggests that heterosexual relationships will never fully satisfy her because the role she was made to play was infantilizing, putting her in a childlike, dependent, helpless state. Her love affairs with women, often nervous and fleeting and shy, seemed to involve less manipulation than her affairs with men, where Nin was always seeking covert ways to achieve power.

Anaïs Nin was bisexual. There is no myth to debunk. To deny it is to erase the bisexuality of another famous figure. Yes, it was an uneven bisexuality, an uncertain bisexuality. She did not make love to June because she was inhibited; despite her quest to have adventures and sleep with whom she liked, it was still early in her marriage when they first met. Nerves, doubt, their husbands' resentment, were all social pressures that held these women back from daring to take that dangerous step. But, it is clear: Nin had strong and romantic erotic feelings for women. Her bisexuality allowed her to express parts of her personality that she struggled to repress in an era in which 'masculine' and 'feminine' personality traits were seen in such stark and stereotypical terms. Her lesbian love affairs gave her a chance to be dominating, different. Being with both men and women allowed her to express a richer range of herself.

5

Susan Sontag

To stay in the closet or to come out of the closet? Susan Sontag took a long time to emerge, finally stating the fact of her sexuality in February 2000, at the age of sixty-seven. It wasn't an easy moment for her. Bisexuality was something she admitted to, rather than announced.

Picture the scene: she's in her living room, being coaxed to confess by Joan Acocella, for an interview for the *New Yorker*. She has no desire to come out, to pin a label on herself. She has staunchly avoided any official declarations of sexuality for decades, despite pressure from friends, from PEN, from the public, although, strictly speaking, one might say Sontag was not hiding but hovering in an ambiguous place, a state of 'queer opacity', the glass closet, neither quite in, nor quite out. Whilst she might have refused to define her sexuality, she has written about gay culture; 'Notes on "Camp"' (1964), is still celebrated as one of her most glittering essays. The shock comes when she receives a letter informing her that Carl Rollyson and Lisa Paddock are working on a biography of her: *Susan Sontag: The Making of an Icon*. And they are planning to include details of her relationships with women. Sontag needs to fight back by having the first word. Joan Acocella, who is interviewing her, has advised her to 'Head them off at the pass and use me for it. Use this article for it. Say you're bisexual and that's that.' But Sontag is fearful. Normally so articulate, so eloquent, and ready to defend herself, she is suddenly lost, childlike. She tells Joan that she doesn't know what words to use. The interview begins. Joan switches on the tape recorder. Sontag manages to respond in what Acocella (and her transcriber) describe as a 'strangulated' tone: 'That I have girlfriends as well as boyfriends is what? Is something I guess I never thought I was supposed to have to say, since it seems to me the most natural thing in the world.' Finally, she has opened the door and reluctantly stepped out.

Later that year, she is interviewed by the *Guardian*. Her discussion of her sexuality is more playful, more confident. She tells Suzie Mackenzie that 'when you get older, 45 plus, men stop fancying you. Or put it another way, the men I fancy don't fancy me. I want a young man. I love beauty. So what's new? . . . As I've become less attractive to men, so I've found myself more with women. It's what happens. Ask any woman my age. More women come on to you than men. And women are fantastic. Around 40, women blossom. Women are a work-in-progress. Men burn out.' She declares that she had been in love nine times, with 'Five women, four men.' However, when asked to respond to rumours that she and Annie Leibovitz are in a relationship, she lies. She claims the rumours are 'without foundation.' She and Annie are just close friends.

Sontag could have announced her bisexuality on numerous occasions before the year 2000: during the AIDS crisis, or in the 1970s, when coming out became more acceptable. Gay activists frequently implored her to go public, and she refused, for complex reasons. After her death in 2004, however, a certain backlash set in. The initial news pieces about her passing didn't include any details of her final relationship with photographer Annie Leibovitz, because it hadn't been verified. Since then, Sontag has been portrayed as a coward in denial, who refused to rally and support the gay community. Writing in *The Advocate*, Allan Gurganus complained: 'My only wish about Sontag is that she had bothered to weather what the rest of us daily endure: I wish she had come out of the closet.

The discrepancy between her professional fearlessness and her actual self-protective egocentric closetedness strikes a questioning footnote that is one blot on her otherwise brilliant career.'

Some critics have even emphasized their dismay by deciding that her bisexuality must be a mask. In the *Los Angeles Times*, Patrick Moore declared that Sontag had outed herself in her New Yorker profile as bisexual, which he interprets as 'familiar code for "gay"'. The *Sydney Morning Herald* ran an indignant piece declaring that, unlike traditional news outlets, 'leading gay and lesbian news organisations announced that "lesbian writer Susan Sontag" had died'. Joseph Epstein, reviewing the memoir *Sempre Susan*, a portrait of Sontag by Sigrid Nunez, in the *Wall Street Journal* in 2011, described her as the 'beautiful young woman every male graduate student regretted not having had a tumble with, a fantasy that would have been difficult to arrange since she was, with only an occasional lapse, a lesbian'. Whilst Epstein's tone is less admonitory than the other examples I've cited, the word *lapse* is such a cringe. We find ourselves returning to that traditional idea that bisexuality ought to be evenly balanced, that if the scales tip too much in one direction, it might be invalidated as an identity. Perhaps the fiercest critic of her reticence about her sexuality is Benjamin Moser, who wrote the monumental *Sontag: Her Life and Work*, for which he was allowed unprecedented access to letters, diaries, friends, colleagues, lovers. The book is beautifully researched; the 'coming out' *New Yorker* moment has come to life thanks to Moser's research. However, the tone of the biography ranges from generosity to hostility, admiration to condemnation. On her reticence about her sexuality, however, Moser is impassioned. He doesn't label her a lesbian, for his biography spans the range of her lovers male and female, from Jasper Johns to Carlotta del Pezzo, Joseph Brodsky to Lucinda Childs. But he does tend to emphasize her unevenness as he makes his case: 'Despite occasional male lovers, Sontag's eroticism centred almost exclusively on women', causing a lifelong frustration with her 'inability to think of her way out of that unwanted reality' and a dishonesty about the issue that lasted 'long after homosexuality ceased to be a matter of scandal'. The words 'lesbian' or 'lesbianism' crop up in the book far more when his anger is evident. In all these articles, one feels that by emphasizing Sontag's lesbianism rather than her bisexuality, her silence becomes an even greater sin: simplification becomes a weapon of condemnation.

'There are so many things in my life now that are more important to me than my sexuality,' Sontag said in the 2000 *Guardian* interview. 'My relationship with my son, David. My writing.' There is a note of defensiveness to this quote, as though chatting about her love life is trivial, gossipy. She echoed Roland Barthes' *Death of the Author* by arguing the case, 'For not caring about . . . the writer and what the writer says and what the writer knows and what the writer's life is like or what the personality is or whether you really like that person or you don't like that person . . . Some very good writers have been rather awful people. Some very good writers are not articulate at all . . . It doesn't matter. What matters, finally, is the work . . . You as readers should try as much as possible to repress or marginalise, put to the side, what you know or you think you know about the person of the writer . . . Make it [about] the work.'

I find myself wondering if I am guilty of this sin myself, by writing a chapter focusing on her lovers rather than her essays. But even Barthes, one of Sontag's heroes, said at the end of his life – rather contrarily – that he had 'sometimes come to prefer reading about the lives of certain writers to reading their works', referencing Kafka's diaries and Tolstoy's notebooks. Those whom we love shape our thoughts, ideas, our language, whether in agreement or reaction. Sontag's development and growth as a writer was inextricably linked to her sexuality. Her first love affair with a female, Harriet Sohmers, liberated her and gave her a sense of being 'reborn'; after experiencing her first orgasm with María Irene Fornés she wrote, 'I feel for the first time the living possibility of becoming a writer'; the exiled Russian Joseph Brodsky shaped her ideas on politics and communism; Annie Leibovitz gave her an emotional support that helped her to develop the fiction career she considered more important than her essays and write *The Volcano Lover*.

*

Susan is sixteen years old when she first meets Harriet Sohmers. She is living in California with her mother, Mildred, her stepfather, Nathan, and her sister, Judith. She has suffered an 'unconvincing childhood'. When she was a child, her middle-class parents were frequently abroad, taking long trips to China for their fur-trading business, leaving Susan to the care of nannies in their Long Island home. One day her mother returned home from abroad without her father, Jack. Four months passed, during which Susan believed her father was still in China: her mother finally confessed that he had died of TB. Susan was five years old at the time.

Mildred is not a loving mother. Alcohol is a greater passion for her than child-rearing; the glass that sits by her bed, which Susan thought contained water, is filled with vodka. Fearful of ageing, Mildred asks her daughter not to call her 'Mother' in public; indeed, Susan often ends up feeling like her mother's mother. After a number of house moves, they settle in a cosy cottage in the San Fernando Valley in California. At the age of twelve, Susan reinvents herself. She changes her surname from Rosenblatt to Sontag, taking her stepfather's name. He warns Susan that she reads too much, advising her that she'll never marry – which leaves her amused rather than concerned. At school a teacher catches her pretending to read a copy of *Reader's Digest*, behind which is a copy of Kant's *Critique of Pure Reason*. She's so precociously smart that at the age of sixteen she goes to university, attending the University of California at Berkeley, for a semester.

It's May 1959: the year in which Susan is 'reborn'. She is keeping a diary in notebooks, part of her project of self-transformation, where she often makes lists: of books read and to read, of gay slang, of ways to behave – *don't smile too much . . . sit up straight . . . think about why I bite nails in movies.* Her 'lesbian tendencies' worry her. The thought of sex with a man is 'nothing but humiliation and degradation'; the power relations between the sexes disturb her, and she dislikes the way that a woman must be passive in the act. At Berkeley, she feels exhilarated to have escaped the 'Lower Slobbovia' of her home, to learn how to pronounce Proust, to soak up the rich intellectual atmosphere. She enjoys a sapiosexual crush on a boy called Allan Cox, whom she describes in her notebooks as 'one of the finest intellects I've yet come into contact with'. She loves to discuss music and philosophy and literature with him, their conversation zinging from Bach cantatas to Mann's *Doctor Faustus* to Einstein's theory of curved space.

She visits a bookstore, Campus Textbook Exchange. There she meets a bookseller with a 'beautiful smile' who seems 'wonderfully, uniquely alive': Harriet Sohmers. Harriet, too, is struck by Susan's beauty, her dark hair, her dark eyes. She recommends *Nightwood* by Djuna Barnes, a literary flirtation. A few weeks later, Harriet takes her out on a night of adventure, to the gay bars of San Francisco. In the early hours of the morning, they take a taxi to Sausalito, holding hands, and around 4 a.m., they end up in bed together, in a narrow cot in the back of the lesbian nightclub the Tin Angel, making love. For Susan, the experience is bliss. The feelings of ugliness that she has suffered seep away. 'To love one's body and use it well, that's primary . . . I can do that, I know, for I am freed now.' Whatever has been cramped and blocked inside her is now released with the revelation that 'bisexuality as the expression of the fullness of the individual'. The norms of the 1950s, with the traditional idea that you should stay chaste until the right person came along, are also something she discards, for it 'limits sexual experience, attempts to dephysicalize it'. She feels she has been 'reborn'. Her life choices change there and then. She will no longer go into academia, she decides, and follow a path where she will end up writing 'a couple of papers on obscure subjects nobody cares about and, at the age of sixty, be ugly and respected, and a full professor'.

And yet: a year later, Susan is married.

×

She is only seventeen. She's known her husband-to-be for just over a week. After winning a scholarship to the University of Chicago, she met sociology tutor Philip Rieff. He is eleven years older than her, 'tall + thin with a skeletal face + a receding hairline', as she describes him in a letter to her mother. She attended his lecture on Freud, he asked her to lunch at the end, and their romance has been on fast-forward ever since. She suggested they sleep together; he suggested they wait until they were married.

There's a photo of Susan and Philip together that year: 1950. It shocked me when I first saw it. I'd only ever seen pictures of Susan in which her intelligence, her beauty, her charisma and her power were manifest. Some of the most iconic ones adorn the covers of her books in the Penguin Classics series. Sontag in New York, cool and charismatic in jeans and a leather jacket, looking both magisterial and studenty, a woman who adorns magazine covers but stays up all night on speed, surrounded by books, crafting genius sentences on her typewriter; Sontag holding up a picture frame, symbolic of her myth-making, the way she sculptured herself as a public intellectual; Sontag with an iconic lightning streak of white in her black hair, which for me mixes associations of Cruella de Vil and Einstein. She was featured so regularly on *Saturday Night Live* that they kept a similar wig in their prop department. Sontag the star, the intellectual, the polymath, the Renaissance woman, the wise, the moral, the powerful.

But in this picture, which makes me wince, Susan sits next to Philip outside. Her hair is partially pinned up, her clothes conservative and she looks so cowed, as though the energy that Harriet released in her has been neatly folded up and tucked away. Even as she married, she knew it was a rash, rushed decision – 'I marry Philip with full consciousness + fear of my will toward self-destructiveness', she wrote in her diary. So, why do it? Some critics have seen the decision as a way of trammelling down her lesbian impulses, an attempt to conform to the time, to be normal: marriage as a mask. After her affair with Harriet, she confided her sexual experiences to her friend, Merrill Rodin, reflecting that she couldn't tell her parents who would be 'shocked'. Merrill's friend, Gene Marum, advised her if she didn't want to be gay, she should force herself to go out with men; her diary includes a list of people, male and female, that she's slept with called 'The Bi's Progress', which Moser interprets as an attempt to 'train herself into heterosexuality' by trying to even up the balance, add more men to her quota. Yet other parts of her diary don't support the idea of Susan crushing her love of women, gritting her teeth and forcing herself to sleep with Philip: indeed, she reflects on the erotic frisson between them, even though that desire fades over time. The physical connection is matched by an intellectual one, the joy of being able to talk and talk and talk. If she hurried into their marriage, then perhaps it was partially motivated by an eagerness to escape the family home where she had grown up so unhappily. And whilst seventeen seems so young to us now, it wasn't for the time – in the 1950s the average marrying age in the US was twenty.

She goes into labour in the middle of the night, not realizing at first what is happening. Susan thinks that she has pissed the bed; Philip has to explain that her waters have broken. She gives birth to their son, David, but it is a difficult experience and afterwards she spends a month in bed, recovering and nursing David with help from a nanny. Gradually, Susan begins to feel suffocated by their marriage. At first they are bound by their intellectual pursuits, discussing Kafka and Freud, working together on a book about the latter called *The Mind of the Moralist*. But Philip is a traditionalist who wants a conventional marriage, whilst Susan is starting to find the domestic space oppressive. When they attend dinner parties with other academics, the wives are expected to leave whilst the men smoke together and share cerebral discussions; Susan, irritated by this convention, stays put and philosophizes with the men. She begins to despise the dulling repetition of her relationship with Philip; the feverish talking which was once such an inspiration now makes her despondent about 'the leakage of talk. My mind is dribbling out through my mouth.' She grows to dislike 'his timidity, his sentimentality, his low vitality, his innocence', but she also finds him an 'emotional totalitarian'. At the age of eighteen, she reads *Middlemarch* for the first time and bursts into tears – realizing 'not only that *I* was Dorothea but that, a few months earlier, I had married Mr Casaubon'.

Susan plots her escape. She applies for a one-year fellowship at Oxford and is accepted; Philip agrees that she should have a 'sabbatical' from their marriage; their son, David, now nearly five, will go to live with his grandparents in Chicago. For Susan, it is a seminal moment: a chance for her to free herself from her stifling domestic existence and discover who she is – 'at least I'll know if I am anything outside the domestic stage, the feathered nest', as she ponders if she has been herself in marriage, or 'am I myself when alone?'

At Oxford, she feels as though she is sixteen again. She discovers the joys of being carefree, flirting, living alone again. However, finding it a fusty place, she only completes a term there before moving to Paris to study at the Sorbonne, enrolling in a philosophy course. It is here that Susan discovers a new approach to intellectual life: the café culture of debate and cerebral conversation; French films; the idea of the French intellectual, all of which will shape her ways of thinking and writing and inspire her to become a lifelong Francophile.

In Paris, Susan reconnects with Harriet Sohmers, who is working at the *International Herald Tribune*. They begin a love affair that is turbulent and cruel, where Susan plays at being the (emotional) submissive, Harriet the master; Susan the masochist, Harriet the sadist. Susan is stunningly beautiful, attracting men and women in droves; on one occasion Harriet, who feels that her 'jealousy reflex' is 'being activated big time', punches Susan in the face at a party. However, Susan does enjoy a certain exhilaration from the turbulence of their affair, reflecting that marital wars are a 'deadly, deadening combat which is the opposite, the antithesis of the sharp painful struggles of lovers'. In the meantime, Susan is supposed to be writing to her husband daily, but notices an 'accelerating delinquency in my writing of letters' and a 'growing reluctance, aversion even' to reading his letters. In one journal entry, written as though she is penning a letter to her husband that she can't send, she muses: 'Seven years is a long time, isn't it, dear one? . . . I have given you my youth, my weakness, my hopes. I have taken from you your masculinity, your self-confidence, your strength – but not (alas) your hopes.' A growing cynicism crystallizes in her that marriage is a 'dull, bourgeois institution', whereas homosexuality is a 'criticism of society', a 'protest against bourgeois expectations'.

When Susan flies back to Boston a year later, Philip picks her up at the airport, warm and welcoming. Before he's even had a chance to put the key in the ignition, she asks for a divorce. A few days later, she moves to New York with David, renting a two-bedroomed apartment in West End Avenue, refusing alimony and scraping by on a frugal existence, working as an editor at a journal before taking up a teaching position at Columbia. For a year after their divorce, she wakes up most days with a smile on her face. Finally, she is free: the end of her marriage marks the beginning of her adolescence, which she later jokes lasted from the ages of twenty-seven to thirty-five. It took her ten days to get married, she reflects, but it has taken her ten years to feel she has a right to a divorce; later she will regard those years as 'a lost decade'.

In 1959, during her first year in New York, she meets María Irene Fornés, a Cuban-American aspiring playwright who is also Harriet Sohmer's ex. Their love affair results in Susan's first orgasm at the age of twenty-six, and an immediate explosive impact on her creative energies: 'The orgasm focuses. I lust to write. The coming of the orgasm is not the salvation but, more, the birth of my ego. I cannot write until I find my ego.' A little while later, they're sitting in a café in Greenwich village, when Susan mulls on how unhappy she feels about not making progress with her writing. Irene replies along the lines of, *let's start writing now, and I'll start too*. And there and then, Susan begins writing *The Benefactor*, which will become her first published novel, whilst Irene starts crafting a play; she will go on to become a successful avant-garde theatre playwright and director. Susan and Irene develop a routine of sitting 'across the table from each other, each at their typewriters, stopping to read to the other a passage they were proud of'. It is a contrast to her marriage to Philip, where they both worked on *The Mind of the Moralist*; Moser has argued that Susan was the principle author of the book but, as part of their divorce settlement, her name was removed as co-author and Philip achieved sole credit.

Philip also fights her hard over the custody of their son. After learning about her lesbian affair, he weaponizes it against her, taking her to court on the basis that she is an unfit mother. Susan is successful, and the judge favours her. The case is reported on by the *New York Daily News*, with the headline *Lesbian Religious Professor Gets Custody*. This was a crucial factor in Susan's subsequent reticence about her sexuality. Her friend the poet Richard Howard recalls that she was shocked and shaken by the experience; though she wins the trial, she is no doubt aware that many other gays and bis have lost custody as a result of their sexuality. He feels that it is a formative moment in Susan's silence about her female lovers from this point on.

*

'The 1950s were perhaps the worst time in history for women to love women.' This, from historian Lillian Faderman, sums up the difficulties of the era Sontag was born into and how it infused her with a sense of shame about her sexuality. In 1948, Alfred Kinsey had published his famous study, *Sexual Behaviour in the Human Male*, in which he had created the Kinsey scale, where individuals were rated from 0–6, 0 signifying exclusive heterosexuality and 6 exclusive homosexuality, creating a strong bisexual space in the middle. 'The world is not to be divided into sheep and goats ... nature rarely deals with discrete categories,' Kinsey concluded. 'Only the human mind invents categories and tries to force facts into separated pigeon-holes.' Kinsey himself moved from a 1 or a 2 early in life to a 3 or a 4 later on. A bisexual, he was married to Clara but enjoyed relationships with men throughout their marriage, with her consent and support. The book was followed by *Sexual Behaviour in the Human Female* five years later. His sensational studies were a revelation to American society – which frowned on masturbation and considered homosexuality a deviance. They revealed not only that masturbation was common, but that over half of men and a fifth of women had had affairs and that at least 37 per cent of the male population had some kind of homosexual experience between adolescence and old age. But the heightened awareness of bi, homo and lesbian leanings resulted in both greater understanding and greater hysteria around the issue.

Following the Second World War, American society had heralded a return to the traditional family structure. In part, this was championed as a defence against the threat of communism: the traditional family unit was depicted as solid, safe, sane in its domesticity. Senator McCarthy's Red Scare had also given risen to the Lavender Scare, tying together 'commies and queers' as a common enemy, both portrayed as perverts seeking to undermine public order and indoctrinate children. The official government terminology for anyone with gay leanings was 'deviant'. In 1953, President Eisenhower signed Executive Order 10450, barring gay people from working in federal government. Queers were susceptible to blackmail by communists, it was feared. As a result, government employees were subject to traumatic investigations, and between 5,000 and 10,000 civil servants and military workers lost their jobs, resigned or committed suicide. The FBI and the CIA conducted surveillance on queer groups; the police regularly raided gay bars, harassing, making arrests, whipping up trouble.

Harry Hay, a homosexual man who read Kinsey's report, was inspired to set up the Mattachine Society in 1950 along with Chuck Rowland. The word *mattachine*, from the Provençal/Italian, refers to a thirteenth-century clown or court jester, who was often homosexual, and was known to speak the truth through riddles and play. Given the fog of collective fear, Hay found it very hard to recruit members at first and the society used the term 'homophile' to describe gay men, fearing the term homosexual had been pathologized. Over in San Francisco, the first civil rights group for lesbians, Daughters of Bilitis, was set up in 1955, evolving from a social club to a political organization (Bilitis was a female character romantically linked with Sappho). However, this was an era before Pride. These groups had to compromise. They seemed to accept the premise they were 'degenerate', or unwell (a diagnosis that the medical and psychiatric profession pinned on them), asking for understanding and acceptance. An attitude prevailed that you could be cured, that you could choose to heal your sexuality, resulting in conversion treatments peaking in the early 1960s. In Matt Crowley's 1968 play *The Boys In the Band*, men gather in a Manhattan apartment for a birthday party, the majority of them gay, many of them melancholic, viewing their sexuality as an illness.

The queer literature that was published in this period, the limitations placed on those writing about gay desire, gives us an insight into the prejudices faced. Lesbian pulp fiction (which was often actually bisexual fiction) was a hugely popular genre, selling in vast quantities in the 1950s and early 1960s. The endings of these stories were notoriously bleak. In order to make such fiction acceptable, the heroines had to be punished and come to a sorry end by death or suicide. Yvonne Keller notes that Radclyffe Hall's *The Well of Loneliness*, the subject of an obscenity trial in 1928, was republished in 1960 as lesbian pulp with *Why Can't I be Normal* splashed in red on the cover. A rare novel depicting a nuanced portrayal of female love which didn't end in death was *The Price of Salt*, Patricia Highsmith's classic (also known as *Carol*), published under the alias Claire Morgan. The book was one of Sontag's personal favourites. It ends with a more optimistic finale than many, for Carol and Therese are reconciled. But the price Carol pays is severe, for she loses custody of her children to her former husband.

Often written from the voyeuristic perspective of a man, a typical lesbian pulp plotline would involve a love triangle where two lesbians are observed by the hero, resulting in a love story where one of them is 'normalized' back into heterosexuality. One such example is *Man Among Women* by lesbian author Randy Salem, where the male protagonist, Ralph, enjoys a moment of voyeurism, watching two women together. The one he most desires is Alison, whom he feels he can seduce away from her female lover because he knows 'firsthand' her 'deep and fiery need for a male'. Despite the fact that the novel is known as 'lesbian pulp fiction classic', what follows is a bisexual love triangle whereby Ralph wins Alison and heterosexuality prevails. Bisexuality, then, is portrayed as a sort of Freudian transitional state, where a woman might pass from immature lesbianism to rich and fruitful fulfilment with a man. Or: bisexuality as a kind of conversion treatment, the subtext reinforcing the idea of the time that 'if you want to change, you can'.

It was against this backdrop that Sontag published her daring essay 'Notes on "Camp"' in 1964 in the *Partisan Review*. Though the circulation of the *Partisan Review* was small and elite, the essay would make her famous, launching her career as a critic and cultural commentator. Dedicated to Oscar Wilde, 'Notes on "Camp"' is a list of fifty-eight jottings, playful, sparkling and erudite, where she defines and explores the aesthetic sensibility of Camp, its quiddity as a 'love of the unnatural: of artifice and exaggeration . . . It incarnates a victory of "style" over "content", "aesthetics" over "morality", of irony over tragedy.' Camp is playful; it dethrones the serious. It puts quotation marks around all that it touches, so that a lamp is 'not a lamp but a "lamp"; not a woman but a "woman".' It also collapses the distinction between high and low art. Whilst the traditional dandy adopted a posture of 'disdain' and 'sought rare sensations, undefiled by mass appreciation', Camp signals 'Dandyism in the age of mass culture – makes no distinction between the unique object and the mass-produced object.' Camp, therefore, includes *King Kong*, Jean Cocteau, Tiffany lamps, Greta Garbo, old Flash Gordon comics. If Camp was once 'snob taste', defined by aristocrats, then their heirs are homosexuals 'who constitute themselves as aristocrats of taste'.

When the essay came out, it caused a sensation and was widely reported and discussed in the American national press. This was an era, after all, where people were actively looking for signs of homosexuality as though symptoms of a disease; instead, Sontag suggested that Camp was 'something of a private code, a badge of identity even, among small urban cliques', as though it was special, elite, rather than anything to be ashamed of. That said, whilst Sontag broke taboos, she was cautious in the way she positioned herself. Benjamin Moser has noted that the first printing of 'Notes on "Camp"' included the line 'I am strongly drawn to Camp, and almost as strongly frustrated by it'; when it was included in her essay collection *Against Interpretation* two years later, 'frustrated' was changed to 'offended'. Sontag sets herself up as the heterosexual translating queer culture to the heteronormative masses: objective, detached, engaged, amused, but not actually part of it.

It was a risky piece to publish. The *Partisan Review* received a flood of letters from readers who were shocked and upset by it; and whilst there was much positive coverage, the *New York Times Magazine* declared that 'Notes on "Camp"' was 'potentially dangerous to society – it's sick and decadent' and the *New York Times* published a letter from a reader fretting that if the concept of Camp were allowed to enter the mainstream of cultural life 'then I think our society is headed for a moral collapse unlike anything we've ever seen'. One of the *Partisan Review* editors, who had not been a fan of the piece, wrote to Mary McCarthy in 1965 lamenting that: 'I find New York quite different from what it was three years ago . . . every kind of perversion is regarded as avant-garde. The homosexuals and the pornographers, male and female, dominate the scene.' Others were greatly inspired, however; a few years on, Andy Warhol would make a short film called *Camp* and as Sontag became a celebrity intellectual, she was invited to sit for his *Screen Tests* series.

At the end of the decade came that pivotal moment for the LGBT population: Stonewall. It was still illegal for bis and gays to drink together, dance together, but the Stonewall Inn (run by the New York Mafia) was one of the few places that welcomed them. There were frequent fines, arrests and harassment from the police, including raids where the officers got rough and brutal. On 28 June, the fury against their violence rose to a frenzy; the LGBT population turned on the police when Marsha P. Johnson and Sylvia Rivera, transgender women of colour, resisted arrest and threw bottles at them. The riots lasted for three days.

Brenda Howard was a bisexual activist who had previously fought against Vietnam and for feminist rights. She organized a march a month after Stonewall called the Christopher Street Liberation Day march where, as the *New York Times* reported, thousands gathered 'proclaiming the new strength and pride of the gay people'. The following year she organized a week-long series of events, which inspired similar parades and marches across the world: it's thanks to Brenda Howard that we celebrate June as Pride Month each year. However, although many bisexuals like Brenda were actively involved in fighting fiercely for gay rights, a crisis in vocalizing their identities ensued; many thought it best to keep quiet about their sexuality and focus on promoting homosexuality as a cause. To claim bisexuality at this time was dangerous, given that it supported the idea that homosexuality was 'curable'.

Over in the UK, 1967 was also the year that the Sexual Offences Act was passed. It is often cited as a landmark moment for gay rights but it took years for life to integrate law, theory to become practice, for a true shift in collective consciousness to take place. During the 1950s, there had been a number of high-profile arrests of gay men. Peter Wildeblood, the diplomatic correspondent for the *Daily Mail*, was sentenced to eighteen months in prison for conspiring to incite a young man to commit 'indecent acts'. At his trial, Wildeblood pleaded that he was an 'invert' (a term harking back to Wilde's era) and that he was suffering from 'arrested development', a reference to Freud's idea that bisexuality was an adolescent state that men and women evolved out of. After his release from prison in 1955, he published the memoir *Against the Law* which detailed the appalling conditions at HMP Wormwood Scrubs and argued passionately for reform of gay laws. The controversy around these arrests led to a government enquiry and the publication of the Wolfenden Report in 1957. It took a decade for the report's recommendation – that homosexuality should be decriminalized in private – to come to fruition.

The two key men who pushed forward the 1967 act were Labour MP Leo Abse and Lord Arran. The latter remarked that the act would enable those 'who have, as it were, been in bondage, and for whom the prison doors are now open, to show their thanks by comporting themselves *quietly and with dignity*'. Leo Abse, on introducing the bill, said that it was required to prevent 'little boys from growing up to be adult homosexuals'. Abse later argued that he'd said these words just to get the bill through; he was a Freudian who believed in the theory that bisexuality was an early, natural stage of development and that homophobia stemmed from the latent homosexuality in all of us. If those opposing the bill feared it would 'open the floodgates', then they were concerned about their own repressed gay desire flooding out, he argued. Interviewed by the *Guardian* four decades after the act, he declared that it was not just about freeing homosexuals but 'a way of encouraging society to come to terms with its bisexuality': 'it was the start of opening up society to be more caring and sensitive. One was battling for all men and women to have a greater freedom.'

*

In 2003, Sontag gave an extended television interview, where she began by asserting that: '. . . a very particular citizenly duty that a writer can choose to have . . . is to be a spokesperson and try to formulate opinions, particularly oppositional opinions . . . to be a gadfly. To say what isn't being said by everybody else.'

She went on to criticize the Bush administration, which was controversial at a time when patriotism and emotions were running high following the 9/11 attacks on the Twin Towers. She had been a prominent activist against the Vietnam War and declared that 'the white race is the cancer of human history'. She fought boldly and hard for causes, for individuals: in 2000, when the poet Bei Ling was arrested on a visit to China for criticizing the regime, she called up Bill Clinton's office and pulled every string she could to ensure his release. She was brave enough to travel to Sarajevo and put on a performance of *Waiting for Godot* in a building with no electricity which was in danger of being bombed (later, the square in front of the national theatre in Sarajevo was named after her). It seems surprising, then, that someone so courageous and articulate, undaunted by criticism in the face of controversial opinions, was so nervous about coming out. However, if you look into the ethos that informed her writing and art, it becomes clearer as to why Sontag wanted to avoid a 'bisexual' tag.

There's a video on YouTube that features a clip of Sontag attending the 1971 debate about feminism at the New York Town Hall. It features a panel of women, including Germaine Greer, and is chaired by Norman Mailer. Sontag, in the audience, stands up and demands to know why Mailer has referred to Diana Trilling, also on the panel, as a 'lady critic'. Mailer looks defeated. He agrees that he'll never use the term again. The clip illustrates how vehemently Sontag hated labels. She did not want to be a gay writer. She did not want to be a lady writer, or a woman writer. She did not want to be a Jewish writer. She didn't even like being called an intellectual, rejecting the epithet when it was applied to her at the start of talks and lectures, insisting that she was simply a 'writer'. She was determined to erase the 'I' from her work. In contradiction to the contemporary vogue for confessional writing, she was 'anti-autobiographical', rarely interested in exploring memoir; only a few autobiographical pieces, such as 'Pilgrimage', remain. *Against Interpretation*, the essay collection published in 1966 that made her famous, favours the abstract; it refuses to temper or support its arguments with the personal, instead opting for a more ambitious universal. Such confidence was not always felt by her; there is an element of play-acting in her prose. In her journal of 1980, she felt, 'I must give up writing essays. I have become the bearer of certainties that I don't possess – am not near to possessing.' Which is not to suggest her work was inauthentic: quite the reverse, for she chose to write about authors, films, art that she had genuine passion and admiration for. However, the erasure of her self was her creative manifesto, her approach to her work. Nor was she interested in representing any cause simplistically. She defended herself as a feminist who chose not to bang a polemic drum, but opted for more subtle arguments: 'I'd like to see a few platoons of intellectuals who are also feminists doing their bit in the war against misogyny in their own way, letting the feminist implications be residual or implicit in their work, without risking being charged by their sisters with desertion. I don't like party lines. They make for intellectual monotony and bad prose.'

Her son, David, noted that rather than referring to 'my work', she spoke of 'the work'. But if there was a tint of gender in her writing, she perceived it as masculine. 'The only kind of writer I could be is the kind who exposes himself,' she wrote in 1959. The cover of *Against Interpretation* reinforces this idea. It's an elegant black-and-white photo of Sontag at a party, in a pale dress, framed by men in dark suits, poised ambiguously in mid-listening or perhaps mid-flow; I imagine her owning the room with her opinions, holding sway over them, like Elizabeth I reigning over her court. It is a photo which says: Sontag has invaded the male-dominated literary world, and she has won her place there. She may well have felt that by coming out, she would have compromised her reach, her power, been pushed into the corner of the room, marginalized, labelled a gay writer who would then only be commissioned to write about gay subjects. Patrick Moore has speculated that 'she may have felt that her true sexuality would limit her impact in the male-dominated intellectual elite', implying that some of her power was derived from her desirability. Edmund White, one of her literary contemporaries, observed, 'If Susan had been publicly identified as gay, she would have lost two-thirds of her readership.' Note – again – that she is being labelled as 'gay' rather than 'bi', though that is also part of the trouble: there is a tendency for bisexuals, when coming out, to be re-labelled 'gay', even in recent times. Or, your sexuality becomes a tag attached to your name that you get sick of until you want to wrench it off, as Jessie J discovered when she came out as a bi in 2011: 'I was honest and then BAM it took over, the word bisexual before my name on almost every article. Instantly I was boxed.' This was a fate that Sontag dreaded, and resisted.

Moser compares her unfavourably to Adrienne Rich, also 'an intellectual of the first rank' who, unlike Sontag, publicly acknowledged her lesbianism – 'by coming out publicly [she] bought herself a ticket to Siberia – or at least away from the patriarchal world of New York culture.' As a teenager, Sontag wrote that her desire to write was connected to her sexuality – 'I need the identity as a weapon to match the weapon that society has against me.' Her literary persona was a shield, and she was not prepared to drop it and make herself vulnerable, suffer the attacks that would follow. That shield was her mythology, her project of self-transformation. Yet there is more of Sontag in her novels, for she felt that, 'The fiction comes from a deeper place and a broader place. I have much more access to myself than I do in my essays.' *The Benefactor* is narrated by an aging aesthete called Hippolyte, and portrays homosexuality as 'a playfulness with masks', whilst in her 1992 novel, *The Volcano Lover*, she explores her thoughts on being female when Eleanor, her protagonist, says: 'Sometimes I had to forget that I was a woman to accomplish the best of which I was capable. Or I would lie to myself about how complicated it is to be a woman. Thus do all women, including the author of this book.'

In 1978, Sontag published one of her most famous and influential works, *Illness as Metaphor*, in which she explored the way that illness is primarily couched in metaphor: diseases are no longer suffered but battled, which can make the sufferer feel as though they have been defeated. Given that we might prefer to dodge the draft rather than take up arms, this can impact our decisions to get tested for illness, 'inhibit people from seeking treatment early enough, or making a greater effort to get competent treatment. The metaphors and myths, I was convinced, kill.' Yet she did not mention in the essay that, three years earlier, she had entered the 'kingdom of the sick' herself, suffering from breast cancer and undergoing a radical Halstead mastectomy followed by 30 months of chemotherapy, musing that such 'a narrative, it seemed to me, would be less useful than an idea'. There is, therefore, a consistency in her refusal to refer to the personal, even when writing from rawest experience.

Her later book on AIDS, *Aids and Its Metaphors*, argued that 'more than cancer, but rather like syphilis, AIDS seems to foster ominous fantasies about a disease that is a marker of both individual and social vulnerabilities.' Upon its publication in 1989, she suffered even greater criticism for failing to include the 'I', a confession of her sexual orientation. Jerome Boyd Maunsell argued that 'the understated autobiographical subtext . . . Sontag's own experience as a bisexual – made her text on AIDs look strangely limp and coy. This is perhaps why the book drew such fire from its critics, especially from the gay community.' Her short story 'The Way We Live Now' was a more empathic exploration of the illness, comprising fragments of whispered conversation from the friends of an unnamed man who lies sick in a hospital bed, which layer and overlap to form a wave of communal grief.

*

Susan felt a strong desire to break free of male/female conventions, the way that patriarchal society had ordered relationships so that male and female were 'dominator and dominated', for women were 'raised to be masochists'. The American academic Terry Castle reflected that 'the few times I saw her with men around, they seemed to relate to her as a kind of intellectually supercharged eunuch . . . She seemed uninterested in being an object of heterosexual desire and males responded accordingly.' Susan was not interested in dressing to impress men, to ensnare the male gaze. But she certainly did experience erotic relationships with men:

she felt attracted to Paul Thek, a bisexual friend who inspired her essay collection *Against Interpretation*, and as friends/lovers, they occasionally slept together during the 1950s; meanwhile, some of her relationships with women might have lacked an erotic charge but they gave her maternal comfort, such as Nicole Stéphane, who played a motherly role in their romance. Benjamin Moser felt that her relationships with women were more emotionally significant for her, on the basis of her journals, where there are fewer mentions of men compared to numerous entries where she's 'tearing her hair out' over a woman. Indeed, some of her love affairs with men, particularly in the 1960s, were fleeting. They ranged from Warren Beatty – which lasted a month; he would call her around 500 times a day and Susan once let her phone ring for three hours straight – to Richard Goodwin, a staffer at the White House, whom she summed up as the ugliest person she had ever slept with, and who was also the best in bed. He gave Susan her first orgasm with a man. The impact on her sense of self was anticlimactic, however: 'Oh shit . . . Now I'm just like everybody else,' she lamented. If her attraction to the opposite sex was a source of shame, it also gave her the cachet of belonging to that secret gay aristocracy she had lauded in 'Notes on "Camp"', whereas heterosexuality represented something altogether more bland and everyday.

However, one of her most significant relationships was with Joseph Brodsky. A Russian poet, he was sentenced to hard labour at the age of twenty-three when his writing was denounced by a Leningrad newspaper as 'pornographic and anti-Soviet'. He was arrested and charged with 'social parasitism' – the Soviet authorities felt that being a poet was not a sufficient contribution to society. When he was sent to an Arctic labour camp, there was such an outcry from international cultural figures that his sentence was reduced to eighteen months. In 1972, he was expelled from the Soviet Union and moved to Vienna, then the US, where he became a cause célèbre. When Susan first met him, she recalled that 'he made a stunning impression. He was so authoritative personally. That would register here as supreme confidence.' Sontag and Brodsky were two of a kind: industrious, confident, cunning, devious, prone to being bullies, which was a quality Susan struggled with – 'he could be very cruel'.

Her friend Richard Howard reported that Brodsky was 'so besotted with Sontag that he even asked her to marry him'. His impact on her intellectual life was profound, inspiring in her a newfound fascination for Russian literary classics and East European literature, and causing her to re-evaluate her politics. 'Think whatever you want about him on a political level,' he said of Solzhenitsyn's *Gulag Archipelago*, 'but what he witnessed, what he describes, are *facts*.' Susan's radical left-wing politics softened and led her to adopt a more liberal position; she suffered a public backlash when she boldly declared that Communism is 'Fascism with a human face.' After their relationship faded, they remained close friends. Susan was heartbroken when Brodsky died in 1996, aged fifty-five, from a heart attack: 'I'm all alone. There's nobody with whom I can share my ideas, my thoughts.' Her son, David, recalls that there were two people Susan recalled on her deathbed – her mother and Joseph Brodsky.

Susan saw homosexual relationships as a way of offering the possibility of 'improvising and breaking away from set conventions of the erotic relationship', whilst acknowledging that 'most homosexual couples' only parody heterosexuals. Indeed, many of her affairs with women did involve Susan asserting power or becoming powerless, the emotionally whipped masochist (with Harriet Sohmers), or the bullying, dominating sadist. In 1969, she fell in love with Carlotta del Pezzo, Duchess of Caianello, a beautiful, bisexual, androgynous model whose previous lovers had included Colette's daughter, Colette de Jouvenel. Her life was the polar opposite to Sontag's; whilst Susan was a workaholic with a voracious hunger for art and books, Carlotta was an indolent aristocrat who had probably never read a book in her life. Whilst Susan indulged in drugs for the triumph of her will over her body, buying speed from W. H. Auden so that she could stay up all night crafting a dazzling essay, Carlotta would imbibe smack for debauched fun, partying and sometimes landing herself in jail. For Susan, the process of falling in love, the process of becoming vulnerable, was frightening in the way we all find it: losing layers, exposing the raw underneath – but particularly so for her because her persona was so well sculptured, so that the beautiful and tough and glamorous Susan wrote in her diary: 'Remember what she said the other day about finding me so different from the way I appeared at first' and reminds herself to try and maintain her cool. Inevitably, Susan couldn't keep up that façade. Her lover resembled her mother, 'weak, unhappy, confused, charming'. When their relationship collapsed after a year, Susan was left burnt and scarred, broken and despairing; when her friend Don Levine suggested that they go for a walk, entreating her to look at the beautiful autumnal trees, Sontag replied: 'Fuck the leaves!'

Susan was fifty-five when she met Annie Leibovitz, at a publicity photoshoot for *AIDS and Its Metaphors*. Annie was thirty-nine, one of the highest-paid and most famous photographers in America, who had photographed Demi Moore naked and pregnant, and John Lennon and Yoko Ono just hours before he was shot. Like Susan, Annie was bisexual; her past lovers included Mick Jagger and *Rolling Stone* founder Jann Wenner (and his wife Jane). Following the photoshoot, Annie went out and bought all of Sontag's books. 'I remember going out to dinner with her and just sweating through my clothes because I thought I couldn't talk to her,' she said. 'Some of it must have been I was just so flattered she was even interested in me at all . . .'

In their first meeting, Susan asserted a certain dominance by advising Annie, 'You're good, but you could be better.' This was a steely nurturing that Annie welcomed, feeling that she had often been compelled to be 'a little silly', whilst Susan encouraged her to be serious in her work. Susan seemed eager to play professorial Pygmalion, to inform and transform her new girlfriend with the same zeal she had employed in her own project of self-transmogrification. But when Annie didn't always keep up, when they argued over her not knowing the difference between the October Revolution and the September Revolution, Susan could be snobbish and cruel. She mocked her lover in public; she chided her for her ignorance of Balzac. Her son, David Rieff, remarked that 'they were the worst couple I've ever seen in terms of unkindness, inability to be nice, held resentments.' People were sometimes shocked by the way that Susan treated Annie, though she had herself noted in her diary, years earlier, that 'sadism, hostility [is] an essential element in love. Therefore it's important that love be a *transaction* of hostilities.'

Annie reflected that 'She was actually a very warm, outgoing person, the opposite of what you sort of expected — just so charming, even childlike in some ways'; she recognized that Susan 'was tough, but it all balanced out. The good things far outweigh the bad things. We had so many great experiences together.' The good included their admiration of each other's ambition; making each other laugh; travelling together to locations such as Egypt, Capri, Venice, where Annie would photograph her lover abroad. Their relationship would last for the next fifteen years, on and off.

By the late 1980s, Susan's finances were a worry as she struggled to afford the rising rents in areas such as Greenwich Village. When she hired a new literary agent, Andrew Wylie, she complained that 'I'm sick of being Susan Sontag. I can't get any work done.' Susan now sought 'the highest form of literature in the empire of the novel rather than the republic of the essay', but she was living like a student, struggling to complete her new novel, *The Volcano Lover*, constantly having to write journalism to pay the bills and getting thirty calls a day asking her to write a blurb, make a speech, support a cause. After Wylie negotiated her a large advance, Susan was able to move into an apartment in Chelsea, in the same complex where Annie lived. Susan then won the MacArthur 'genius grant', which would provide funds for the next five years; Annie also bankrolled her, paying for first-class travel, a private chef and maids, spending over $8 million on her over the course of their relationship. Annie saw 'childlike' qualities in Susan, wanted to take care of her, mother her: 'I felt like a person who is taking care of a great monument.' Susan was finally able to focus on *The Volcano Lover*, which she fell into 'like Alice in Wonderland', working for twelve hours a day in 'a delirium of pleasure'. Upon publication in 1992, it received the critical acclaim Sontag had been craving for her fiction writing for years.

They were known as a couple among close friends. But never in public. Susan even denied the relationship to her sister and when her assistant asked about it, she said she hated 'labels'. In interviews, Susan would sometimes assert that they were friends in her determination to resist coming out – and even when she finally did come out, she denied being with Annie, putting her bisexuality safely into the past, obfuscating the present. Annie went along with this for a time. After Susan's death, she reflected, 'words like "companion" and "partner" were not in our vocabulary. We were two people who helped each other through our lives. The closest word is still "friend".' Eventually, however, Annie was left feeling 'frustrated and upset because she was proud of the relationship'; it seemed as though Susan was ashamed of her. Richard Howard and other members of PEN put pressure on Sontag to come out 'in the hope that it would increase public acceptance of lesbians and gays', whilst Michelangelo Signorile, who had a column for *OutWeek* magazine in which he regularly outed celebrity figures as gay, 'called Leibovitz's studio day after day, asking her and Susan to comment on their relationship. Neither returned his calls.'

In 2000, Annie decided to have a baby at the age of fifty-one, which led to their final split. Initially, Susan mocked her, feeling scared that she was losing someone important to her; but nine months on, when baby Sarah was born, Susan was by her side in hospital.

'Endings in a novel confer a kind of liberty that life stubbornly denies us: to come to a full-stop that is not death.' This is Susan in 2004, mulling on ways to end a novel, as though she sensed, on some level, that danger was lurking; in March of that year, she developed myelodysplastic syndrome (a precursor of acute leukaemia). She had suffered cancer twice before, and survived it twice before, but this time it was terminal. Annie took several months off work to help care for her. Susan chose to undergo a brutal bone marrow transplant, even though success was unlikely, despairing that: 'There are still so many things I have to do, I'll never be able to forgive myself if I don't do them.' She was devastated when the transplant failed and her leukaemia returned. Annie took a number of final photos of Susan, as life slowly seeped out of her: her stomach bloated, her black hair now white and cut short. Susan's son loathed the pictures, saw them as 'carnival images of celebrity death', particularly because Annie went on to publish them. I find them very moving to look at. My mother died of cancer at the age of sixty-five, and spent her last ten days on a hospital bed in our living room; I took photos, and gazed at them obsessively after she had gone. Her face had been fraught with tension until the moment of death, when a look of euphoric release adorned her face; to look at it over and over was a repeated reassurance that death had been a tragedy for us but a release for her. Susan once wrote that 'to photograph is to appropriate the thing photographed'. I wonder if, for Annie, those last images were possessive, a way of asserting the love they had shared, conveying what she hadn't been allowed to say in words: *I am the one who was closest to her, who was with her in the end, and here she is, stripped of her persona, her armour: my lover.*

Annie didn't publicly knowledge their relationship until long after Susan's death; *The Daily Show* mocked her for acting as though Susan was 'only a friend'. Finally, in 2006, in an interview with the *San Francisco Chronicle*, she confessed, 'It was a relationship in all its dimensions. It had its ups and downs . . . I mean, we helped each other through our lives. Call us "lovers" . . . I like "lovers". You know, "lovers" sounds romantic. I mean, I want to be perfectly clear. I love Susan. I don't have a problem with that.'

*

I think of Annie when I look back on my liaison with Z, on the frustration of being in a relationship that feels too private, lacks the validation of a public dimension. When I read interviews with him in the papers, I would search for some hint of our affair like a watermark in the page. I felt frustrated that I could not introduce him to friends and family.

Our liaison – or our friendship, or our flirtation, for I was still unsure – continued with daily emails that were long and intimate. He disappeared to the US for a publicity tour. By googling him, I could follow his events, his interviews, where his wit sparkled, his wisdom impressed. He was spinning a persona with flair, casting himself in a lineage of Great Male White Writers: a hint of Amis's provocative panache, the grandeur of Hemingway, the moral seriousness of a Victorian great. Like Sontag, he knew personas were important; he too regarded them as a shield to hide a private self. Once we'd discussed how I might build a persona, what it might be like. But I'd floundered at such a suggestion. I felt that mine needed to erase most of who I was until, like one of those censored documents you see in movies, there were more blacked-out lines than ones you could read. Erase my background from a working-class family; hide my gender (which was easy, given that I was Sam), for there was still a literary atmosphere presiding that women wrote for the masses and male writers won the prizes. Whilst I knew what I wanted to erase, I did not know what I wanted to build. His persona glittered out from prestigious publications and, because I craved love's illusions, I worshipped him all the more for his lies as much as his truths.

Our patchy email correspondence went on for six months. Every so often he'd mention that he was keen to meet, but nothing ever materialized. I lived in hope. A launch party for his new book loomed. I had learnt (from Google) that he did indeed have a partner, thought I wasn't sure if she was part of the persona; my editor told me that nobody at the publishing house had ever seen or met her at any event or party Z attended, and she was a complete mystery. On the night of the launch, there was no partner. But there was a glamorous blonde. I had to spend much of the night watching her sitting on his lap, kissing him. That night, I sent him a crazed email and he replied nervously, and then furiously, wondering why I was trying to pin him down. He told me that he was surprised by my passion, my possessiveness: you seemed such a cool customer, he said, and I thought of how Clara had said I never let people in, and wondered at myself, my perspective shifting 180 degrees, wondering how I might seem to a lover, at how much I kept buried and internalized, unable to translate it into action and speech.

This humiliation ought to have been the full stop; our love affair as a short story, with a bitter ending. But we carried on emailing, day in, day out, and it became a habit, and the months went by, and then the years, and he was the biggest constant in my life. Sometimes the emails were just a few lines – a joke, an anecdote, an update on the day's writing, and sometimes lengthy paragraphs, intimate as a post-coital chat, detailing childhood memories, fears, thoughts on religion, the afterlife, the point of it all. He had once spoken, I recalled, about the regret that came from fucking up and letting good people go. Our passion had died – his passion had died – and this was, I supposed, our beautiful friendship.

*

Four years passed.

I had a brief fling with an Irish actor. I had a few meetings with men from Guardian Soulmates which were farcical, like awful dates from a bad romantic comedy. One claimed he was five foot eight when he was four foot eight and I spent the date looking into the space above his head as though hoping he might unfold himself; another spent the date telling me about all the women he had met on dates who wanted him but he rejected with sadistic delight. I was unable to allow anyone else in. No other man or woman quite had Z's wit, his beautiful mind, his insights (often so throwaway, in an email, like casual genius), his panache. Without wanting to admit it to myself, conscious of how humiliating and humbling it was, I was playing a waiting game, as though I was standing by a shore and Z was far, far out; my heart persuaded me that he must return, that the tide would roll back one day. All I could do was stand there, in sun and wind and rain, and every sound like a distant hush might turn the tide of the sea.

Finally our reunion night came: a rendezvous at a hotel in Europe. Half an hour before our meeting, I had gone to the toilet and seen a stain of red flower in horror: my period had arrived five days early. It was like an omen for the doomed night, which had a feeling of disconnection, anticlimax, years of expectation becoming smoke. I fell into a despair the next day. But to my relief, I was not alone: the night had evoked a frustration in him too, a hunger to recapture the feverish nights of our first summer together, when we had been intoxicated with each other.

In 2010 we drove across Scotland, crossing the border from north to south, the lights in houses coming on as dark descended, silhouettes of lovers and families moving, intriguing. The trees became wild with an oncoming storm. We talked and talked and he told me how beautiful my profile was. He had a night energy but I had to struggle against my tiredness, hungry to savour each moment and commit it to memory. Something had changed, I realized: the seesaw between us no longer heavy with my weight and light with his lack of care. It had come into balance. We ended up in a hotel room, stayed up until around three or four in the morning, having sex and going to dark places together, followed by tender post-coital hugs. When I got up and went to the bathroom, I was surprised by my reflection in the mirror. The glow in my pupils, starry complexion, made me look so alive: but he had made me so, it all belonged to him. He said, *I want to mark myself into your psyche, your soul, so that in decades to come you remember this night.*

In 2012, I published a novel that had taken over a decade to write, *The Quiddity of Will Self*. It aimed to be the literary equivalent of *Being John Malkovich*, with Will Self as its centre of fascination; it was weird and wild and filthy. The epigraph I chose to put at the start of the book was Self's quote: 'It was Cocteau who said that all artists are hermaphroditic.' I suddenly became aware that publication was going to be very different from my previous books, aimed at YA readers: I was being reviewed in the *Sunday Times* and the *Guardian*, whilst disgusted female critics were unfriending me on Facebook. I wanted Z to come to the launch. He was busy, he said, but he barely seemed interested, and so I berated him. I felt like Annie Leibovitz: tired of being someone's guilty secret. But Z did not want to be open about us; for him, the secrecy was the thrill.

I was becoming aware that times were changing. The cult fiction displays in bookshops were no longer solid blocks of male writing; female titles were starting to creep in. Quirky female authors from the past, such as Brigid Brophy and Rachel Ingalls, whom you had to pay a fortune for to pick up second-hand on Amazon, were being reissued. Pink covers lazily marketed to women were being replaced by edgy designs, such as the thick fur on *Bear* by Marian Engel, about a woman who goes to work on an island and has a hot love affair with a bear. Love stories were no longer implicitly about heteronormative relationships; bisexuality hovered in the margins of Sally Rooney's romances. I knew that I was no longer in danger of going to a literary party and having to suffer being introduced to a male editor who 'wasn't really interested in female authors', as I had done in 2006. Z, along with various other male writers, were being toppled from their pedestals – not that it stopped his devotion to writing, nor dimmed his love for his craft. But, as society shifted, my perspective on our love affair shifted. I had read all his books; he'd never read one of mine. He had given me permission to quote from our emails after he died, as though I could only ever be the sidekick, the narrator of his genius. It was a role I had savoured playing, but now it was one I had grown out. I had more confidence in my own writing abilities. I no longer need his approval; now I loved him as an equal.

When I began to pull away from Z, a few years on, it drove him mad. He chased me with a fervour. I was beginning to feel that our relationship fed me in certain respects but still left me constantly hungry: and that was the point. By maintaining a stasis, by seeing each other only a few times a year, if that, the passion could not burn out, we could not end up, as he dreaded, 'in domestic strife'. Whereas I had once been happy playing the mistress, now I found myself maturing, wanting more, even though I dreaded that any relationship might compromise my first love: my writing addiction. I pulled away because I entered more serious relationships, though we continued to email every day, and now it was Z's turn to wait for me, to be patient until they had ended and we could meet again.

And then came the day when he sent me an email with a phrase that leapt off the screen:

Thanks, I love you. This is a picture of the beautiful Wilson's Bird of Paradise of Papua New Guinea. I bequeath this bird to you.

I realized then that though our affair had begun as something messy and superficial, it had evolved into a relationship I would always treasure.

*

There are different theories on the origins of the term *coming out*. One is that the term refers back to the debutante balls of the early twentieth century, where young women would 'come out' into society, ready for marriage; a term echoed at drag balls which elite gay men would attend, thereby announcing their sexuality. 'The coming out of new debutantes into homosexual society was an outstanding feature of Baltimore's eighth annual frolic of the pansies', reported the *Baltimore Afro-American*. The metaphor also has connotations of secrecy: the skeleton tucked away in your closet; the closet as a dark, safe space where you can hide. In James Baldwin's novel *Giovanni's Room*, a small room in Paris, formerly a maid's quarters, is a place where two men, both bisexual, can meet and love in private, where 'time flowed past indifferently above us; hours and days had no meaning'.

Nicholas de Villiers has argued that the stars of the 1950s, such as Andy Warhol, resisted the modern pressure to 'come out' by existing in the closet of opacity. He quotes Barthes, writing in the preface to the gay classic *Tricks* by Renaud Camus, declaring that the 'one thing that society will not tolerate' is 'that I should be . . . *nothing*, or, more precisely that the *something* I am should be openly expressed as provisional, revocable, insignificant, inessential, in a word irrelevant'. De Villiers considers this not as a strategy of silence, of invisibility, but of opacity, in the figures of Michel Foucault, Barthes and Andy Warhol. Villiers also points out that insisting on someone coming out can be the manifestation of homophobia in another form, 'demanding transparency to the gaze of the interrogator', suggesting a fear of the hidden and the unknown. As David Halperin writes: 'If there is something self-affirming and indeed *liberating* about coming *out* of the closet, that is not because coming out enables one to emerge from a state of servitude to a state of untrammelled liberty. On the contrary: to come out is to precisely expose oneself to a different set of dangers and constraints.'

I can think of so many public figures who are secretive about their heterosexual relationships. I remember those years of specu- lation that accompanied the *Twilight* films, as to whether Kristen Stewart and Robert Pattinson were lovers offscreen: the sneaked paparazzi photographs which caught them chatting in a lift, kissing, the buzz and the gossip and the 'are they, aren't they' excitement. A heterosexual star never has to suffer the pressure of being a spokes- person for love and relationships. They might be condemned for conducting a love affair as a publicity stunt or shamed for infidelity. But to be silent about their loved ones might even be seen as a form of gravitas, particularly for male stars, serious actors, who are above such things. Not so for bisexual or gay stars. To be silent means you are ashamed. To be silent is to make yourself a blank page, to enact a betrayal. When Ellen Page came out as gay in 2014, she said, 'I am tired of lying by omission.' (She later came out as trans and became known as Elliot Page.)

Sontag wrote that 'it is the author naked which the modern audience demands, as ages of religious faith demanded a human sacrifice', and this is doubly so for the bisexual or gay author or artist. You must represent the community, play politician – a pres- sure that many bisexual figures have struggled with, from Sontag to Bowie to Jessie J. Sontag felt that her love life, as a whole, was a failure. Relationships were a struggle; her relationship with Annie Leibovitz was fraught. So should we condemn her for protecting it in the manner that heterosexual stars do, when they draw a line around their private spaces? Judith Butler questioned the idealized notion of coming out of the darkness (the closet) into a supposed 'illumination'; indeed, for Sontag such illumination would not have involved the soft lighting of friends and family smiling congratu-lations, but a spotlight of searing intensity. 'Coming out' implies a sense of bold ownership, of saying, 'this is me, this is my narrative', but too often for bisexuals, it then gets rewritten: Amber Heard came out as bisexual and then attracted headlines about how she had announced she was gay. Bisexuals do not step out of the closet into an open, free space; as the academic Clare Hemmings has noticed, bisexuals are often characterized as existing in precarious geographical landscapes, and so they often end up being seen as 'sitting on the fence', neither here, nor there.

Before her confession in 2000, Sontag had moments of regret and uncertainty about not coming out. Terry Castle recalls the following about Sontag: 'in some way I felt the subject of female homosexuality – and whether she owed the world a statement on it – was an unresolved one for her', and 'was there some way, I wonder now, that she wanted me to absolve her?' In her essay collection *Under the Sign of Saturn*, Sontag celebrated the author Paul Goodman, whom she regarded as 'our Sartre, our Cocteau', writing that she admired 'his courage . . . one of the most admirable being his honesty about his homosexuality in *Five Years*, for which he was much criticised by his straight friends in the New York intellectual world'. There is, perhaps, a note of wistful envy here. In the end, I believe she carried the past with her. Such is the nature of this kind of trauma: I am aware of all the gains women have made across my lifetime, but the chauvinism I endured in the noughties still lingers and co-exists. Fears that might now seem irrelevant still inform my feelings. Richard Howard felt that for Sontag the shock of nearly losing her child stayed with her; the prejudices that she grew up with seeped into her and became an internalized homo-phobia. When her assistant Karla Eoff, witnessing Sontag in crisis in the late 1990s about her sexuality being exposed, asked her, 'So you're bisexual. Own up to that. What does it hurt?', Sontag's reply belied a coming-of-age in the 1950s: 'I don't think that same-sex relationships are valid.' Karla recalled how she then 'came up with all of these things that you hear from these awful people who call themselves Christian: "The parts don't fit."' Interviewed after Sontag had died, the actor Fran Lebowitz defended her passionately, saying, 'That must be the only thing I ever defended Susan about', arguing that, 'This is completely unfair . . . This is an age thing. To someone my age, this seems to me like a private thing. Why is it a private thing? Because for someone my age, for most of your life, it had to be a secret thing.' And so I disagree with Benjamin Moser when he declares, 'inauthenticity was the price Sontag paid for maintaining her cultural centrality'. I don't blame Sontag; I blame the society she grew up in, which left such a strong character feeling weak with shame, rendered such an eloquent and articulate woman silent on the subject of her sexuality.

6

David Bowie

My mother took me to see the film *Labyrinth* when I was eleven years old, along with my younger brother. We loved it so much we went back for a repeat performance. David Bowie, then in his late thirties, played the film's antagonist, Jareth the Goblin King, who steals sixteen-year-old Sarah's baby brother and challenges her to fight her way through the labyrinth to rescue him. This was the first time I had encountered Bowie's androgyny. His Goblin King persona is both deeply masculine – sporting a thick leathery jacket and tights so tight that his codpiece is a hilarious, notorious bulge – and sinuously feminine, with beautiful eye make-up and long, sweeping blond locks reminiscent of his 1970s glam rock phase. (When I saw the film later in life there were cheers and wolf whistles every time the bulge appeared on screen; the end of the film was met with rapturous applause.)

Brian Froud, the film's concept designer, said that the Goblin King was influenced by Heathcliff, Mr Rochester, and the Scarlet Pimpernel; one of his costumes was inspired by a character from Grimm's Fairy Tales: a knight with worms eating through his armour. He is an uncomfortable, disruptive presence in the film, introducing a dangerous sexuality into a childish world of puppets and colourful sets, luring a young Jennifer Connelly into biting a forbidden fruit that leads her into a glass bubble of decadent fantasy. It's the most memorable scene in *Labyrinth*: Connelly, dressed in a beautiful, fairy-tale ballgown, her hair a dark halo decorated with stars, enters a ball and pushes through eerie, masked dancing figures, searching for King Bowie, who is always a little out of reach, enigmatic and alluring, until he finally steps forward and dances with her, fixing his steely gaze on her. The scene represents a latent sexual awakening – and stirred lovelust in hundreds of young fans who went to see the film and, like me, experienced their first film crush. I had no idea then that the Goblin King was a rock star, or that he had been one of the UK's most famous bisexual figures in the 1970s.

In the late 60s, the modern idea of bisexuality as an identity began to take shape. In America in 1972, the bisexual activist Don Fass founded the National Bisexual Liberation Group in New York, which published the first bi newsletter, *The Bisexual Expression*. In the UK, Charlotte Wolf published a key book in 1977, *Bisexuality: A Study*, when she interviewed over 150 bi men and women, concluding that bisexuality – which she deemed the natural state – was much more prevalent than society realized. Even so, in the fight for queer rights and progress during the early 1970s, bisexuals were often discriminated against, erased or actively rejected by the gay community.

At the start of the 1970s, homosexuality was still listed in the American Psychiatric Association's handbook *Diagnostic and Statistical Manual of Mental Disorders*. Stonewall might have sparked a riot, queers might be gaining a voice, but there existed a lingering belief that they were suffering from neurosis/mental aberration. In Sweden, a spate of workers telephoned in sick. Their illness? 'Homosexuality', they'd reply, using absenteeism as a form of protest and satire. Although homosexuality had been decriminalized in Sweden in 1944, being gay was still classified as a sickness by the National Board of Health and Welfare.

In the UK, although the 1967 Sexual Offences Act decriminalized homosexuality for anyone over the age of twenty-one – so long as they kept their sexuality private – it actually introduced harsher penalties for public acts. This reflected the mood of the nation. When the *Daily Mail* ran an opinion survey in October 1965 for their readers, 63 per cent disagreed that homosexual acts in private should be deemed criminal, but 93 per cent believed that such men were in need of psychiatric help. Bis and gays were no longer sinners or wicked men to be loathed. Now they had the nation's pity; the attitude was, 'let them get on with it, as long as it's behind closed doors'. Queer men, therefore, couldn't chat each other up outside, couldn't exchange telephone numbers in a public place because this would be 'opportuning for an immoral purpose'. It was still hard for a gay couple to rent a flat together; men would need to find a gay-friendly solicitor, whilst lesbians had to find a guarantor.

Queer people were expected to be seen and not heard, as though they might spread their sexuality like a virus if they were too public about it. In 1967, the Rolling Stones recorded the song 'We Love You' after the arrests of Mick Jagger and Keith Richards for drug possession. The video for the song was a cheeky reimagining of Oscar Wilde's trial, with Jagger as Wilde, heavily bound in chains, Marianne Faithfull as Bosie, and Keith Richards playing a grim judge, his wig made up of absurd rolls of paper. The BBC refused to play the video on *Top of the Pops*. It seemed that queer love was still one that dared not speak its name.

If you had walked down Harley Street in 1971, you might have seen members of the Gay Liberation Front demonstrating against the psychiatric profession. The GLF, as they were known, weren't prepared to shut up and hide their sexuality and sit quietly whilst prejudices raged across the media. Freud might have argued that bisexuality was innate, but from the 1940s to the 1970s, various members of the psychiatric profession disregarded this viewpoint and felt that homosexuality could be cured. Dr Irving Bieber, for example, declared that 27 per cent of patients were 'converted' in his clinic. When the American psychiatrist David Reuben published the bestseller *Everything You Always Wanted to Know About Sex* (*But Were Afraid to Ask)*, the queer community was disgusted by its prejudice: lesbianism was seen as 'immature' and gay men 'were trying to solve the problem with only half the pieces'. The GLF reacted by leafleting WH Smith and composing a letter of complaint, inviting members to contribute key points; two points about bisexuality were initially on the list, but never made it into the final letter.

The GLF were engaged in a political fight that revolved around an ideological binary. The 'straight' population represented conservatism, preserving the traditional family unit and gender stereotypes, supporting the patriarchal family. In contrast, the gay community was progressive, and aimed to tear down such conventions and create a new way of living. Since many bisexuals ended up in heterosexual marriages, they could reinforce the very power structures the GLF wanted to bring down, and were therefore regarded with a degree of suspicion. Lesbian feminists were also suspicious of female bisexuals because they were seen as 'sleeping with the enemy'. In the previous decade, numerous psychiatric theories had argued that children were made queer by their parents – girls who weren't encouraged to play with feminine toys would become lesbians, for example. Gay Pride in the 1970s fought back by asserting that homosexuality was not the result of a bad upbringing, but a choice. But that also meant that bisexuals could be seen as traitors, by actively choosing to marry the enemy.

I was surprised to discover, however, that the GLF did regard bisexuality as an ideal of human sexuality. As Steven Angelides has noted, 'a particular temporal framing of bisexuality has cast bisexuality in the past or future, but never in the present tense.' Freud, after all, located it in the past, a state we evolve out of. For the GLF, bisexuality represented a utopian future – one to be embraced once compulsory heterosexuality had been abolished. Bisexuality was often a starting point or an end point, but it rarely managed to anchor in the present.

The Campaign for Homosexual Equality was another important organization fighting for queer rights. Earlier in the 1970s, they were more sympathetic to bis. Initially, the CHE were less radical then the GLF, more moderate, and more willing to promote a homosexual way of living that was 'private and respectable'. If in the Victorian era you donned a mask and hoped it wouldn't slip, then now there was a greater awareness and acceptance that theatrics should be performed, that you should slip on your heterosexual mask and only remove it once you were indoors and the curtains were closed. LGBT rights campaigner Lisa Power recalled how bis and gays grew tired of having to wear a suit. It was as though it had become the costume for proving that you were a vital part of a capitalist society, earning a living to support your family, and any hint of indolent, dandified, decadent rebellion remained hidden behind cufflinks and smart collars. The image of 'being in the closet' suggests you leave the clothes that might describe who you really are in that dark place, in order to don the boring suit and blend in with the masses, to say goodbye to your individuality, be part of the crowd who flow over London Bridge under the brown fog of a winter's dawn.

And then along came David Bowie in 1972 and – in the words of critic Rupert Smith – 'blasted the closet door off its hinges'.

*

Around 14 million people – over a quarter of the British population – watched Bowie on *Top of the Pops* on 6 July 1972. He bounded on stage as Ziggy Stardust and played an androgynous bisexual alien who had come to Earth to warn the planet of an impending apocalypse. His hair was dyed red and spikey, his face made up pale, his costume bright orange and kingfisher blue, quilted and slithery against his skin, inspired by *A Clockwork Orange* and Japanese kabuki theatre. He curled his arm around his guitarist, Mick Ronson, with affection and eroticism – a queer gesture of wild daring. Here was bisexuality being performed under surveillance – cameras everywhere – with joyful abandon: bisexuality noisy and furious, bisexuality bright and bold. Bowie came right up to the camera, pointing a finger, singing 'I had to phone someone so I picked on youuu' as though seducing the viewer, initiating them into his decadent and joyful world. Parents were shocked; young people were enthralled. As the journalist Dylan Jones recalls, 'the next day Bowie was all anyone was talking about.'

Bowie was born in Brixton to Peggy, a waitress at a cinema, and John, a promotions officer for the children's charity Barnardo's. He'd grown up in the grey suburban conformity of Bromley. A whole generation of repressed young people could now fuck conformity, unleash and explore their queer fantasies. On the album, Ziggy is referred to as a 'mama-papa' (gender fluid), 'the space invader' (heterosexual) and 'a pink-monkey bird' (gay slang for receiving anal sex). Ziggy the alien represented the outsider, the shameful role so many gays and bis had been cast into – but now being the outsider was glamorous. For a society still afflicted by a lingering homophobia, bisexuality represented a liminal place which was a little more acceptable.

Bowie was, after all, married. His wife was the model and actress Angela Barnett. And he was a new father; their son, Zowie, was just a year old. For years they had frequented gay clubs together, such as the Sombrero Club in Kensington, where Angie would dress in a suit and Bowie would flirt with men such as the costume designer Freddie Burretti. But, as a man who cavorted on stage and then went home to his family, Bowie represented both daring and safety, transgression and tradition. As CHE argued in their fight for gay rights, bisexuality offered 'a bridge between the gayworld and the straightworld'.

The *Top of the Pops* performance substantiated a provocative interview Bowie had given to *Melody Maker* a few months earlier, where he declared he was 'gay' and always had been (later he said he was misquoted, that he'd said he was bi and they simplified this to 'gay' – a problem familiar to many bis). It was an interview that celebrated Bowie's sexuality and his androgynous dress – 'camp as a row of tents', the copy cooed, 'rock's swishiest outrage'. Bowie had worn drag prior to Ziggy, draped across a couch in a Mr Fish dress for the album cover of *The Man Who Sold the World*, influenced by his time as a mime artist with Lindsay Kemp and kabuki theatre, where the *onnagata* actors – the men who impersonated women on stage – were encouraged to dress as women in real life too.

The *Melody Maker* piece was published in the same year that John Berger's *Ways of Seeing* came out, exploring the male gaze in art. Bowie turned the gender tables, revelling in his role under the spotlight and being an object of desire for the male and female gaze. Grayson Perry recalled how liberating this was, how at the time 'the social texture was very straight' but 'it felt like Bowie was giving me and a whole generation of kids permission to explore the dressing up box.' 'Gender-bender' was the term the press affixed to him that year, a lurid term for gender fluidity and bisexuality; though it was, at times, used with affection and admiration too. Later in the 1970s, Charlotte Wolf noted that the meaning of the term 'bisexuality' still shifted between sexuality and androgyny, just as it had at the start of the century. You can see this in moments such as Bowie's interview with the fusty television presenter Russell Harty in 1973. Harty keeps giving Bowie quizzical glances; you feel as though, like the doctors of the Victorian era who were called in to examine the 'criminals' of the Cleveland Street scandal, eager to find signs of what a gay was, the presenter wanted a shortcut: he wanted to pin down and recognize a bi. He glances down at Bowie's outrageous pink and orange sparkly platforms and says, 'Are those men's shoes, or women's shoes, or bisexual shoes?' Bowie responds:

'They're shoe-shoes, silly,' rousing laughter from the audience. Harty's question suggests that bisexuality sits in a hermaphroditic realm between male and female.

There's another moment in this interview where Harty asks Bowie why bisexuality has become so fashionable. Bowie stares intently at the camera as though delivering a political manifesto, his charisma mesmerizing; he explains that his father's generation had been happy to settle with a good job for life, but 'now people want to have a role in society, they want to feel they have a position, they want to be an *individual*, and there's a lot of searching to find the individual inside oneself.' *An individual*: an interesting choice of word, given that the campaign for queer rights around this time was so often about finding safety in numbers, lobbying as groups. The critic Camille Paglia has noted that Bowie's dressing was particularly subversive at the time because, since Stonewall, gay men had adopted a macho uniform of jeans, lumberjacks and moustaches; Bowie's dress was disruptive. But Bowie understood that his championing of bisexuality signalled a shift in collective consciousness. He represented all queers in this epochal moment, later reflecting that: 'I think we took it on our shoulders that we were creating the twenty-first century in 1971. We just wanted to blast everything in the past, question all the established values, all the taboos.'

'There is a new vibration to spring this year. While the birds and the bees are striking up their vernal hum, so are the boys and the boys and the girls and the girls. Bisexuality is in bloom.' This was *Newsweek* in 1974 which, along with *TIME*, ran articles on 'bisexual chic'. Numerous pop stars had come out as bi, including Elton John and Marc Bolan. In the US, famous female bisexuals included Janis Joplin, and Maria Schneider (who starred in *Last Tango in Paris*). *TIME* magazine cited the psychologist John Money's view that 'the single major cause of the new acceptance of bisexuality was the invention of mass birth control, which separates recreational sex from procreational sex and influences attitudes toward "every part of sexuality". But the article ended on a note of sheer prejudice, demonstrating that the psychiatric community were even more damning about bis than gays; psychologist Natalie Shainess is quoted as saying 'that bisexuality and homosexuality are symptoms of "developmental damage"' during childhood. A homosexual, she notes, grows up distrusting the opposite sex; a bisexual is in a sense in a worse plight because he distrusts both sexes.'

For all these criticisms, bisexuality was in vogue: associated, once more, with decadence, transgression, beauty and danger. According to the journalist Cosmo Landesman, it was an era when he first heard the claim 'everyone's bisexual' from a girl on a date (Cosmo wasn't happy about this). 'Bisexuality was so fashionable that it seemed that everyone I knew was either bisexual or pretending to be,' he grumped. The novelist Robertson Davies sums up the moment when he remarked that 'the love which dare not speak its name has become the love that won't shut up.' A cynicism set in, however, that all these glam rock stars were capitalizing on a trend, using it to sell records and widen their fanbase, sweeping in gay as well as heterosexual fans. In a 1979 TV appearance, Bowie is interviewed by a woman who asks him if he is bisexual. 'Yes,' he replies. But she won't accept the answer. She asks again and he gets snippy, rightly irritated by her scepticism, her refusal to accept his sexuality, shutting down the discussion by retorting: *I've answered the question.*

'Stars are beings that partake at once of the human and divine, they are analogous in some respects to the heroes of mythologies or the gods of Olympus, generating a cult, or even a sort of religion.' This quote, from French philosopher Edgar Morin, reminds me of Bowie's commentary in the 2022 *Moonage Daydream* documentary, released a few years after his death. The film begins with Nietzsche's famous proclamation that God is dead, felled by man, which 'led to a terrifying confusion: for if we could not take the place of God, how could we fill the space we had created within ourselves?' Early on in the film, there is a mesmerizing image of Bowie on stage as Ziggy, haloed in red light, looking like some sort of crimson deity, guiding his audience on a journey of beauty and mysticism. Bowie's voiceover comes in as he narrates Ziggy's genesis: 'I believe that there was some unconscious need to create a high priest form, from the line of the Greek gods who could procreate themselves, somebody who was at a super level to we regular mortals, because of his androgynous nature, being somebody who incorporated both feminine and masculine attributes.' Indeed, Bowie and other queer gay icons are something like a postmodern pantheon for the twentieth century, echoing the gods and goddesses of the Greek era in their androgyny and sexuality. The gods Apollo, Poseidon, Hermes, Dionysus, Pan and Zeus were all bisexual. Zeus, the protector and father of all gods and humans, was married to Hera, but fathered children with numerous mortal women; he also fell for the beautiful Ganymede, 'the fairest of mortal men'. Zeus famously turned himself into an eagle and abducted Ganymede, inviting him to become his cup-bearer on Mount Olympus, which has been depicted countless times in art: pottery, sculpture and paintings. In the Philippines, before the Spanish colonization occurred, Animism was the flourishing religion, and the shamans, or *babaylans*, was a feminine role that might be occupied by women, or men in feminine clothing. Academic John Izod has drawn parallels between 'the rocker and the shaman: a "traditional" rock concert functions as a mass, a gathering of the tribe around the medicine man. The visionary singer takes his audience to another universe', which sounds to me like an apt description of a Bowie concert.

And so, for a time, it seemed as if Bowie was the ultimate bisexual icon . . . *but* . . .

*

Fast-forward to 2002. Bowie is sitting on the sofa on *The Jonathan Ross Show*. By now, Bowie has been asked about his sexuality in interviews for decades and grown tired of it. Ross joins in, both softening and sharpening his question with humour: 'What's the deal? You were gay for a while, then you were not gay, but were you bisexual, were you pansexual, were you tri-sexual? Because I thought being gay was like being in the Foreign Legion – once you joined, I didn't think you were allowed back in?'

Bowie – as he often did when asked this question – looks on edge even as he jokes with Ross, laughing and replying, 'I just got my leg over a lot . . . I was incredibly promiscuous and I think we'll leave it at that.' His unease sums up the awkward cultural position he ended up occupying: the first bisexual music superstar who did more for gay culture than anyone in the 1970s, who may or may not have been bisexual.

Having once boasted to William Burroughs that he embodied 'the spirit of the Seventies', Bowie retreated, flirted, teased and then back-tracked about his sexuality. Following the 1972 *Melody Maker* interview, he confirmed his bisexuality in an interview with *Playboy* in 1976, playful and flippant: 'for one thing, girls are always presuming that I've kept my heterosexual virginity for some reason. So I've had all these girls try to get me over to the other side again: "C'mon, David, it isn't all that bad. I'll show you." Or, better yet, "We'll show you." I always play dumb.' He also described how, at the age of fourteen, he had slept with 'some very pretty boy in class' who he 'neatly fucked on my bed upstairs'. Despite the fact that Bowie was openly proclaiming his bi status, not everyone was convinced – and nor, it seems, was Bowie himself. In the same year that he gave his *Playboy* interview, he also told a journalist that his bisexuality was 'just a line'; meanwhile, the *Boston Phoenix* asserted that he was 'an authentic gay superstar, authentically a superstar and authentically gay at the same time – for the first time in our culture since Oscar Wilde'.

Was it all a publicity stunt? After a decade marked predominantly by failure, where his only hit was *Space Oddity*, of singing in
bands such as the King Bees, the Mannish Boys, the Lower Third,
of releasing songs that went nowhere, dabbling with different
styles, miming at being a mime artist, releasing two solo albums
that tanked, being dropped, firing managers, and wondering if he
should jack it all in, Bowie had released *Hunky Dory* in 1971. The
cover is a perfect illustration of how he embodies both definitions
of bisexuality, both ancient and modern, bisexous and bisexual, his
pose inspired by an album of Marlene Dietrich photographs.

Hunky Dory is one of my favourite Bowie albums. Written after
he had spent years striving for success, neglected by his manager,
Bowie experienced a surge of creativity and optimism as he set
aside his guitar and composed the album on an old grand piano.
It includes 'Oh! You Pretty Things', 'Changes', and the album's
magnum opus, 'Life on Mars'. I saw Bowie perform the song live
around 2002, at a small, intimate venue in London, and I've never
forgotten how it prickled tears in my throat whilst evoking surreal
colours in my mind. And yet, when it was released in December
1971, it didn't sell well. It looked as though Bowie was in danger
of another flop despite critical acclaim; it also seems astonishing
now that 'Changes', released as a single in the spring of 1972,
failed to soar. For Bowie, the *Top Of The Pops* performance was a
moment where all his skills coalesced, where he combined theatre
and music and mime in a glorious cocktail. It was a breakthrough
for gay rights – and a personal breakthrough for him as his *Ziggy*
album shot up the charts and his other, overlooked and underrated
album, finally took off too.

*

The word 'kaloprosopia' means transforming your personality by
living your life as a work of art. Bowie's chameleon reinventions
hark back to Wilde and his penchant for living as a work of art.

Bowie was subversive in reinventing himself over and over, using personas as a way of exploring parts of his psyche and creating masks he could hide behind, making his characters simultaneously intimate and elusive. 'David was a person who collected characters,' Alan Yentob reflects, 'and also because he was sort of propelled by curiosity', embracing his own uncertainty as to who he was and who he wanted to be. It meant that his fans could also collaborate in this process of creating, explore their dimensions in his dimensions; Bowie reflected that, when it came to Ziggy, 'fans contributed more information than I put into him.'

In his publicity, he refused to be pinned down, embracing the ephemeral, acutely aware that ambiguity was part of his game. It electrified his fans, who were seduced by the way he contradicted himself in interviews, declaring that he was going to retire from music one day and then going on to do a three-month tour the next, shedding persona after persona like a hyperactive snake. 'Nothing matters except whatever it is I'm doing at the moment,' he told *Playboy*. 'I can't keep track of everything I say. I don't give a shit. I can't even remember how much I believe and how much I don't believe. The point is to grow into the person you grow into. I haven't a clue where I'm gonna be in a year. A raving nut, a flower child or a dictator, some kind of reverend – I don't know. That's what keeps me from getting bored.'

And so Ziggy Stardust was killed off in 1973, much to the horror of both his band and his fans. Bowie undulated through identities, Ziggy morphing into Aladdin Sane, a lightning bolt painted bold on one eye, to Halloween Jack of Diamond Dogs who sang 'plastic soul' to the fascist, ghostly Thin White Duke, to his final persona, the Blind Prophet, blindfolded with button eyes. His 1970s personas had a common theme of androgyny and gender fluidity, from Halloween Jack's eye-patched pirate to the elegant tailoring of the Thin White Duke, whose slender silhouette echoed Marlene Dietrich's famous pose. He told the *Daily Express*, 'I'm Pierrot. I'm

Everyman. What I'm doing is theatre and only theatre . . . What you see on stage isn't sinister. It's pure clown. I'm using myself as a canvas and trying to paint the truth of our time on it.' Bowie's acting was heavily stylized, highlighting its own theatricality. Yet who could say where Bowie left off and a character began, whether his bisexuality was bleeding into Ziggy or Ziggy was merely an experiment in a sexuality he did not enjoy in his private life?

In a 1976 interview he said: 'Most people still want their idols and gods to be shallow, like cheap toys. Why do you think teenagers are the way they are? They run around like ants, chewing gum and flitting onto a certain style of dressing for a day; that's as deep as they wish to go. It's no surprise that Ziggy was a huge success.'

But Bowie is – self-consciously and playfully – selling himself short. He painted a lacquer of irony onto his lyrics, but they were layered with a richness of reference, a depth of thought, a passion for film, theatre and reading. Watch any performance and what is striking is not just the costume, or the sets, or the enigma of his adopted character, but the sincerity of his performance, the sheer soul in his singing, the passion of his delivery, which remains a constant beneath the shifting personae. And so it was hard to simply dismiss Bowie's bisexuality as mere theatre, given the personal element underlying each creation. His fans revelled in the joy and frustration of playing the guessing game. They would buy songs and attempt to dissect the lyrics 'to find out about Bowie's sexuality'. In 'John, I'm Only Dancing' – described as a 'bi anthem' – Bowie assures his jealous male lover, 'She turns me on' but he's only dancing, whilst in 'Rebel Rebel' he crooned about having your mother 'in a whirl' because she's uncertain if you're a boy or a girl. As the journalist Jon Savage sums up, 'Bowie invented the language to express gender confusion.'

*

The denial came in 1983. Bowie appeared on the cover of *Rolling Stone*, with the shock headline: *David Bowie Straight*.

Bowie declared that his *Melody Maker* interview of 1973 had been 'a mistake'. His bisexuality phase had just been adolescent, fleeting: 'Christ, I was so *young* then. I was *experimenting*'. In 1993, he would reiterate this sentiment, in another interview with *Rolling Stone*, asserting that it wasn't really him, it was Ziggy: 'I was always a closet heterosexual . . . I was physical about it but frankly it wasn't enjoyable'. His bisexuality was not sexual, it was cultural, he emphasized: 'I was more magnetised by the whole gay scene, which was underground. Remember, in the early 70s it was still virtually taboo . . . I like this twilight world'.

For many of his fans in the 1980s, the confession was a shock. The timing seemed cruel, coming as it did on the eve of the AIDS crisis, when gays would be vilified and bisexuals condemned as deviants who carried the disease to the heterosexual population. Bowie had liberated them and now he was deserting them just when the glam and glitter were fading. Even so, not everyone was convinced. One fan, Alan McGinty, writing in *The Body Politic*, felt Bowie had helped 'thousands of sexually confused kids like me, trapped in middle-class suburban high schools'. He noted that though Bowie might be shying away from bisexuality in his music, it was still present in the film roles he was choosing, such as *Merry Christmas, Mr. Lawrence*. He wondered if it was all part of Bowie's 'old game of keeping the public guessing' and was left 'completely perplexed'.

Bowie's predicament was partly self-created and partly the result of a public grappling with the new queer phenomenon. When he pronounced he was bi, not everyone believed him; when he went on to deny it, not everyone believed him. He existed in a liminal state, spinning confusion, frustrated by it, revelling in it.

*

Was Bowie straight, then? It doesn't seem so: in those promiscuous days in the Seventies, he slept with far too many men and women for this to seem plausible. 'He was semi-straight, and semi-gay', says

Mike Berry, a rather wordy and less committed description than bi: a blurry, uneasy definition of Bowie's sexuality. Berry worked at Sparta Records, Bowie's music publisher; their professional relationship began in the mid sixties, bled into friendship, evolved into 'fumblings', but mostly they would just 'talk about things', suggesting a homoerotic intimacy that was creative, emotional and physical.

Wendy Leigh, one of his biographers, felt that Bowie's sexuality was 'a bisexuality of ambition', switching on and off his willingness to sleep with men depending on how useful they were to his career. Lionel Bart was one such example, she attests. Bart, the composer of *Oliver!*, gave Bowie business advice and acted as a mentor – Bowie only slept with him 'because it was expedient to do so'. She doesn't necessarily judge or condemn him for this, pointing out that the casting couch is normally the domain of women and so it is 'refreshing' that Bowie was willing to play the game. There is certainly some truth in Leigh's claim about the link between his sexuality and his desire to become a superstar. His sexuality could be like a weathervane that span according to the winds of opportunity; early in his career, when he was in the Mannish Boys, the group was playing at the London Palladium when a promoter for the (gay) Star Club in Hamburg asked, 'Which way do you swing, Davie?' It was a residency the group were keen to get, and so Bowie replied, 'Boys, of course.'

But it's simplistic to conclude that Bowie was sleeping with men when it suited him solely in order to get ahead in his career – not given the way he lived life as art. He was hard-working, passionate, obsessive; there was no separation between a private life and his music. If his male lovers helped him to progress, then equally his female lovers were often muses, inspiring and shaping his career. A creative magpie, he was constantly sifting, ingesting, thieving, turning it all into great art. Amanda Lear, an American singer whom he dated in the 1970s, recalls how she told him about

William Burroughs' novel *Naked Lunch* and the next day Bowie rushed out and bought a copy, leading him to adopt Burroughs' cut-up technique when writing *Diamond Dogs*; after she took him to see Fritz Lang's *Metropolis*, he developed a passion for German Expressionism. Bowie is sometimes accused of being selfish and manipulative in his career, of using people and then discarding them as he climbed ahead, but others argue that he was fuelled by a passionate enthusiasm, a man who could inspire other musicians 'to reach inside themselves and come up with ideas buried deep within their consciousness'. It seems that joyful hunger was raw in his early years, emerging in a voracious desire for making music, for fame and for sex – with both sexes. We have to bear in mind that the men of this era were the ones with power in the music industry: men who owned the record labels, who managed bands, who shaped their media images, whilst at the other end of this power spectrum were female groupies, often underage, who were an accepted part of the rock and roll scene, seeking their taste of glamour from sleeping with the greats. If Bowie gained more obviously from men during this time, then it reflects those gender structures. It no doubt also helped Bowie's career to date famous women such as Susan Sarandon, his co-star in the bisexual vampire film *The Hunger*, but there seems to be more cynicism about the men he slept with, a lingering determination that Bowie's uneven bisexuality ought to tip in one direction, and therefore his straight relationships were sexually sincere and the homosexual ones false.

Calvin Mark Lee, a Chinese-American A & R man at Mercury Records who spotted Bowie's talents and was keen to sign him, was another of his lovers. It was Calvin who introduced Bowie to Angela Barnett, who was big-egoed and beautiful, with a fierce intellect and a powerful personality. They were both dating Calvin when they got together, a detail they rather relished repeating to the press. Notoriously, both were late for their wedding because they were having a threesome the night before with a female artist friend that led them to oversleep. She played a vital part in his career. She was business manager as much as lover, encouraging him to come out as bi, helping to drive him towards success. She has been described as Bowie's Lady Macbeth but she deserves credit for helping him to flourish after years of failure. Later in life, Bowie downplayed the contribution she made to his career.

David and Angie lived out their bisexuality publicly, theatrically, enjoying the edgy status of being a bi couple in the spotlight. The singer Ava Cherry recalls being seduced by Bowie and waking the next morning to find Angie knocking on the door – shocked to discover he had a wife and subsequently to be introduced to her. The Bowies' living room had a large, fur-lined bed called the Pit, where threesomes and orgies took place. Bowie is said to have watched Jagger making love to Angie, and there are numerous reports of a love affair between Bowie and Jagger, but it's hard to know if there's any truth to this or if it's salacious gossip. In the end, the open nature of their marriage became a strain, exacerbated by Bowie's descent into drug addiction. His relationship with his manager, Tony Defries, ended at the time his marriage began to collapse. He moved to LA.

'There was something horrible permeating the air in LA in those days,' he recalled. 'The stench of Manson and the Sharon Tate murders.' John Updike's comment that 'Celebrity is a mask that eats into the face' seems to encapsulate Bowie's experience at this point. He was becoming sick of his personas; though early on he relished the way they gave him 'room to work in', now the mutating character of Ziggy/Aladdin/Jack had become claustrophobic. Glenn Hughes, one-time bassist of the band Deep Purple, had what we might now call a bromance with Bowie at the time, a deep and intimate friendship that involved them holding hands and kissing on the neck, sleeping in the same bed, doing drugs together. So many drugs: mountains upon mountains of cocaine. Bowie kept his curtains drawn, became obsessed with the Kabbalah and magick, kept his urine in the fridge to protect him from spells, watched reel upon reel of the Nazis. A walking skeleton, he survived on milk and red peppers. This was such a deliciously, disturbingly odd detail that when I read about it back in my late twenties I incorporated it into the novel I was writing, where a character suffering a schizophrenic breakdown lives off this food and covers his walls with Will Self covers and art, just as Bowie scrawled pentagrams on his walls.

The product of this shadowy, paranoid, jittery period was an extraordinary album, *Station to Station*, performed by Bowie's new persona, the Thin White Duke. But Bowie was falling apart. One night he overdosed on coke and friends saved his life by putting him in a warm bath in order to keep his circulation moving. He grew so paranoid that he became convinced that the Devil was alive in his swimming pool and ended up having an exorcism conducted on it. His friend Iggy Pop was also suffering from drug addiction, and had ended up institutionalized. They both travelled to Europe to sober up and get straight.

In Berlin, Bowie enjoyed being able to walk about, paint, browse bookshops; he relished being able to travel by bike or on foot and remain anonymous. It was here that he enjoyed a love affair with the famous transsexual Romy Haag. Romy, born Eduard Frans Verbaarsschott, suffered bullying for his effeminate body, and became a woman in his teens. In 1974, at the age of twenty-six, she set up the cabaret club *Chez Romy Haag*, which became one of the capital's most popular nightclubs, frequented by figures such as Freddie Mercury, Bryan Ferry, Lou Reed and Mick Jagger. Haag was a significant influence on Bowie's 1979 single 'Boys Keep Swinging'. It's one of Bowie's lesser-known songs, recorded for his *Lodger* album, the last in his 'Berlin' trilogy. Bowie appears in the video in multiple gender guises, singing before a mic in a set based on Romy's Berlin club. For each verse, he is dressed in a suit, exuding male power and privilege, singing lines such as 'Nothing stands in your way when you're a boy.' In the choruses, Bowie appears in drag in triplicate, and with each finale he tears off his wig and smears off his make-up, an anarchic gesture he appropriated from Romy, who used to finish her acts with this climax. It's a disturbing, fascinating song which Bowie described as an exploration of the 'colonisation of gender'. But Bowie's audience seemed less enamoured of Bowie in drag than they had of Bowie as an alien, or Bowie's vivacious lines from 'Rebel Rebel' – here was 'gender-bending' without the glamour and the glitter. The single was selling reasonably well until the video was released, provoking a torrent of complaints when the BBC showed a clip. When Bowie performed the song in America, on *Saturday Night Live*, NBC muted the line 'when you're a boy/Other boys check you out'. His American label RCA feared that US audiences would be put off by such sexual ambiguity and they didn't release it at all, putting out 'Look Back in Anger' instead. All of which helps to explain Bowie's shifting feelings about his sexuality, not least the regret that followed his boldness.

In a 2002 interview with *Blender*, Bowie reflected on why coming out as bisexual had ended up being the biggest mistake he'd ever made. His concern was the impact it had on his career: 'I don't think it was a mistake in Europe, but it was a lot tougher in America.' Bowie insisted that he didn't want to be a spokesperson for gay culture or 'hold any banners' or be political. First and foremost, he wanted to be an artist, 'a songwriter and a performer'. And his queer persona had caused problems in the US: 'America is a very puritanical place, and I think it stood in the way of so much I wanted to do.'

The critic Nick Kent recalls that, early on in Bowie's career, there was a difference between Ziggy concerts on both sides of the Atlantic. In the UK, fans would dress up in grandiose outfits, the concerts akin to a glorious and grotesque fashion show, but in the US it was much wilder, 'like Fellini's *Satyricon*', with fans fucking in the toilets: 'that was Bowie's audience, as somehow it was more radical to be sexually ambiguous in America.' Tony Zanetta, who worked as Bowie's tour manager, confirms this: 'At the time, the English were very different sexually from Americans, because even though we were fucking everything in sight, we were still very repressed. The English weren't. They were a lot easier with it, and bisexuality wasn't a big deal.' When Bowie toured as Ziggy in 1973, he faced both fan adoration and homophobic backlash, because 'for most of America bisexual just means gay'. There were protests held against him performing and, when he toured in the South, the Ku Klux Klan turned out in huge numbers to protest.

Elton John was another pop star whose career in the US was hampered by coming out. In 1976, he gave an interview to *Rolling Stone* where he declared, 'I think everyone's bisexual to a certain degree.' Following this interview, music journalist Darryl W. Bullock observed that his career 'hit a major trough . . . and *Blue Moves* would be his last Top 10 album in the States until 1992's *The One*'.

Denying his bisexuality brought Bowie rewards in terms of record sales and career. He disavowed it just as he was about to do his Serious Moonlight tour of the US and *Let's Dance* was released. It was a triumphant commercial success and for the first time, Bowie acquired a huge American following. Whilst Bowie's frustration is understandable, the loss of his nerve is disappointing. His provocative bisexual persona was the key that helped to unlock fame and notoriety for him, that got him the attention he deserved, that enabled him to have a long career after a decade of being overlooked and underrated. To switch it on and switch it off, to play it up and then backtrack, may be part of Bowie's reinvention, the ephemerality of his play-acting, but it also seems cynical, even cowardly. Bowie once declared that he was a canvas on which he was painting the truth of an era; if so, then his mainstream early 1980s attitude reflects Bowie bowing to a transatlantic mood of prejudice. There was growing homophobia, epitomized in the ruthlessness of Reagan and Thatcher, the latter of whom would go on to introduce the 1988 Section 28 amendment to the Local Government Act which prohibited local authorities and schools from promoting homosexuality. On the other hand, some fans argued that his reaction was not his fault but a painful, legitimate reaction to the biphobia and prejudice he was suffering. To be fair to Bowie, if we rewind to that first *Melody Maker* interview, it's emphasized right from the start what he's about: 'As it happens, David doesn't have much time for Gay Liberation . . . That's a particular movement he doesn't want to lead. He despises all these tribal qualifications . . . it's individuality that he's really trying to preserve.' Bowie's devotion was not to any cause but to his journey an artist.

*

The academic Martha Robinson Rhodes has noted that during the 1970s, 'rather than being an independent identity', bisexuality was often seen as a 'synthesis of identities': a sex of two halves – homosexuality and heterosexuality, where many judged themselves in terms of ratios. She cites the example of George Melly, who, in 1972, declared, 'I'm 75% hetero-, 25% homosexual.' This, perhaps, was a reflection of Kinsey's influential study, which tended to see sexuality in terms of a scale. In the late 1970s, along came Fritz Klein, an Austrian-born bisexual psychiatrist, who tried to seek out books about bisexuality and was disappointed at the dearth. In 1974, he set up the world's first bisexual group, the Bisexual Forum, and would go on to found the *Journal of Bisexuality* and the American Institute of Bisexuality. When he published *The Bisexual Option* in 1978, he included a useful tool: the Klein Sexual Orientation Grid. This was intended to be a learning tool to help you think about your sexuality, rather than a diagnosis. It was far more nuanced than the Kinsey scale, with seven categories which covered sexual attraction, sexual behaviour, sexual fantasies, emotional preference, social preference, lifestyle preference, and self-identification.

By including past experiences and future desires, it illustrated how your sexuality might fluctuate over time. Furthermore, it expanded on Kinsey's focus on sexual acts, adding social and psychological dimensions too.

My sexuality has regularly gone through cycles of traditional, monogamous phases and more adventurous polyamorous ones. In the summer of 2017, I discovered the complications of 'unicorns' and expectations around bisexual threesomes when I joined OkCupid. I flitted through profiles and images crafted with earnest kaloprosopia, and I felt a flicker of unease, wondering if this face, that face, concealed a psycho underneath. This was the issue: I didn't want to date, which would have been a slower, safer way of meeting strangers; I wanted a fling, which involved far more risk and trust. The thought of a serious commitment repelled me. I was still feeling raw from the dissolution of a relationship that had lasted for years and ended with an echo of my parents' marriage, with me replicating the physical and emotional exhaustion my mother suffered. In the innocence of your twenties, a poor relationship can be bad luck, a fluke, but as the decades pass and you begin to know yourself, patterns set in, signalling character flaws and tendencies. This can leave you suffering the sense of a loss of free will: that you are fated by unseen forces that were absorbed in early years, genetic tendencies that wind back over centuries. I had decisively carved a path in life that was the opposite of my mother's and yet still I had performed the cliché, circled back to fatal imitation.

In 2015, I also became a carer to my elderly, widowed father. This interfered with relationships, restricting my ability to travel, causing clashes of loyalty, until I lost confidence that I could combine duty and romance. After a year of my dad being in and out of hospitals and liaising with doctors, things had settled down, but a midlife crisis was assailing me, an equation of pleasure with youth, a desire to mess around like a teenager again. When I looked in the mirror, I pictured a future Sam: wizened and wrinkled.

Now was my last chance, a panicky voice advised. I had read in an article somewhere that the thing people missed the most in old age was sex. I had been monogamous for years, followed the traditional path; now I craved wild abandon. There's a moment in Hanif Kureishi's *Intimacy* where the narrator reflects that once you're over the age of forty, a feckless one-night stand is no longer possible: emotion will bind you. Which led to my paradox: I did not want an empty, drunk-hazy one-night stand with a man or woman who would forget my name by morning. I wanted a fling that meant everything and nothing, that had the intensity of *Last Tango in Paris* and the sweetness of *Brief Encounter*, to compress intimacy into a potent concentrate.

My profile, I found, was easier to construct than anything I had crafted on social media to promote my writing. The Sam I created was bisexual and sapiosexual. She was me and she was not me: she was me narrowed down to a profile that looked playful but (I hoped) not trivial. Within forty-eight hours I had over 200 emails from interested men. It was a welcome boost, though I soon found out that this was simply the norms of the game. Dating apps work in women's favour; women are far more selective than men: on Tinder, for example, a guy has a 2.8 per cent chance of finding a match compared to 35 per cent for a woman. A common male strategy, therefore, is to play a numbers game, and send out dozens of emails a day, many just cut-and-paste jobs, to woman after woman, in the hope of a response.

I chose men and women in their late twenties. It was as though I wished their youth might seep into me by osmosis. To a degree, this worked. Since I had lied about my age, I had to become healthy, and the boring, virtuous diet I adopted took years from my face, left me looking shiny and bright. I began to forget my real age, in fact, and became convinced I really was thirty-five. This confused men, who couldn't understand why I was interested in no-strings flings; presumably because they thought my biological clock was ticking. 'Are you real?' was a question I was often asked by people suspicious that a woman seeking sex might be a scammer. I met a Turkish man in Southwark and back at his flat he poured me an Aperol and confessed that he was not really thirty-nine as his profile claimed, but forty-one. He looked at me glumly and said how he envied me, at only thirty-five. 'Your midlife crisis awaits you,' he warned me, and I smiled smugly into my drink.

The 'are you real?' question also spoke of the complications of our #MeToo age. It has been a movement of many positive gains, but one misconception that has begun to arise is that women don't like sex, when in fact we simply don't like being *harassed* for sex.

A young Italian man I met was handsome in a way that differed from his online profile, which exuded movie-star charisma; he was exquisitely beautiful, with sharp cheekbones and chestnut eyes, but his teeth were awful, a flaw that endeared him to me. When we sat down together in a pub in Vauxhall, our conversation was halting, and I found myself staring into my drink more than his eyes. I drank alcohol on my Internet dates whereas I normally avoided it in everyday life, which meant I was tipsy very quickly from low tolerance, and worried that my survival instincts would be blurred. He was tall and very muscular, and as I followed him up the stairs to his flat, a habitual fear came over me. As each fling came and went, I suffered a constant underlying unease that this was all wrong, that all the films I had watched and the TV crime series that began with women killed and discarded in woods indicated that women could not get away with this sort of thing, that we could not simply enjoy visiting strange men's houses and luxuriate in random flings because some sort of divine punishment was inevitable: sex must be followed by death.

In his bedroom, there was a series of coloured bulbs on the wall that he played about with. As a sickly red light flooded the room, I made an appalled objection: was I supposed to be in a red-light district? He giggled, 'Oh, I am the prostitute.' And he became so silly with nerves that I was endeared to him again. 'I have some-thing to show you, Sam,' he said and I felt some trepidation again – but it was only his cock, which he felt very vulnerable about showing to me, as though making sure approval was gained from the start, that I would not be startled halfway through and feel cheated at some lack of size. I gave him assurances, and soon we were making love and suddenly he stopped halfway through, star-ing down at me, smiling. He was amused and delighted, he told me, by the shift from the shy, nervous woman I had been in the pub to the passionate woman in his bed. Afterwards, we lay side by side and I wondered if the laughter I was sharing was more therapeutic than the sex. I slept poorly, as I always did in a strange bed, and returned home hazy, napping in the day. During the afternoon, I saw that he had been looking at my profile. The thought that he was also savouring an afterburn made me smile.

And what of the women on OkCupid? I wondered. I'd had far fewer approach me. Would they be up for flings too? Or were they – as the men claimed – only interested in relationships, commitment and anchors?

It turned out that the women were often interested in some-thing else. It wasn't until I joined OkCupid that I learnt what the term 'unicorn' means.

It was one of the top frustrations that bisexuals face: that every-one assumes you must be up for a threesome. The word 'unicorn' was coined to sum up that elusive third party who will join a couple hungry for adventure.

One day I received a message from a woman asking me if I would join her and her boyfriend in bed. I looked at a picture of her: at her beautiful features, pale blonde hair and blue eyes. I looked at a picture of him: several years older, balding, pallid skin.

I find you very attractive, I messaged her back, *but I am in all honesty not very keen on your boyfriend.*

She was hurt and I felt a little guilty, so she attempted to resolve the problem by suggesting *why don't we make love and he can watch us?* If she had suggested we would be watched by say, another woman, I would have felt safe. But a man made me mistrustful. I thought he would video us and there was a danger he could post online; or else he would become too excited and attempt to join in and I would be cajoled into something I wasn't sure of; or that they might drug me. This last fear was pure paranoia, but paranoia might save me from terrible things. All the time that I was navigating the site, I relied on my intuition and the moment someone seemed the slightest bit dubious, I cut things off abruptly.

So I said no, but the woman had planted a seed. A few weeks later, I had a fling with a civil servant in his late twenties called Avyaan. Trust built up between us, and he eventually suggested that he could organize a threesome with a friend of his.

We met at a pub in Clapham Common. I greeted Avyaan and Sophie, who had long fair hair and a sweet smile. I had dressed up; she had dressed down. She wore jeans and a top and a loose, casual jacket, which made me feel self-conscious in my dress and heels. We exchanged introductions, titbits of character. I learnt that Sophie was a scientist conducting experiments on bees. The conversation wandered through boxsets, books and films, yet beneath our chat was a nervy self-consciousness, jolted moments where we caught eyes and looked away, and a glee too that we looked like every other group in the pub, out for a drink. There was no erotic anticipation on my part. I could not make a connection between the normality of the here and now and what was to come, which seemed surreal, unfeasible. How could we make the transition? The gap felt like a chasm. I didn't believe it would really happen. We would chicken out, laugh the idea off, postpone it for another day.

As darkness fell, we walked back through suburban streets to Avyaan's house. In the lounge, we sat on the sofa, bunched up tight with Avyaan in between Sophie and me, sipping drinks and listening to music. We argued playfully over what to choose, naming songs we loved and simply must listen to, delaying, delaying. I wondered if, like so many experiences in life, anticipation might be better than the act itself, if we should stretch out and savour the moment forever. Another part of me was impatient to smash through the inner boundaries that made me want to jump up and run out of the door before I lost my nerve. I decided I needed more drink; I was still too sharp and clear-edged when I needed to become blurry. More alcohol burned down my body, pooling in my stomach. Giggles assailed us as though we were teenagers. I thought of that line from *Atonement*, when the young Cecilia and Robbie are fucking in a library; Ian McEwan writes how they needed to become 'strangers'. That was what needed to happen now; we needed to undo the 'getting-to-know'ness of the pub to become intimate. Avyaan kissed my cheek, and then my lips. Then I watched him kiss Sophie. Her hair glittered under the lamplight, golden-streaked like a summer day. *It's finally happening*, I thought in joy and in panic.

Avyaan stood up and reached out one hand to each of us: 'Let's go upstairs.'

The next morning I woke up gazing at a white ceiling, aware of a warmth beside me. The night before was still hazy inside me; *I've had a threesome*, I thought in surprise, in pride, conscious that it already felt better as a memory, an anecdote. In the present, it had often been overwhelming: 'too many things going on at once, too much multitasking involved,' I would joke. It had been more about novelty and surprise than ecstasy. But Avyaan, who had more experience in these matters, felt we should be proud: our threesome had been diplomatic, kind, unselfish. There are delicate emotions involved too: nobody wants to be left out.

We were in balance until Sophie got up and went to take a

shower; Avyaan and I found ourselves kissing, and soon we were having sex. There was an exciting, furtive feeling about this: as though we were both married to Sophie and having an affair behind her back. Then Sophie entered, wearing a towel, immediately upset. She felt left out. She felt Avyaan had favoured me, that he was now spent, would have no energy left for her pleasure. I was suddenly dismayed, feeling greedy, guilty; and the make-up sex she then had with Avyaan made me relieved, as though our apology was being played out through his lovemaking. Harmony was re-established at breakfast. We munched on toast and laughed again at how surreal this all was, to be sitting here, chatting away as though we'd spent the evening in the cinema.

Afterwards, Avyaan was keen to organize a repeat performance. Perhaps with practice, I thought, I might get better. If I felt less fazed and shocked, the pleasure would be heightened. But I didn't want to dilute my experience. By keeping it a off-one, the memory seemed more special. It remained my sole threesome, and I was happy to keep it as that.

*

Some bisexuals hate the stereotype that they are ripe and ready for a threesome, the implication that they are greedy, promiscuous, decadent. Just as some women end up feeling like bad feminists, you can feel like a bad bisexual for vocalizing your experience. The good, virtuous bisexual that you ought to be projecting, for the sake of the movement, is one who behaves, who is monogamous, who has a moderate appetite! (Which is not dissimilar to the way that gays in the 1970s felt obliged to put on a suit, to project a good image for their cause.) But whatever your sexual orientation, it's normal to go through cycles, to have periods where you're more adventurous and want to explore, and phases when you just want to settle down and commit. Following my summer of decadence, I entered a traditional, monogamous, long-distance relationship with a man.

The trouble with being bi, however, is that any promiscuous phase might be immediately interpreted as a superficial 'symptom' of your sexuality rather than a complex expression of your personality. Take Bowie, when he was young and Bacchanalian, joking that, 'Any society that allows people like Lou [Reed] and me to become rampant is pretty well lost . . . [it's the] herald of western civilisation's terminal decline.' However, it would be far too simplistic to link this purely to his promiscuity, as with all the icons in this book. Bowie reflected that his affairs were not necessarily fuelled by desire – 'I do fall in love quite quickly. And once upon a time I used to fall in love quite a lot.' Being in love was also creative fuel for him: 'I think love is very important for my writing.' But when asked by the interviewer if he was willing to commit to someone, he looked wary, musing that 'love can't get quite in my way', because his true love affair was with his music and he didn't want to sacrifice or compromise it by settling down – he needed the freedom to travel, to adventure, to wander into uncharted, uncomfortable territory.

That was Bowie in 1979. Iman would be the partner who changed everything.

David Bowie met Iman in 1990. They were set up on a blind date in LA and for Bowie, it was love at first sight: 'I couldn't sleep for the excitement of our first date. That she would be my wife, in my head, was a done deal.' They wed in a private ceremony in Switzerland in 1992. It was a committed, tender and loving relationship, one in which they enjoyed the everyday, walking together, taking their daughter to school – 'it was a beautiful ordinary life,' Iman reflected. For some, Bowie's happy, monogamous marriage is seen as him becoming 'straight' in both senses of the word – as though heterosexuality is the steady, orderly state, whilst bisexuality is a kinked and decadent path. He did continue to explore bisexuality in music, such as 'Hallo Spaceboy'. But, once married, Bowie was pinned down as heterosexual and his bisexual years were sometimes dismissed as a phase.

This is the challenge of heterosexual marriage for bisexuals: it can end up being a negation of your identity, as though it draws your sexuality to a conclusion – if you marry someone of your gender, you were really gay all along; if you marry someone of the opposite, you were just experimenting. Gays and lesbians can come out once and that is enough, but bis often have to 'come out' over and over to affirm that being in a relationship hasn't magically simplified their orientation. And this was something that Bowie, increasingly sick of being asked about his sexuality, was never going to do.

So whether or not Bowie was a lifelong bisexual, or whether his bisexuality was a phase, we don't know. But so what if Bowie's bi years were a phase, or an experiment, or an exploration? The *Advocate* cites a list of celebrities who are bisexual, adding the accolade that 'they're not just experimenting'. It reassures us that they are the Real Thing, authentic, just as people who claim to be the real fans of a band can cite a list of concerts they attended in their early days. Why is 'confirmed' a superior status to 'experimenting'? If we are to explore our sexuality we will all go through phases which may be cautious, tentative, before we adopt a label, come out, announce. Experimentation is a crucial phase, not a dilly-dallying weakness showing flimsy character, but an important step on a journey of sexual exploration and identity. Once again, it creates a dichotomy between the 'good' bisexual, whose orientation remains static, and the 'bad' bisexual, who fluctuates – when both are fine, depending on your nature, the period of life you're going through, and all those rich complexities that govern a love life.

A phase need not be fleeting. It can be richly rewarding, evolutionary; you can learn much from it about yourself. You cannot find out what your sexuality is unless you explore and, even if you later lean in a new direction, there should be no condemnation for this. Nor does it undo the tremendous gains made in 1970s for the bi and gay community, aided by Bowie regardless of his intention, from the first Gay Pride March in 1972 to Sweden declassifying homosexuality as a mental illness in 1979.

*

David Bowie died from liver cancer on 10 January 2016, at his Lafayette Street home in New York. In Brixton, grieving fans laid flowers, records and messages in front of the iconic Aladdin Sane mural that the artist Jimmy C painted, just around the corner from Bowie's childhood home. Tony Visconti commented that Bowie's 'death was a work of art', for his swan-song album, *Blackstar*, was released two days before his passing, a final gift to fans. There was an outpouring of grief all over the world, and so many from the LGBT community spoke movingly of how he had not only changed their lives but saved their lives. Guillermo del Torro tweeted, 'Bowie existed so all of us misfits learned that an oddity was a precious thing. he changed the world forever.' Folk singer-songwriter Mary Gauthier said: 'David Bowie showed this queer kid from Baton Rouge that gender outlaws are cool. Androgyny=rock&roll, not a reason to kill myself.' Kris Kneen: 'He helped me understand myself as bisexual. He helped me accept myself.' Checkmark Becks: 'Many cis or straight folk loved Bowie but he saved LGBT lives. He gave us a reason to keep fighting. He means something special to us.'

On his final album, Bowie was still preoccupied by and playing with themes of sexuality and gender; in 'Girl Loves Me', he includes Polari, the secret language gays used in the Sixties, combined with the Nadsat slang of *A Clockwork Orange* – '*cheena so sound, so titi up this malchick, say/Party up moodge, nanti vellocet round on Tuesday*', which translates as 'girl so sound, so pretty up this boy, say/Party up man, no drugs on Tuesday'.

One of the most interesting books to follow Bowie's death was Dylan Jones's *Bowie: A Life*, an oral history that blends together snippets of people who knew, loved, loathed and worked with Bowie across the decades: producers, music journalists, lovers, groupies, musicians, fans, forming a chorus of voices, carefully structured, so that as you read you feel you simultaneously know Bowie more and more and less and less. Was he manipulative or kind, selfish or generous, a genius or a thieving collager of other people's ideas? Was he bi or was he straight? These are all hotly contested issues. As David Bailey, who photographed Bowie on many occasions, says: 'I don't think I ever got him, not in a picture.' Bowie remained a private man hiding behind a range of public personas. Yet if Bowie remains characteristically elusive even in death, even if we can't know how sincere or cynical his bisexual proclamations – or denials – were, he made a significant and concrete contribution to improving the lives of bisexuals.

7

Jean-Michel Basquiat

My boyfriend surprises me by telling me that he encountered Basquiat when he was a teenager. It was the summer of 1982. He and a friend travelled to the Lower East Side, New York, for the holidays, sixteen-year-old punks with V-sign hair, piercings, and ripped clothes.

It was a daring place to seek adventure at such a tender age. New York was the crime capital of the world and had been close to declaring formal bankruptcy. Traditional structures and hierarchies had broken down, including those dictated by the housing market. The Lower East Side was a wasteland, occupancy so low that from time to time landlords would set fire to their properties because it was more lucrative to claim the insurance. Graffiti was a relatively new art form – or an eyesore that swept brickwork and subway cars in a neon rash – depending on your perspective. The Puerto Rican artist Lee Quiñones recalled that he would be spray-canning a train at night, enjoying artistic rapture, whilst hearing the terrifying sound of gunshots close by.

Unfettered by rents, young people were free to be creative. Everyone was an artist or a poet or a musician or a writer or mostly likely a combination of all four. Trendy clubs were springing up, mixing dance, art and performance. There was Club 57, Area, and the Mudd Club, the last of which was the first club in New York that was both nightclub and gallery. It had a strict door policy:

'poor chic' was welcome and 'rich chic' would be turned away. *People* magazine reported that 'For sheer kinkiness, there has been nothing like it since the cabaret scene in 1920s Berlin.'

'What was he like?' I ask. I have seen pictures of Basquiat, tall and charismatic, dreadlocks framing his beautiful face. I imagine him and I imagine my boyfriend and the possibility of attraction between them. It creates a strange frisson.

The anecdote becomes anticlimactic. My boyfriend and Basquiat were both in a group of people, hanging out in a bar. They didn't speak, for Basquiat was very quiet and shy.

He goes on to tell me about how the fun he had was shadowed by a prevailing atmosphere of unease; whispers of a strange disease that you got from having sex. He was tempted to sleep with a woman who made it clear that she liked him, but he was warned that she was like a black widow: men who went with her never recovered . . .

Vincent Van Gogh, Pablo Picasso, Jackson Pollock: a line of art kings, an all-white lineage of talent that Jean-Michel Basquiat interrupted when he burst onto the art scene in the 1980s, becoming the most successful Black artist to join their ranks. During his lifetime, he received both acclaim and backlash; in a 1986 interview with Tamra Davis, he reflected with frustration on the critical ambivalence towards his paintings: 'Most of the reviews have been more reviews of my personality, more so than my work.' Race played a part in this, with his complex, enigmatic art lazily described as 'primitive', naïve or childlike. But as the decades have passed, time has sifted talent from hype and Basquiat has gradually achieved the recognition he deserves. The Whitney rejected his work when he was alive, but ran a hugely successful retrospective four years after he died. In 2017, Basquiat's *Untitled (Skull)* was sold at a Sotheby's auction for $110.5 million. It hit the headlines across the world, a record-breaking sum: the highest ever paid for an American artist.

Once, when Andy Warhol was asked what he was working on, he replied, 'Death'. He was referring to his iconic prints of Marilyn Monroe. Death as a performance piece, that moment where celebrity solidifies, where immortality might begin. Many biographies of Basquiat begin with his end, so tragic that it overshadows his existence: in the summer of 1988, at the age of twenty-seven, he was found dead in his apartment, having overdosed on heroin. His life was one of fall and rise and fall, from being a homeless wannabe who sold postcards on the street to a millionaire art star who blazed across the cover of the *New York Times Magazine*. A life that was glitzy on the surface, including a love affair with Madonna and a collaboration/friendship with Andy Warhol. Beneath that veneer, however, were intense, painful struggles with drug addiction, with fame, with the challenges of being 'a black man whose fate twisted with the whims of an all-white jury of artistic powers'. And he matured during a decade when the art world was one of dealers, hype and hustle, an era of greed and speed. As artist Richard Marshall sums up: 'Jean-Michel Basquiat became famous for his art, then he became famous for being famous, then he became famous for being infamous – a succession of reputations that overshadowed the seriousness and significance of the art he produced.'

Why, then, write about Basquiat's love life at all? Oscar Wilde might have quipped, 'I put all my genius into my life; I put only my talent into my works', but is this also relevant to Basquiat? Is it trivial, gossipy, to consider the men and women he slept with, rather than divorcing the artist from his work and simply dissecting the enigma of one of his paintings? Look at *A Panel of Experts*, however, and you'll see a depiction of a love triangle Basquiat was involved in, a story of who fought and which woman won him. Look at *Eyes and Eggs* – a 1983 painting of a Black man in a chef's hat holding a frying pan, two eggs gazing out of the picture as though the yolks are pupils – and you'll savour the title of the painting chosen by his girlfriend at the time. One of the paintings that Basquiat admired from a young age was Picasso's *Guernica*, which was heavily influenced by Picasso's own turbulent love life. There's an evolution in Basquiat's painting, a path that can be traced from the vibrant colours and thick brushstrokes of masterpieces like *Charles the First* and his skull paintings to the stark beauty of *Riding with Death*, none of which would have happened without the support of the partners he loved and was loved by in his short life.

I remember attending an exhibition of Vincent van Gogh at Tate Britain a few years ago. His biography was an important part of it; that collective grief we feel when we stare at *Starry Night over the Rhône*, knowing he failed to sell a single painting in his lifetime. It is almost Christian, the moral behind his biography: that even if you are overlooked in this life, you will be rewarded in the next. In the accompanying notes his death was presented as a suicide, without any mention of the counterclaim, well researched, that Vincent was accidentally shot by two young men. It lacks romance, the incidental murder; we prefer the suicide, which seems a more fitting ending. How we present and shape an artist's life says a lot about the social attitudes of the time. Once an artist dies, they might be understood with more nuance, but their life might also be simplified. Basquiat's fame has intensified to the degree that even the crown motif which he favoured in his art has become a brand. His life has been dramatized in film (Julian Schnabel's *Basquiat*), covered in documentaries, turned into a play (*The Collaboration*, spring 2022), and more film biopics and TV series are due. As an illustration of how we might start to favour fiction over fact, one recent *Guardian* review of *The Collaboration* contrasted the play to the Julian Schnabel biopic, comparing lines, scenes, echoes – but didn't compare it to Basquiat's actual life.

'Basquiat is represented . . . as the stereotypical black stud randomly fucking white women,' writes bell hooks. Much of the coverage about him has simplified his love life, and in that process his bisexuality has been erased. In the films, the documentaries, the articles, his female lovers are always present, sometimes as a chorus, sometimes condensed into one figure, such as Claire Forlani's character in *Basquiat*. The male lovers are absent. Basquiat was prone to crossing out words in his paintings; his male exes seem to have been painted over by the media, blacked out until there is nothing to be seen, and I found myself wondering: why? What does it say about us, his fans, his critics, his public, that we have rewritten his narrative in this way: what's so hard about acknowledging that Basquiat was bisexual?

*

It's the late Seventies and Jean-Michel Basquiat is seventeen years old. His hair is dyed blond and cut into a Mohican; he wears a garish overcoat. He's homeless in downtown Manhattan. Sometimes seduction is necessary for survival: sex with a man or a woman means a bed for the night. In the evenings, Jean-Michel frequents the Mudd Club, picking up loose change from the floor to feed himself.

He and his friends form an experimental band called Gray. One of his bandmates, Vincent Gallo, is surprised to meet Jean-Michel's father one day: a middle-class accountant, wearing a suit and swinging a tennis racket. Soon enough Jean-Michel will be stereotyped as an artist from the ghetto (a myth he sometimes contributes to as he rallies against the bourgeoisie). In fact, his background is affluent and privileged. His father is Haitian, his mother Puerto Rican, and by the age of eleven he is fluent in three languages: French, Spanish and English. Yet here he is, fleeing that comfortable four-storey brownstone in Boerum Hill, Brooklyn, for a life on the streets, because his childhood has not been an easy one. There are scars and bad memories: beatings, rows, school rebellions, parental breakdown, divorce, pain. A mark left on the skin of his buttock; fading bruises on his body.

His love of art has been instilled in him from a young age. Matilde, his mother, would regularly take him to galleries; by the age of six he had a junior membership to the Brooklyn Museum. After the visits they would lie down on the floor, propped on their elbows with paper in front of them and they would draw together, Matilde encouraging him. She has been a loving mother but depression set in deep and now she is in a psychiatric ward. When Jean-Michel put his underpants on back to front, she would beat him, as if sensing some deviant impulse inside him. After the divorce, he went to live with his father and two sisters, but life got harder still. His father found him in a bed with a male cousin, stuck a knife into his buttocks, left a scar. Jean-Michel fled, shaving his head so he wouldn't be recognized, hanging out in Washington Park Square and dropping acid. When he returned home, he was enrolled in a school for gifted, contrary children called City-As-School. The teachers saw that he was a talented pupil – and an angry one. He would turn up with bruises, the dark aura of father/son rows shimmering about him. He brooded, raged, burning with ambition: he wanted to be famous. He wanted to be rich. At graduation he played a daring prank and threw a box of shaving cream at the principal as he was giving his speech. He was expelled and never finished school.

That's when he leaves home. He ends up on the wild side of New York, a time and place that is creative, chaotic and dangerous. A new graffiti tag starts to attract attention. It's innovative, more poetry than image, satirical and subversive in the tradition of Graeco-Roman graffiti:

SAMO © AS AN ALTERNATIVE 2 'PLAYING ART' WITH THE 'RADICAL CHIC' SECT ON DADDY'S FUNDS

SAMO © . . . AS AN END TO THE 9 TO 5 'I WENT TO COLLEGE' 'NOT 2-NITE HONEY' . . . BLUZ . . . THINK . . .

SAMO © 4 THE SO CALLED AVANT GARDE

SAMO © ANOTHER DAY . . . ANOTHER DIME . . . HYPER COOL . . . ANOTHER WAY 2 KILL SOME TIME . . .

SAMO © . . . FOR THOSE OF US WHO MERELY TOLERATE CIVILIZATION

Gossip flies about, the *Village Voice* runs a piece: is SAMO the work of a successful but disillusioned conceptual artist?

Jean-Michel is tickled, enjoying the buzz, for SAMO is the tag he and his collaborator Al Diaz have created. They thought it up one night whilst stoned: SAMO (same old shit), a fake, guilt-free religion, 'a tool for mocking bogusness', as Jean-Michel describes it. When they are revealed as the authors of the tag and enjoy their fifteen minutes' of fame, Jean-Michel's ambition sharpens. The art world close by in SoHo is undergoing a thrilling transformation. Traditionally, it has been a landscape of 'white walls, with white people drinking white wine'. Now Reagan's tax cuts have created an economic boom and a new urban professional: the yuppie. Money has poured into the art world, paintings are being sold for millions, the city is abuzz with dealers looking for the next breakout artist. The new generation of artists, developing their work via the graffiti scene, are attracting attention: artists like Keith Haring and Kenny Scharf.

Jean-Michel tells Al Diaz that he's going to be a famous artist and that he's going to die young.

In late 1979, he moves in with Alexis Adler, who lives on the top floor of an abandoned building. Jean-Michel's inspiration and passion for his painting is unstoppable. Unable to afford canvases, he will paint on anything and everything: refrigerators, doors and windows brought in from the street, pieces of foam, a cigar box, a lab coat, cardboard boxes, a mirror. Adler sometimes gets up and finds her feet landing in wet paint; on one occasion she buys a gold lamé coat only to find Jean-Michel has painted over it. He likes to listen to music as he works, carrying around a red cassette player, his favourite albums being Bowie's *Low* and *Heroes*.

Perpetually broke and living hand-to-mouth, Jean-Michel sells hand-painted T-shirts and postcards on the street. He sneaks onto the subway without paying in order to travel. Al Diaz notices that every once in a while Jean-Michel disappears, then shows up with new shoes, which means that he's been hustling: 'One time he told me he was messing around with someone who worked at the Eighth Street Playhouse. They had a master-slave relationship and Jean would walk him around on a leash. He told me he enjoyed sex more with men.'

There's a sleazy bar in Manhattan called Night Birds that Jean-Michel frequents. He doesn't buy a drink – he can't afford to. Instead he feeds coins into a juke box, picks out Eartha Kitt's *My Heart Belongs To Daddy*, stands by the wall and stares at a beautiful dark-haired woman serving behind the bar. This goes on for months. Normally he falls quickly, easily, into bed with women; this is an uncharacteristically slow-burn courtship. Eventually, finally, he buys a drink and introduces himself. She is Suzanne Mallouk: half-Palestinian, half-British, a painter living in the East Village. Soon Jean-Michel has moved in with her. They share confidences; Suzanne learns that his first homosexual relationship occurred when he was about fourteen, when he ran away and lived for a while with a DJ who worked for a local radio station. Suzanne quits her bar job when the owner tells her that she should look for a white boy as her boyfriend.

Though Jean-Michel was bisexual, his more committed relationships tended to be with women. Stonewall had been a liberation but it was still common to be reticent about being gay, to exist in a liminal space, half in, half out of the closet. Living with a man was not as easy nor as common as it is today. Andy Warhol began a relationship with Jon Gould around this time. Though they lived together, Gould would never publicly admit that he was gay and when they went to visit his family a mutual female friend would be called on to play 'girlfriend' and act as a beard. Jean-Michel wanted to be mothered and women, perhaps, were more willing to play this role. Certainly, the story of his girlfriends at this time shows a repetitive pattern: drawn to his charisma, talent and beauty, they would end up looking after him, both financially and emotionally, playing the role of muse and nurturer, allowing his artistic talent to ripen, only to find the love they received in return was passionate but unreliable.

Jean-Michel's ambition rendered him childlike. Suzanne was the breadwinner, working as a waitress and paying the bills so that he could paint, paint, paint. They'd row and she'd tell him to get a job but when he tried it only lasted a day. He loved her and she was special to him, but monogamy was not in his nature. He'd cheat on her with the same unbounded energy that fuelled his painting, going to the Mudd Club to pick up boys or girls, disappearing for days. In *Widow Basquiat*, Suzanne reflected that:

> *It was clear that his sexual interest was not monochromatic. It did not rely on visual stimulation, such as a pretty girl. It was a very rich multichromatic sexuality. He was attracted to people for all different reasons. They could be boys, girls, thin, fat, pretty, ugly. It was, I think, driven by intelligence. He was attracted to intelligence more than anything and to pain. He was very attracted to people who silently bore some sort of inner pain as he did, and he loved people who were one of a kind, people who had a unique vision of things.*

There was no neat separation between his painting routine and his daily life. His art would cover the floor and he would scribble lists and phone numbers on top of it or casually walk across it, leaving sneaker marks (there was a running joke at the time that you could date his work by the tread). He liked to paint surrounded by stimulation: music playing, especially Boléro and bebop, the TV blaring, stacks of novels, non-fiction and textbooks, all of which would fuel his colours and ideas, giving his work the feel of scratch and sample music from the 1980s, or the intuitive, improvisational flow of a jazz harmony. Once, when he was asked how he painted, he replied that it was like asking Miles Davis 'How does your horn sound?' Next to his paintings were piles of cocaine, another of his muses, along with the joints he smoked whilst his brush danced and swerved. Like Haring, he favoured motifs as vocabulary: the crown, a skull, and the copyright symbol. This was a reference to Charlie Parker, the jazz musician ripped off by white corporations because he never copyrighted his music. Ernest Hardy captures the paradox of his art: 'Basquiat's work was about exploding formula and convention, about harnessing the energy and vision of the street (low culture), even as he was a serious and learned student of the masters (high culture) with whom he wanted to be counted.'

Suzanne would often be referenced in his paintings via the name VENUS. Their love life flavoured his paintings: *Arroz con Pollo* depicted a dinner scene, a chicken he and Suzanne had shared. Much of his artwork was untitled and Suzanne would often give them names: she christened *Eyes and Eggs*. She was close to throwing him out of her apartment when he had a career breakthrough. His work was shown prominently at the New York/New Wave exhibition of 1981. Organized by Diego Cortez, it was a show that celebrated raw, rising talent, so popular that queues for entrance snaked down the block. The most promising artists displayed were Keith Haring, Kenny Scharf, and Basquiat, with Jean-Michel singled out for particular praise in reviews. The trio became the rising stars of the lively new art scene. Gallery owner Annina Nosei offered Jean-Michel the use of her basement as a space to paint, buying him canvases and materials. He would play

Ravel's *Boléro* over and over as he worked, until she complained that she was being driven mad by it. From time to time collectors would troop down and watch him as he worked. Jean-Michel was angered that New York gossip stereotyped him as a 'wild monkey man' (his words), chained up in her basement; 'if I were white, they would just call it an artist-in-residence,' he asserted.

It was a racism he encountered over and over. There was the everyday prejudice he suffered: not being able to hail a cab unless he was with a white guy, or being on a date with a woman and the police asking her if Basquiat was bothering her. And then there was the racism he experienced as the sole successful Black artist in a predominately white art world. In one interview with Mark Miller, he was asked if his style was 'some sort of primal expressionism' and he shot back: 'Like a primate? Like an ape?' In another, he pointed out that whilst Keith and Kenny had managed to move on and be taken seriously, he was still being labelled 'a graffiti artist'; whilst Keith got a show at the Whitney, they rejected Basquiat's work.

Suzanne reflected that, like the jazz artists of the past who could not even walk through the front door of the hotels/clubs they were playing in, Basquiat had to creep into the art world through the back door. Sometimes he would react with wit and satire – he wore African garb to openings organized by white collectors to mock and satirize their stereotyped perceptions of him. But he also found himself in an angry, paradoxical place where he wanted approval from a virtually all-white art world that he simultaneously wanted to give the finger. He was hugely ambitious, frequently using sports metaphors to describe the art scene, telling Haring he wanted a boxing match, declaring he wanted to be number one; but he was also self-destructive, contemptuous of art dealers, and once turned up to a posh dinner and offended everyone by putting his Walkman on and listening to it throughout. Suzanne pointed out that much of his crazy behaviour seemed like that of an *enfant terrible* when it was just a normal reaction to racism he suffered.

One of his most famous pieces is *Defacement*, painted in private on the wall of Keith Haring's studio: a reaction to the murder of Michael Stewart. Michael was a young artist graffitiing an East Village subway station when police attacked him; he was beaten so badly that he lay in a coma for thirteen days in hospital before dying. 'It could have been me,' Basquiat reflected furiously. *Defacement* was his powerful lamentation, an outpouring of rage, depicting a black silhouette in the centre of the canvas, both dignified and vulnerable, with a policeman on either side, faces pink as meat, batons a threat, smears of blood framing them.

It's October 1981 and for the first time Basquiat's paintings are being shown inside a SoHo gallery. Annina Nosei has organized a group exhibition called the Public Address Show, exhibiting works by Keith Haring, Barbara Kruger and six paintings by Basquiat. Basquiat turns up in a pinstriped Armani suit, the pants splattered with paint. The first night is a huge success for him: all his paintings sell. He and Suzanne move into a big loft on Crosby Street, paid for by Annina. It's the age of the art star: famous for both their talent and the headlines they create, the whispers in gossip columns, the brand that shimmers around their surname. It's as dizzying for Suzanne as it is for him, to witness his ascent from homeless hustler to millionaire celebrity who travels in limos and paints in Armani suits. Basquiat doesn't even have a bank account. When tidying up at home Suzanne regularly stumbles across wodges of money stashed behind a couch cushion or tucked into the pages of a book. In 1982, his career goes stellar on the international circuit. He becomes the youngest artist to have his work shown in the *Documenta* exhibition in Germany.

Basquiat is unfaithful to Suzanne, sometimes cruel, and their relationship crumbles. In the autumn of 1982, he visits the Lucky

Strike art bar and is introduced to an attractive dark-haired singer. She's called Madonna and she's recently released her first single, 'Everybody'. She's not yet famous, though when Basquiat introduces her to his art dealer, he proudly declares that 'She's going to be huge.' He falls for her hard, admiring her work ethic, her ambition, her talent. They start a relationship. Armon Stewart, a good friend of Basquiat at the time, recalls that Basquiat 'loved the fact that she truly didn't care what people thought of her, that she was her own woman and that she seemed on her way to great success without kissing ass'. Madonna, in turn, finds herself waking in the middle of the night to see her lover awake and lively: 'he'd be standing, painting, at four in the morning, this close to the canvas, in a trance. I was blown away by that, that he worked when he felt moved.' Within a few weeks, Madonna has moved into Basquiat's loft.

In 1982, Basquiat paints *A Panel of Experts*. In the first panel there is a scribbled name, VENUS, with MADONNA © crossed out underneath. ('I cross out words so you will see them more; the fact that they are obscured makes you want to read them,' Basquiat says.) Beneath that are two stick figures, boxing, a representation of a fight between Madonna and Suzanne that unfolds when they all run into each other at the Roxy club in Chelsea. Suzanne, raging with jealousy, kicks it off, attacking her rival. Madonna's name is copyrighted to suggest her blossoming fame, but crossed out because Suzanne wins the fight. Basquiat was generally adored by women despite his bad behaviour; he liked to wake up with one woman and go to bed with another. He liked to be fought over.

The cracks start to show. There is a dissonance in their routines, their addictions. Basquiat smokes dope to paint, snorts so much cocaine that he develops a hole in his septum. Madonna doesn't do drugs. Her loves are yoga and carrot chips; she likes getting up early, going for a run on the beach and calling her agent. Basquiat doesn't wake up until the afternoon. She is ambitious and so is

Basquiat, but for Madonna ambition dictates a disciplined routine, a more structured way of living. Having once dated an addict myself whilst being virtually teetotal at the time, I can recognize all the signs and problems: like Basquiat, my boyfriend would party till midnight and sleep throughout the day. He was charming and charismatic, sweet and smart, but over time I began to see that the drugs were dictating his life, making him dance to their rhythm, from his routine to his neglect of his talents and his career.

On New Year's Eve 1982, they stay in Los Angeles, at a beach house owned by the art dealer Larry Gagosian. After a day of meetings, Madonna returns to the beach house to find it strewn with drugs, her lover accompanied by four women, possibly prostitutes – 'They weren't choir girls, I only knew that much.' A huge row ensues: Madonna accuses him of fucking them and Jean-Michel insists the women are just his friends. She storms out, goes to a hotel; by the time they return to New York they are growing apart.

Madonna leaves a note for him. It tells him that their relationship was a mistake, not meant to be. And then she gets back together with her ex, the musician John Benitez, better known as 'Jellybean'.

Basquiat isn't used to women leaving him. He has seen Madonna as the love of his life. He responds by drinking a bottle and a half of rum in an attempt to kill himself. He forces her to give back the paintings he gifted her, then paints over them in black.

*

When it came to Basquiat's male lovers, the details are less clear. Only Phoebe Hoban, in her 1998 biography of Basquiat, has preserved this element of his sexuality through her interviews with his friends and contemporaries.

We know that he had a relationship with Klaus Nomi, a performance artist who once played a supporting role as one of David Bowie's backing singers. Klaus became a gay icon and a 'key staple of the city's new wave scene'. Performance artist Joey Arias, a friend of Basquiat's, has recalled witnessing 'a naked and aroused Basquiat walking out of Nomi's bedroom'. Basquiat loved it when Klaus spoke German, but he gave his lover gonorrhoea and Klaus got angry that he wouldn't offer any help with his medical bills. In 1983, Klaus died of AIDS at the age of thirty-nine.

We know that he had an affair with the artist David Bowes, whom he met in the early 1980s. Basquiat had broken up with Suzanne Mallouk and he had several relationships with men and women that overlapped. He was also seeing a model called Laura (as described in Phoebe Hoban's biography, this was a name to cover her real identity). When they broke up, Basquiat turned to Bowes for solace: 'He was all inside out, run ragged and raw.' Bowes was also having a difficult relationship and the two 'commiserated, finding consolation in each other'. They were lovers for three weeks. Interviewed by Hoban, Bowes reports that 'Basquiat was comfortable with his bisexuality', explaining that: 'He was this kind of truly exotic creature and had a kind of omnidirectional passion.'

Whilst Basquiat's ex-girlfriends are regularly interviewed for documentaries, the same can't be said of his male lovers. In the years since Basquiat's death, the lack of attention given to his male exes is a comment on his acquaintances and critics, on their tastes, their feelings about his sexuality, rather than on him. As Ernest Hardy, *Village Voice* critic, says, critics 'turn squeamish or disingenuous when speaking of Basquiat's queerness'. His girlfriends are at the fore, under the spotlight; his boyfriends remain in the shadows.

We have far more detail about his relationship with Warhol, which Ronnie Cutrone, an artist who was once Warhol's assistant, called 'like some crazy art-world marriage', but even that is ambiguous.

Basquiat's relationship with Warhol was one-sided to begin

with. Like many of his contemporaries, Basquiat worshipped Warhol. Julian Schnabel's film *Basquiat* depicts their first meeting in 1979. The young Basquiat, played by Jeffrey Wright, is penniless and still trying to make it. He approaches his idol, played by David Bowie, who is dining with a friend, and succeeds in selling him a couple of hand-painted postcards. Bowie gives a fine performance as Warhol, capturing his quirky essence; both were enigmatic men who constructed personas and hid behind them – as Basquiat would also come to do once he was successful.

Basquiat wanted to connect with Warhol but when he turned up at his studio, the Factory, Warhol told his minders not to let him in. Warhol was a little scared of Basquiat. He became wary of strangers after Valerie Solanas had attempted to murder him in 1968. Then Basquiat met Paige Powell, who was working at Warhol's *Interview* magazine as an advertising executive. 'He exuded this highly creative, highly sexual energy', she remembered. Basquiat wanted her, but she was in a relationship, was put off by his drug use, and wanted to keep things on a professional footing, since she was organizing a show which featured some of his work. Soon, however, they were a couple – and a complex emotional love triangle with Warhol ensued.

'What's Andy doing now?', 'What did he have for lunch?', 'What's he wearing now?' Basquiat would ask her. When Paige told Warhol that Basquiat needed help, he was uncertain – 'Well, gee, he just wants to be famous.' The art dealer Bruno Bischofberger eventually brought the artists together, introducing them over lunch. What happened next is the stuff of legend: Andy took a Polaroid of them together, Basquiat exited early, went home, painted the pair together, named it *Dos Cabezas*, and sent it back to Andy via his assistant, the paint still wet on the canvas. Soon they were collaborating, forming a trio with Francesco Clemente, then duetting in a separate, secret collaboration that their dealer didn't know about. Basquiat was delighted by the fact he'd inspired Warhol to pick up a brush for the first time in years. They worked together on epic canvases, Warhol often kicking off with a logo, Basquiat painting on top, sometimes riling his mentor-rival by erasing his work. There was a playfulness to their collaboration, a banter between mentor and protégé. 'Gee, I think he's better at painting than me,' Warhol wrote in his diary. And: 'He's the best.'

Warhol's diaries of 1983 onwards record a fascination with Basquiat's love life, often making more commentary about Basquiat's than his own (Warhol was, at this time, in a relationship with Jon Gould). Warhol enjoyed playing voyeur, matchmaker, therapist and disruptor as he observed Basquiat and Paige Powell's love affair playing out like a soap opera. Paige was not only dating Basquiat at this point, but managing his career. She organized a lecture for him in Vassar; Basquiat told Warhol that he wanted to go alone to fuck girls up there. This left Paige 'hysterical' (Andy's term) and furious, declaring she'd never do anything to help Basquiat again; Warhol advised her 'that's the way life goes'. But the relationship continued in a turbulent fashion. Basquiat asked Warhol if he could marry Paige; Andy agreed, but only if she kept working at *Interview*; Warhol wanted Basquiat and Powell to have a baby that he could then adopt. In his diary entry of 17 August 1983, Warhol ponders about the couple having sex; the next week he photographs Jean-Michel in a jockstrap. Soon Warhol and Basquiat's relationship was so intense that Powell began to feel shut out, especially when Jean-Michel began to cancel dates because Andy was coming over.

Suzanne Mallouk experienced a parallel scenario in her over-lapping, on-off relationship with Basquiat. She recalled how Warhol would stir up tensions between them, telling Basquiat about the beautiful models who were attracted to him right in front of her, or provocatively suggesting that Suzanne become a lesbian. Hurt and upset, she learned to feign indifference. Suzanne reflected that: 'Andy couldn't stand to share Jean-Michel in any way.' Yet the paradox of this scenario was that Warhol seemed to crave a third presence to play off against, the sharp points of a love triangle. When Paige tried to break up with Basquiat, tired of his infidelity and drug-taking, she would find Warhol dragging them back together; she'd be on a date with Warhol and he would confess that he was so embarrassed but he'd double-booked himself, asked Basquiat to be his date too. Suzanne reflected that when Andy assured her of Jean-Michel's infidelities, he was on some level 'talking to himself, trying to console himself'.

Warhol had a lifelong aversion to touching people and being touched. This may have originated from him suffering from attacks of St Vitus's dance as a child, which caused involuntary shaking movements and kept him off school for weeks at a time. Warhol referred to those periods as 'nervous breakdowns', which left him supersensitive. But watch Warhol and Basquiat together in 1983, being interviewed about their artistic collaboration, and you'll see Basquiat sitting on a chair and Warhol standing next to him, his arm curled around Basquiat, Warhol gazing down at him with such love: a mixture of paternal affection and protective desire. Basquiat is different in this interview compared to the others I've seen; his smile is boyish, a little shy, a little embarrassed, and he seems much younger, perhaps in response to Andy playing the father figure. His gaze is affectionate too, and a little awed.

Another photo, taken by Steven Greenberg at a party at the Rockefeller Center in September 1985, shows Basquiat standing behind Warhol, his arms curled around his waist, both facing the camera. It's a pose for the public, yet there is a sweetness that emanates from the picture, a sense that they make each other happy. American art dealer Mary Boone recalls that around Warhol, Basquiat was less inclined to take drugs, more to be sober and happy. Warhol, who was ahead of his time in documenting every little moment with a Polaroid, took numerous shots of Basquiat, detailing the tender minutiae of their friendship: Basquiat grinning whilst they have their nails done; Basquiat in a hotel room, looking miserable, having told Warhol he felt suicidal after no sleep for four nights; Basquiat getting out of bed; Basquiat shaving; Basquiat trying on clothes in a changing room. Then there is Basquiat in a jockstrap; whilst Warhol despised his own body, he celebrated Basquiat's. 'Jean-Michel had a nice big schlong,' Warhol would tell his assistant Benjamin Liu. 'Can you imagine? That's why all those girls liked him.' Over dinner, he would ask Basquiat how many times he came. As Bob Colacello – the former editor-in-chief of *Interview* magazine – recalled: Warhol 'was infatuated with Jean-Michel in both a paternal and a homosexual way'.

Were they lovers? Warhol denied to Paige that they were. When she accused of him of starting up his gay affair with Basquiat again, he cited Basquiat's lack of hygiene and regular baths, saying he was too dirty to go to bed with. Warhol famously claimed to not be interested in sex, confiding in a friend that he found it 'messy and distasteful'. But Basquiat would tease Suzanne by saying that he wouldn't reveal if they were sleeping together. The ambiguity is intriguing, especially given that Basquiat would boast about the women he went with; he may have been less comfortable talking openly about his male relationships given that Andy lived with Jon Gould, and with the backdrop of the AIDS crisis.

In 1982, Warhol mounted a Polaroid of Basquiat on canvas, coated it with copper, and pissed on it. It was one of a series of his 'piss paintings', where he used his urine for the oxidation process. His body fusing with Basquiat's portrait: his stains on his protégé's skin. The result is a portrait that is dreamy and energetic, the blotches (created by the interaction of urine and copper sulphate) like splashes from a storm. Basquiat had it on his wall in the apartment he rented from Warhol – the only picture that wasn't one of his own. But he also fretted, with some paranoia, that the picture was a comment on his skin condition. Basquiat's face was covered in blotches which were most likely related to his toxic drug use (and he lacked a spleen due to a childhood accident), his body struggling to process the overload. He worried that people might think he had AIDS. One night he showed up at the club Nell's and danced the night away wearing an aluminium foil mask on his face.

*

AIDS was slowly creeping up on them. In his diaries, Warhol records being called by a member of his family, oh-so-casually asking if he was ill. At once he intuited the subtext: are you HIV positive? When he attempted to clarify this, they quickly assured him they were referring to the flu. Initially known as 'gay cancer', the AIDS virus swept through New York, which had one of the largest LGBT populations in the world. Homophobes used the illness to justify prejudice: Republican senator Jesse Helms declared it was a punishment from God for homosexuality. I have vague memories of seeing the warning adverts on TV when I was a child, of the enormous tombstone that comes thundering down from a boiling sky (the stone like a commandment; the sky apocalyptic, like something from the last book of the Bible). It made the spread of the disease look like a horror film, AIDS as a plague, as a zombie curse, a fatal vampiric kiss. As prejudice intensified, Warhol speculated: 'I wouldn't be surprised if they started putting gays in concentration camps. All the fags will have to get married so they won't have to go away to the camps and marriage will be like a green card.' People were afraid to shake the hands of gay people; David LaChapelle recalls the story of a gay person at a dinner party who ended up being served their food on a paper plate whilst all the other guests dined off china. Keith Haring's work became politicized after his diagnosis in 1988. His 1989 painting *Ignorance = Fear/Silence = Death* explores public reluctance to engage with AIDS. He included the image of the pink triangle – historically used to mark homosexuals in the Holocaust.

In the US, the Reagan government was silent on the subject of AIDS. In 1984, the Republicans won the election by a landslide, with Reagan elected on a promise to 'resist the efforts of some to obtain government endorsement of homosexuality'. In the UK, Section 28 prohibited the 'promotion of homosexuality', causing many gay and bi student support groups to close. This meant that a teacher at a school couldn't even address an issue of homophobic bullying for fear of losing their job. The word 'queer', once a slur, had been taken back by activists; groups like Queer Nation conducted a campaign of 'politics of provocation', with a slogan of *We're Here, We're Queer, and we'd like to say hello!* Section 28 was based on the idea that being gay was a choice; the government believed that if people saw positive images of homosexuality, they might be inspired to become gay. Bis and gays were no longer apologizing, asking to be pitied, promising to assimilate; now their stance that their sexuality was a choice was weaponized against them.

AIDS created more unity within the LGBT community, for lesbians and gays joined together in sympathy and campaigning. But for bisexuals, it meant further ostracization just when acceptance had started to bloom. Following on from the suspicions they faced from the gay community in the 1970s, bisexuals began to petition in the late Eighties to add a 'B' to LG groups.

It wasn't always easy. In 1985 at the San Francisco Lesbian and Gay Freedom Day parade, the bisexual contingent were dressed as famous bis, such as Janis Joplin, and held up placards with slogans such as *Bi All Means*, only to find themselves booed by the crowds. In Northampton, Massachusetts, the debate over bisexual inclusion for its Lesbian and Gay Pride March and Rally became infamous. There was a large concentration of queer people in Northampton and it was known for being a tolerant place, but when bisexuals asked to be included in the rally, the bi word was added in 1989 but dropped in 1990 with angry backlash within the lesbian/gay community, who felt their 'safe space', their territory, was being diluted and impinged on by bis. In the UK, the London Lesbian and Gay Community Centre banned bisexuals, for the lesbians felt threatened by bisexual men. In 1985, in the feminist magazine *Spare Rib*, a fiery debate unfolded in the letters column, where lesbians argued that bisexual women were sleeping with the enemy. And the singer Tom Robinson, who had once sung the gay anthem 'Glad to be Gay', found himself booed during a concert in 1987. The reason? Tom had discovered he was bi; he had married a woman but declared he was still queer and didn't feel he had to be strait-jacketed into his sexuality. His declaration of bisexuality was seen as a betrayal.

Despite these setbacks, bis had also made progress in gaining acceptance and recognition. They were also passionately involved in the fight against AIDS. Cynthia Slater, a bisexual and BDSM activist who was HIV positive, set up the first women's HIV/AIDS information switchboard. She died of AIDS in 1989, aged forty-four, and was one of those commemorated in the AIDS memorial quilt created by Cleve Jones in San Francisco, where each panel represents someone lost to the disease. A recurrent problem that bisexuals have faced over the decades has been a lack of proper data collected from studies; they are too often lumped in with gays/lesbians. Bisexual activist David Lourea campaigned for two years for the San Francisco department of Public Health to include bi men in their official statistics for AIDS; in 1984 he finally achieved victory. Following this, health departments throughout the US began to recognize bi men as a category on their own.

Just as bisexuals were becoming more accepted, they were scapegoated, mythologized even, becoming the bridgeway between two sexual populations, passing the disease from gay to hetero-sexual and back again. In 1987 *Newsweek* ran an article deeming bisexual men as the 'ultimate pariahs' of the epidemic. In 1989 *Cosmopolitan* carried a piece that stereotyped bisexual men as corrupt, dishonest villains who were spreading the disease. In retaliation, the New York Area Bisexual Network set up a ferocious letter-writing campaign, and *Cosmopolitan* didn't run any further pieces along these lines. But the damage had been done – and it was a damage that lingered, not just during the AIDS crisis years, but for decades thereafter. Even as late as 2014, the *New York Post* ran a piece that declared three-quarters of women with new HIV infections had got it from bi men, ignoring statistics that showed women could also get the illness from heterosexual men.

William Burroughs claimed that Basquiat told him he had AIDS. Basquiat was convinced he was going to die of it and friends such as Glenn O'Brien felt that this made him more reckless, treating his life more lightly, more loosely. Basquiat hadn't always practised safe sex; he had given a number of his past lovers diseases: as well as infecting Klaus Nomi with gonorrhoea, he gave Suzanne Mallouk a pelvic infection that left her unable to conceive. In actual fact, despite his lifestyle, Basquiat hadn't contracted the illness.

*

Warhol and Basquiat's relationship was dealt a tragic blow when their joint exhibition, *Paintings*, opened at the Tony Shafrazi gallery in 1985. Basquiat thought that it would bring him the respect and recognition from the establishment that he had been seeking. Instead, the critics panned it – and patronized Basquiat in the process. A *New York Times* piece asked, 'Who is using who here?' and sneered at Basquiat as Warhol's 'mascot' who 'comes across as the all too willing accessory' to Warhol's 'manipulations'. Not a single picture sold.

'I asked him if he was mad at me for that review . . . and he said no,' Warhol's diary entry reports. But Basquiat was devastated. He left New York, stung and depressed. He had aligned himself with one of the contemporary icons of art, and for him, Warhol had represented acceptance: 'it wasn't just a father, it was also the professional approval of a white artist who was one of the masters'.

The pair did not collaborate artistically again. Whilst it wasn't the end of their relationship, it created distance between them. There is a sad entry from Warhol's diary that comes a few months later: 'Jean Michel hasn't called me in a month, so I guess it's really over.'

On 22 February 1987, Andy Warhol died of a cardiac arrest after gallbladder surgery. The artist Nancy Brooks Brody witnessed the agony of Basquiat's grief when she saw him weep over Warhol: 'I never saw him cry before.' 'I ran into him at a club a few days after Andy died, and it was really sad,' Fab 5 Freddy recalled. 'He's standing in the middle of the dancefloor, crying in agony and leaning his head on a wall. He couldn't even talk.' Barbara Braathen, one of his later girlfriends, remembers how she visited Basquiat to find him attempting suicide with a knife, which she had to wrestle away from him.

'Andy dying might have put the idea in Jean-Michel's head that you could die, even if you were seemingly immortal, because Andy always had this air of immortality about him,' Glenn O'Brien reflected. Once Basquiat was told by sculptor Arden Scott, 'You can either be a great artist or a great tragedy', to which he replied, 'Why can't I be both?' Jean-Michel became more reclusive and Bischofberger recalls that his drug-taking intensified, became 'the centre of his life'. In early 1988, friends began to be shocked by Basquiat's appearance. He had lost teeth; his remaining teeth were covered with a yellow film; his dreads were matted; his face covered in sores that he kept picking at. And he had become as thin as a skeleton. Vincent Gallo, a former bandmate, said that when he saw him, 'I thought he had AIDs.' And so the rumours flew about. His paranoia had deepened, and he was hostile; when Suzanne tried to discuss his addiction with him the drugs would speak through him, resisting intervention with a terrifying anger. Friends and lovers fell away, carved him out of their lives. Collectors avoided him. Basquiat would curl up and weep with loneliness. Suzanne visited him, bathing him with love, and he asked why she left him:

'Everyone has left me,' he lamented. She was shocked: 'it was the first time I had ever seen him feeling sorry for himself. He was usually so gutsy.'

He told a friend that he no longer enjoyed painting. He zig-zagged desperately through new futures: he might become a writer, he might open a tequila business. With one final spurt of energy, he painted a series of new pieces for what would be his final show, held at the Vrej Baghoomian gallery. His style was simplified, looser, darker. One standout piece is the astonishing *Riding With Death*, which depicts a black man, a stick figure, on the skeleton of a horse, against a stark brown background. There is a sense of foreboding, of beautiful decay in the painting. The horse's eyes are gashed out and the black scribbles over its disjointed bones suggest disintegration; 'horse' was slang for heroin. Another is *Eroica*, which translates from the Italian as 'heroic'. In this painting Death slays the hero; MAN DIES is repeated over and over, accompanied by stick men that look like half-formed figures in a lost game of Hangman. Black spots fray and bleed like bulletholes; red smears on the canvas are like blood; the scratchy repetition in *Eroica* looks like the desperate scrawled refrain of a prisoner caged in a cell. Death is such a presence in the work – fuelled by Warhol, the AIDS crisis, and a sense of his own death to come, of his body breaking down, a gradual ruination.

Basquiat told a friend that since Warhol had died, all he could think of was killing himself. A trip to Hawaii in the summer of 1988 was briefly redemptive; he returned telling friends that he had kicked his drug habit, but it wasn't long before he fell. His addiction became a slow suicide. On 12 August 1988 he was found unconscious in his Great Jones Street loft by his girlfriend, Kelle Inman. The air-con had broken and the room was 'hot as a furnace'. The ambulance was called; they attempted to resuscitate him. He was rushed to hospital and there pronounced dead on arrival. He was twenty-seven years old.

*

Keith Haring wrote an obituary for his friend, celebrating his life and reflecting sadly, 'Greedily we wonder . . . what masterpieces we have been cheated out of by his death.' He painted *A Pile of Crowns*, an artwork that shows Basquiat's iconic crown motif enclosed within a red-rimmed triangle, like a warning sign. In the bottom corner was a copyright symbol, another of Basquiat's signature motifs.

Since his death, Basquiat's name and work have not only survived but thrived. He is now more celebrated than his contemporaries, soaring past Julian Schnabel, Keith Haring and Kenny Scharf. His paintings have undergone a corporate appropriation that would have probably evoked both his disgust and his delight. The cosmetics brand Urban Decay used his crown iconography on their eyeshadow palettes; Beyoncé and Jay-Z posed in front of his blue *Equals Pi* painting for a Tiffany ad. Alexis Adler was 'horrified' by the latter, declaring that 'the commercialization and commodification of Jean and his art at this point—it's really not what Jean was about.'

The political nature of his work feels more relevant than ever. In the Black Lives Matter protests of 2020, a mural by Trina Merry painted in memory of George Floyd featured a portrait of George with Basquiat's crown. It echoed Basquiat's *Defacement* and we hear Basquiat's words – on hearing the news of Michael Stewart's death – with a chill: 'It could have been me.' *Defacement*, painted in 1983, and the mural, four decades on, show how little has changed – and how urgent the change was, how important the protests were.

As Basquiat achieves the reputation he deserves, however, the erasure of his bisexuality remains ongoing. As Kenny Scharf has reflected in an interview: 'When it comes to Basquiat, I tell some stories, and they don't wanna hear it. One of the things you couldn't bring up was . . . any hint of non-heterosexuality. And he was a lady's man. He had a lot of girlfriends, but he also liked guys, and they just don't wanna talk about that.' A 2014 *Vanity Fair* article fleetingly refers to Basquiat having 'a brief fascination with bisexuality' in his early twenties, despite the fact that Basquiat lost his virginity to a man in his teens, suggesting an inclination that had gone on for years and was hardly 'brief'. Both of the films that depict his life, Schnabel's *Basquiat* (1996) and the documentary *Radiant Child* (2010), portray Basquiat as a stud who womanizes rather than a man who was attracted to more than one gender. Ernest Hardy has compared Basquiat with Malcolm X – both important Black figures that he feels have been straightened out by mainstream media – arguing that such 'straight-washing' occurs because Black radical artists are fetishized as subversive in their lives; following their deaths, they are depicted in palatable ways that don't disrupt the status quo.

8

Madonna

'Like A Virgin': that was the song that made me fall in love with Madonna. I first heard it a few years after its release in 1984. I was experiencing my first sexual stirrings, though at this stage in my life, boys were my only interest. During my last year of primary school, I had to wear braces to straighten my teeth. I felt ugly; boys teased me for being a 'metal-mouth'; I remained static in games of Kiss Chase. At the age of thirteen, everything was different. Suddenly I was blossoming, aware that boys were looking at me.

Madonna has often described how her attitude to sex was shaped by her strict Catholic upbringing. In the iconic video for 'Like A Virgin', she alternates between two selves, parodying the virgin/whore dichotomy. There is 'virginal' Madonna in a wedding dress, adorned with a lacy veil, gliding around a room and whipping away white sheets to reveal furniture; and then there is 'sexy' Madonna in a gondola, wearing black, her midriff exposed as she writhes and sings. The latter Madonna is hardly a 'whore', more a woman celebrating her sexuality. But this splitting up of innocence and experience resonated with my teenage self. There was still a lingering hangover of conservatism from the 1980s era of regression and repression: it felt necessary to cover any bad-girl tendencies with a good-girl veil. I was studying at a girls' school, where my life naturally fell into two halves: austere days of school and homework, and colourful weekends where we partied with teens from the local boys' school. We frequented over-eighteens nightclubs, creating fake IDs to gain entry, where in the heady mix of coloured lights and euphoric dance beats we sought the male gaze, craved it: for us it meant power, acceptance, affirmation. My love life was simultaneously promiscuous and chaste: I had numerous boyfriends, but refused to sleep with any of them, hanging onto my virginity like a badge of honour, as though to reassure myself that I was still innocent. People would often comment on my girlishly sweet face, my butter-wouldn't-melt persona, which I continued to adopt into adulthood as a sort of shield that disguised a fascination with sex I felt furtive about.

During the early 1990s, I suffered from poor mental health. Transcendental Meditation was helping to heal my fractured mind, but I also felt a need to confide in someone about the worries fizzing inside me. I went to see a counsellor on a weekly basis. A few sessions in, I told him that I wanted to be like Madonna when I grew up. His reply was slightly dismissive: 'She goes around flashing her boobs and her bum – she's certainly very famous.' I think he assumed that I craved fame too, but it was more subtle than that: like many teenage girls, what I loved about Madonna was her power. I read an interview around this time in which she said, *I'm in control, I know what I'm doing*, words which had thrilled me; I was feeling so fragile that I wished I could see life as something to be conquered rather than a force that was overwhelming me.

'Flashing her boobs and her bum': such crude words. They made me shudder, for I couldn't connect them with my perception of Madonna. I associated her with beauty, elegance, danger, excitement, transgression, provocation, glamour. In those pre-Internet days my only access to her was in flashes and fragments: in CD covers, glossy magazines I flicked through, illicit TV clips, all of which left me hungry for more. The 1990 single 'Vogue' had signified Madonna's peak. The single had hit number one across the globe, a sultry dance smash in which she does an elegant rap that lists all the gods and goddesses of old Hollywood who had 'style and grace': Garbo, Dietrich, Monroe, Jimmy Dean, with the implicit sense she wanted to join that roll-call of greats.

My friends and I all went to the cinema to see her documentary, *In Bed With Madonna*, filmed when she was on her Blonde Ambition tour. It was shot in black-and-white and it captured Madonna in a range of 'everyday' situations: sipping soup and calling up her father, recalling being finger-fucked by a childhood female friend, performing fellatio on a water bottle, mocking Kevin Costner and playing Truth or Dare with her dancers. She came across as bitchy, scary, endearing, magnetic. As a result of watching it, I liked her more, I liked her less; and I was even more fascinated by her.

Her next studio album, *Erotica*, was her most raunchy yet, and it was accompanied by the publication of her infamous *Sex* book. This was the climax – for want of a better word – of Madonna's sexy era. She had always been playful and flirtatious; after all, 'Like a Virgin' had been one of the biggest hits of the mid-1980s, and the accompanying album made her a superstar. She had played a sexy dancer in 'Open Your Heart'; in 'La Isla Bonita' she salsa-ed in a Spanish dress and captured the yearning of a holiday fling that's stopped too short; 'Like a Prayer' had caused controversy when the video depicted her kissing a Black Jesus. But 'Justify My Love', followed by 'Hanky Panky', followed by *Erotica* followed by *Sex*, showed that Madonna's latest reinvention was breaking new ground. She was exploring her sexuality with a degree of daring that no music star before her had ever risked.

Madonna recreated herself as Mistress Dita, a persona based on Dita Parlo, a German silent film star of the 1930s. Photographed by Steven Meisel, *Sex* was inspired in part by Brassaï's 1933 book *Paris by Night*, which depicted the underground nightlife of the city: prostitutes and pedlars, illicit lovers on the margins of society. *Sex* was A4 in size, spiral bound, with a metallic cover made of aluminium with a warning stamp on the cover; it was sheathed and sealed in a silvery Mylar envelope with a print of Madonna's face; her ecstatic expression rippled as you opened it up. Fans queued overnight to buy a copy. In the UK, 100,000 copies were released and all were sold by the second day; in the US, it went straight into the *New York Times* bestseller lists.

At the age of sixteen, I never saw an actual copy, but I did have an older boyfriend who described some of the images to me, and I managed to peek at others by flicking through magazines in the newsagents. I remember one shot of her that I particularly loved: she was admiring herself in front of a mirror, her top lifted up above her naked breasts, blonde hair mussed as though she'd just had sex. I wouldn't obtain my own copy of *Sex* until my early twenties, when I discovered that the book celebrated sexuality of every hue. There was a photo of Madonna with Ingrid Casares, both dressed up in male drag, kissing passionately. There were shots that were disturbing, such as Madonna being threatened with a knife, or held down by two men in a school gymnasium, and shots that were comic, of Madonna in a ballgown, crouching down by handsome men in suits, gazing up like a Cinderella craving an orgy with her Prince Charmings. There were shots which challenged ageism: Madonna sitting in her underwear on the lap of an elderly man with white hair, kissing him. Shots of Madonna with her head arched back, throat being kissed by butch lesbians covered in tattoos; Madonna, naked and vulnerable, being held by Isabella Rossellini in a man's suit. These were some of the first images of bisexuality that I'd ever seen, and I was enchanted. The shots taken in Miami felt more personal, as though her persona slipped and her true self came out – Madonna rising naked from the ocean, Aphrodite hair flowing down her back; sitting naked in a pizza parlour, attracting shocked glances; and the infamous comic hitchhiker shot, where

Madonna, wearing nothing but a cigarette dangling from her lips, tries to flag down a car on a palm-fringed street.

A year before *Sex* came out, Madonna had given an interview with *The Advocate*, an LGBT magazine in the US, and declared that 'Everybody has a bisexual nature.' Madonna's celebration of bisexual and gay sex in her music, videos, film and book in this era was hugely significant. Bowie had done it twenty years before, in the early 1970s, but the AIDS scares of the 1980s had done so much damage to the gay community that sex, and particularly gay sex, was a nervous subject once more; in 1992 HIV infection was the leading cause of death for men aged twenty-five to forty-four in the US.

Madonna wasn't nervous. The dancers on her Blonde Ambition tour were nearly all gay. In the game of Truth or Dare, filmed in her documentary, two of those dancers, Salim Gauwloos and Gabriel Trupin, lose a dare and French kiss onscreen. There's nothing shocking about this for a contemporary audience. But back then, for many teenagers, it was a watershed moment comparable to Bowie's *Top of the Pops* performance, arm curled around Mick Ronson. 'It was the first time I'd ever seen that, and it was very liberating for me,' reports one guy who had a conservative upbringing on a farm in Michigan, interviewed twenty-five years on. In decades to come, Salim would go on to receive thousands of messages from people all around the world who told him their lives were changed by watching that kiss.

'It's hard to think of another film about a nongay subject in which the presence of gay people is not only normal and accepted but treasured,' *The Advocate* praised the film. It depicted dancers Jose Gutierez Xtravaganza and Luis Camacho hanging out with Queer Nation at a New York Gay Pride march, as well as showing how Madonna's sole straight dancer, Oliver Crumes Jr, overcame his homophobia. When asked by *The Advocate* why the music industry is so homophobic, Madonna's reply was firm: 'They're not going to be by the time I've finished with them.' As Matthew Todd reflects: 'The 1990s were still a time when homophobia was rife, but things were starting to change. Madonna, by then the biggest star in the world, brought gay culture directly into the living-rooms of the public.' The TV presenter and writer Matt Cain, struggling with his sexuality as a teenager, found redemption in Madonna: he feared 'everyone would hate me if it ever came out', that he was carrying around 'this dirty little secret', and so he would go to his room, listen to Madonna, watch her videos and feel 'like she was the only one who was on my side, sticking up for me'.

Madonna had explored different facets of herself in previous albums and films: 'In true post-modern fashion,' says the *Advocate*, 'she is drawn to complexity, contradiction and ambiguity over harmony, clarity and simplicity. She embraces a fragmented wardrobe of personas . . . rather than a false, integrated persona.' Perhaps one of the reasons that people reacted so vehemently against her *Sex* art was that Madonna was a more unified figure, which made her exploration more bold. If we compare her video for 'Erotica' to 'Like a Virgin', there is no Madonna split into two, with a virginal side to balance out the sexiness, to act as an apology or soften it. This time round, Madonna was sexy in concentrate. Perhaps this also shocked people because it made her more human, flesh and blood; the writer Georges-Claude Guilbert has argued that stars are inherently vamps i.e. an attractive, dangerously flirtatious woman, and that 'the vamp is an object of desire, but she is untouchable, like a virginal deity.' Madonna was no longer a fantasy figure, but a woman exploring *her* fantasies, and as Ariel Levy wrote in *Female Chauvinist Pigs*, the 1990s encapsulated a culture that valued 'the appearance of sexiness, not the existence of sexual pleasure' in women.

I had very little awareness of the backlash that was being unleashed on Madonna around this time. The words 'cancel culture' were not in vogue then, but this was precisely what was happening to Madonna. The Vatican ordered Roman Catholics to boycott the book, deeming it 'morally intolerable'. Madonna was called a whore, a witch, a heretic and the Devil. She received hate mail and death threats. Journalists wrote indignant pieces with titles such as 'Has Madonna Gone Too Far?', and *The I Hate Madonna Handbook* was published, a nasty little book aimed at slut-shaming Madonna and taking her down for being 'under-dressed, over-heard, over-exposed'. A letter to *The Harvard Crimson* from this era, by a fan called Thomas S. Hixson, is so self-righteous that it makes me laugh: 'What can I say? I've been your most loyal fan. I have all your albums, all your biographies and videotapes of all your world tours. You were my idol. But, also, no longer . . . The book (*Sex*, Warner Books, $35) was the final straw, of course. It's disgusting. No, not provocative or titillating. Disgusting.' Madonna paid the price in poor record sales. In the 1980s, she had sold superstar quantities of her albums – 25 million copies of *True Blue* (the bestselling album of the 1980s by a female artist), 15 million of *Like A Prayer*. Her *Erotica* album dived, selling 2 million in the US, a low for her. For the first time, she released a single, 'Bad Girl', which failed to make the Top 30 of the Hot 100 in the US. Even Madonna, who liked to be provocative, to push buttons, to 'rub people up the wrong way', felt the sting of the backlash, reflecting later on that she 'lost confidence in humanity'.

Even Madonna's biographers feel uncomfortable about this moment in her career. For J. Randy Taraborrelli, the book was supposed to be 'adult' but was 'childish and impetuous'. Lucy O'Brien claims that *Sex* was partly inspired by the assault that Madonna suffered during her early twenties, when she first moved to New York and was raped at knifepoint, that she stripped her body bare 'as a mode of confrontation as much as eroticism'. She declares that Madonna was driven by 'white-hot anger'. But this suggests that *Sex* is a product of warped creativity, a painful response to trauma, whereas in fact the book is informed by playfulness as much as anger; Madonna herself felt this was a misunderstood component of the book, telling the journalist Barbara Ellen, 'It was never meant to be this incredibly hot, arousing, erotic piece of porn. In fact, I was poking fun at everyone's prejudices about other people's sexualities and their own sexuality.' And in her ongoing celebration of bisexuality, she defended herself against an accusation of 'sexual irresponsibility' in an interview with *Nightline* with the reply: 'Why are images of degradation and violence towards women okay, almost mainstream, yet images of two women or two men kissing taboo?'

In her next album, *Bedtime Stories*, the single 'Human Nature' – a hissing, slithery, angry song – bemoaned the public reaction to the book and declared that she was not the one with a problem. She suggested that people might have found her exploration of sexuality easier if she was a man. After all, there were plenty of raunchy male figures in the 1990s who never faced equivalent criticism: at the 1991 MTV Video Awards, Prince wore an assless pantsuit, whilst Jon Bon Jovi loved to show off his muscly body.

As teenagers, my friends and I were vaguely aware that Madonna was attracting disapproval, which only made her more alluring and fascinating. Adults and teachers were silent on the subject of sex, whilst Madonna had a megaphone. Nobody at school had any advice for us, beyond a policeman advising us on how to deal with a rapist in the street. Red-faced and giggling, we bought a copy of Nancy Friday's *Men In Love*, which detailed male sexual fantasies, which I then hid behind a layer of books on my bedroom bookshelf. Books, films, music: these were our only way of working out how love and sex worked, but too often a disappointing gap cleaved open between life and art; boys failed to behave like the charming, sensitive heroes of *Sweet Valley High* and other romances. Madonna was refreshingly sex-positive, saying it was fine to have sex (as long as it was safe), to experiment, to enjoy it, to explore your bi side. As she argued herself: 'the problem is, everyone's so uptight about it [sex] . . . If people could talk about it freely, we would have more people practising safe sex.' It wasn't a dark message: looking back, the backlash itself is far more shocking than Madonna's art.

'Bisexuality is in bloom,' *Newsweek* magazine had said in 1974; now it repeated itself in 1995. The magazine cover looks unintentionally comic now: three people, one dressed in a suit with her arms crossed, all looking stern and serious. The headline reads: *Bisexuality. Not Gay. Not Straight. A New Sexual Identity Emerges.* Bisexuality was hardly 'new', but the headline signalled that the 1980s prejudice against bisexuals was starting to heal, that the social mood was changing.

Following the exclusion of bisexuals from gay/lesbian groups in the 1970s, bisexual activists had created their own groups in the 1980s. The 1990s built on this: there was a great flourishing of new bisexual groups, magazines, marches, zines, newsletters, and, as the Internet came into vogue, websites. In the US, the first National Conference on Bisexuality was held in San Francisco in 1990. In 1993 came a watershed moment. Lani Ka'ahumanu, bisexual activist and founder of the BiPOL (the first bisexual political action group in America), was on the bill to speak at a Washington rally/march for gay rights. She was the only speaker to represent bisexuality, but she'd been billed as the last of eighteen speakers; and then, when she finally did get to the podium, she was told to cut her speech short. 'Aloha, my name is Lani Ka'ahumanu,' she started as she took the mic, 'and it ain't over til the bisexual speaks.' Her speech was a triumph. 'Recognition of bisexual orientation and transgender issues presents a challenge to assumptions not previously explored within the politics of gay liberation,' she stated. 'What will it take for the gayristocracy to realize that bisexual, lesbian, transgender, and gay people are in this together, and together we can and will move the agenda forward. But this will not happen until public recognition of our common issues is made, and a sincere effort to confront biphobia and transphobia is made by the established gay and lesbian leadership in this country.'

The writer Sue George notes that between 1977 and 1990 there were no titles listed in the copyright section of the British Library on the subject of bisexuality. But in the early 90s there was a flourishing of bi books: George wrote *Women and Bisexuality* (1993), and anthologies such as *Bi Any Other Name* were published. Author and bisexual activist Dawn Atkins has remarked that the drive for a bisexual movement came primarily from women: 'Women played a major role in the formation of "bisexual identity" and "bisexual politics". Women were often in leadership roles – sometimes the only leaders of – bis organisations. They edited newsletters, and wrote many of the books on bisexuality . . . I suggest that never before has there been a movement composed of and for the benefit of men and women that was predominantly and publicly led by women.'

She argues that the movement was created in response to lesbian-feminism and the prejudices against bi women in the 1970s/1980s that deemed that they were 'sleeping with the enemy'. When bi women were allowed into lesbian groups – and often they were not – they were seen as invading a territory they did not belong in, diluting its ethos, eroding its principles.

Indeed, 'bisexual chic' in the 1990s seemed to revolve far more around women than men, which helped to give rise to the expression 'lipstick lesbianism'. There was Madonna and *Sex*. A *Vanity Fair* cover where k. d. lang is dressed in a suit, face covered in shaving cream, and Cindy Crawford is shaving her. Sharon Stone in *Basic Instinct*, playing a sexy, smart writer (and possible murderer), though the film has attracted complaints that it builds on the age-old depiction of queers as sociopathic. Hollywood was heavily male-dominated in this era; female directors were rare; and the focus on female bisexuality was perhaps the product of male fantasy as much as anything. The film *Chasing Amy*, about a lesbian who falls for her male friend, was much praised, although there was still an uneasy undercurrent of him 'converting' her and the film focuses on his story rather than hers. If there was a more prominent depiction of bisexuals in the arts, it wasn't always positive; in season 3, episode 4 of *Sex and the City*, a discussion on bisexuality included the line, 'It's just a layover on the way to Gaytown.' Tom Hanks played a gay character suffering from AIDS in *Philadelphia*, which received multiple awards and nominations. When it came to Hollywood, gays got more serious, sympathetic treatment, whereas bis were depicted with more frivolity.

At the age of seventeen, I was at a house party with friends, out in the back garden on a sultry summer's evening, when gossip rippled through the crowd: 'Laura and Becky are kissing.' We stood on tiptoe; a sea of heads turned, formed an audience. I caught sight of them sitting on a wall, kissing under a curved wisteria branch. Yet we remained cynical. They hadn't come out as lesbians; one of them was dating a boy. They were kissing in public to get attention, we concluded later: because it was shocking, and because the boys were watching. Looking back, our condemnation feels unfair, but we were trained to define ourselves and our actions through the eyes of heterosexual men, and to regard bisexuality as fashionable but frivolous.

Even so, the sight of them together on the wall lingered in my mind, like an exquisite painting or a shot from a film that stirs a sense of beauty inside you. When my friend kissed me a few months later, after dropping me off from a club, I felt as though a seed had been planted.

*

Imagine Madonna at the age of fifteen. It's 1974. She wants to see David Bowie in concert, but her father has forbidden her from going.

Madonna is in a rebellious mood. At the age of five, she lost her mother to breast cancer. She suffers from insomnia and feels as though 'ants were crawling over her heart', beset with worries that she will die from cancer like her mother did. Her father, an Italian Catholic, is a middle-class engineer with a strong work ethic. He brings up Madonna and her siblings single-handedly, imposing strict order on them. Having grown up without a female figure in her life, Madonna has often adopted a maternal role herself, which has brought out a bossy streak in her. She is also free to behave as her brothers do, to run wild and chase boys in the playground; 'I know that some of my lack of inhibition comes from my mother's death,' she reflected later. 'For example, mothers teach you manners. And I absolutely did not learn any of those rules and regulations.' She has a growing awareness, however, that the Catholic Church comes down harder on women than men. Her grandmother advises her 'not to go with men, to love Jesus and be a good girl'. At school, boys think she is weird and she feels like a misfit. Her teen idols are female creative icons such as the dancer Martha Graham and bisexual artists like Frida Kahlo and Georgia O'Keeffe.

She is also unhappy when her father finds a new female partner, Joan Gustafson. Unable to accept her, Madonna is forever answering back and breaking the rules. And so she ignores her father's dictate: she goes to see Bowie. Dressed in platform shoes and a long silk cape, she sneaks out when everyone is asleep, meets her best friend and hitchhikes to the Cobo Arena, Detroit.

For Madonna, it is a seminal, wondrous moment. She gazes up at him on stage, frozen, thinking, *Oh My God*. His set is spectacular. His androgyny thrills her. She sees in him both the 'male and female spirit'. She admires his beauty and his elegance, his music and his theatre. Back home, her furious father grounds her for the rest of the summer, but the concert was 'worth every minute' of the punishment. All of a sudden she feels as though Bowie has given her a licence to 'dream a different future' for herself.

Another life-changing moment occurs when Madonna visits a gay club for the first time. She once made the lovely, tongue-in-cheek quip that 'Behind every great man is a great woman, and behind every great woman is a gay man.' She starts ballet lessons as a teenager, guided by a gay teacher, Christopher Flynn. He is a tough teacher, but he also nurtures her; holding her face in his hand, he tells her that she is beautiful. Madonna has been feeling ugly, a misfit, a freak; boys at school are intimidated by her. For the first time, she begins to like herself. A new goal – to be a great dancer – awakens her determination and gives her direction. It is Christopher who takes her to Menjos, a disco club in Detroit. As with the Bowie concert, there is a sense of revelation: 'Oh God, I've found it,' she thinks. 'For the first time I saw men kissing men, girls dressed like boys, boys wearing hot pants, insane, incredible dancing and a kind of freedom and joy and happiness that I had never seen before.' She realizes that until that point, she has viewed herself through 'macho heterosexual eyes' – but that's not the way it has to be. She's not a freak. It's fine to be different.

In 1978, Madonna dropped out of college and moved from Michigan to New York. The story has become legend now; she had just $35 in her pocket, and when she arrived, she asked the taxi driver to take her to the 'middle of everything', so he drove her to Times Square. She lived poor and rough, working as a nude model for art classes and manning the Dunkin' Donuts stand, staying in an apartment that was regularly broken into and robbed. But it was a magical place to grow as a creative: 'I felt like I had plugged my finger into an electric socket.' She slept with men; she slept with women – 'Everyone was doing it,' one of Madonna's friends recalled. As in Michigan, Madonna fell in love with gay clubs and culture. But there was a downside: she was forever falling in love with gay men and found that 'I was so miserable that I wasn't a man.' When she lived in the East Village in New York, most of her friends were gay, from the bartender Martin Burgoyne to Keith Haring. Madonna said that, 'I didn't feel like straight men understood me.

They just wanted to have sex with me. Gay men understood me and I felt comfortable around them.'

Dancer Pedro Gonçalves has noted that Madonna opted for diversity from her early career, favouring Black, Latino, gay and trans dancers for her videos. Her camaraderie with gay men stems from the fact that she feels 'their persecution. They are looked on as outsiders, so I can relate to that. On the other hand, I feel that most gay men are so much more in touch with a certain kind of sensitivity heterosexual men aren't allowed to be in touch with.' Boy George has described her as 'a gay man trapped in a woman's body'. Like many bisexual icons, she embodies androgyny; once, in a Reddit chat, when she was asked the question, *if you were a gay man, would you be a top or a bottom*, she replied: 'I am a gay man.' This is played out in her 'Express Yourself' video, one of her other iconic 1990s hits, directed by David Fincher and inspired by Fritz Lang's *Metropolis*. Madonna plays the wife of a factory owner; half-way through she slips out of her evening dress and dons a black, businesslike suit (the type her husband might sport), aggressively yanking open its lapels to show off her lacy bra and grabbing her crotch. The monocle that she plays with is both part of her performance – she is mimicking a powerful captain of industry from the late nineteenth century – and a wink to the lesbian clubs of the 1920s. Critics debated whether she was 'arguing for gender fluidity as a road to gender equality'.

In 1989, Madonna released her fourth album, *Like A Prayer*. Following on from *True Blue*, it signalled a new maturity in her songwriting, mixing exuberantly joyful tracks such as 'Cherish' with more melancholic, soulful songs that explored her relationship with her father and the Catholic Church, the death of her mother, and her failed marriage to Sean Penn. The cover was scented with patchouli oil to mimic the incense of a church, and it included a leaflet inside, 'The Facts About AIDS'. It began with the statement 'People with AIDS – regardless of their sexual orientation – deserve compassion and support, not violence and bigotry' and ended with the advice to wear a condom. Madonna lived through an administration, led by President Reagan, which labelled HIV a 'gay plague' and was apathetic and slow to supply funding, support and research; through an era when the Catholic Church condemned the use of needle exchanges and condoms.

Unlike Bowie, Madonna didn't shy away from her bisexuality during the AIDS nightmare. Instead, she came out in full force and did her best to help the gay community. She attended a charity dance marathon in the US to raise money for people who were HIV positive. She smuggled experimental drugs across the border from Mexico to help friends suffering from the illness; she visited hospitals and hugged HIV patients: 'I came home smelling like shit and vomit and death and defiance. I came home smelling like gratitude.' She lost good friends to AIDS, from Christopher Flynn, her ballet teacher, to Keith Haring and Martin Burgoyne. She dedicated the final date of her Blonde Ambition tour to Haring and threaded these lyrics into 'Get Into the Groove' to remind her audience: 'Don't be silly/Put a condom on your willy.'

Jean Paul Gaultier organized a charity fashion event in connection with amfAR, the Foundation for AIDS research. Madonna was to be the star act, the finale of the show. She was supposed to strut down in trousers, jacket, and top – but lost the top at the last minute, and came down the runway bare-breasted, her nipples peeking out from her red trouser braces. The stunt captures the paradox of Madonna, the way in which she can be wonderful and irritating all at once: it guaranteed amfAR column inches, and it guaranteed her column inches. But there's no doubt that her activism was sincere and impassioned. Like Elizabeth Taylor, another supporter of AIDS victims, Madonna was the subject of speculation that she had the illness herself, as though it was some sort of punishment for her supposed transgressions and racy lifestyle. In 1991, when she was honoured by amfAR for her activism, she said: 'Now I'm not

HIV-positive. But if I were? I would be more afraid of how society would treat me for having the disease than the actual disease itself'; and, 'Instead of pointing the finger at people and having witch hunts and ostracising each other for lifestyles and sexual preferences, we should all be uniting to fight this disease.' Gradually, the public mood began to shift from fear to sympathy; the Clinton administration offered more support and funding, and celebrities began to don little red ribbons on their lapels that signalled their support for AIDS sufferers. Still, long before it became acceptable, fashionable to do so, Madonna was sticking up for them.

*

Madonna's bisexuality is uneven. Her first sexual experiences occurred when she was about seven or eight years old, and she described how, 'All of my sexual experiences when I was young were with girls. I mean, we didn't have those sleep-over parties for nothing. I think that's really normal: same-sex experimentation. You get really curious, and there's your girlfriend, and she's spending the night with you, and it happens.' However, she has stated that she tends to only have crushes on women, whereas, 'I think I've only been in love with men, because ultimately the approval I seek is my father's.'

Madonna suggests that she has sought relationships with father figures, men who echo her father Tony Ciccone's personality: tough, old-fashioned, hard-working, determined, a man who says what he thinks. But the statement is ambiguous, and may also imply that she longed for a traditional heterosexual marriage that her father would be happy with. In that same interview (with *The Advocate*), she also declares that 'I suppose people would say, "You emasculate men in what you do." Well, straight men need to be emasculated. I'm sorry. They all need to be slapped around.' In the 1980s, she was known as the Boy Toy, with its meaning inverted: it's clear that she wasn't the toy, but the one doing the toying with boys. Anyone dating Madonna would have to contend with her immense ego, power, fame, wealth, with entering a room with her and immediately being sidelined as all crowds flocked to speak to her. As Madonna herself famously said: 'I wouldn't wish being Mr Madonna on anybody.'

Her first marriage, to the actor Sean Penn, had foundered in part due to this issue. He had hoped that Madonna would settle down and have children with him, retreating from the spotlight. Madonna hadn't been willing to sacrifice her stardom and artistic journey. As their marriage broke down, Madonna enjoyed a flirtatious friendship/relationship with the comedian Sandra Bernhard. Sandra was bisexual, loud, brash, witty, bold; they connected when Madonna came to watch her one-woman show *Without You I'm Nothing*. Together, they appeared on *Late Night with David Letterman*, wearing matching outfits of white T-shirts and jeans. They were loud and lairy, constantly flirting with each other, talking over Letterman, who looked increasingly lost as they took over the show. 'We split each other's split ends,' Sandra quipped mockingly, adding, 'We frighten everyone out of the room.'

As the press began to speculate on whether they were lovers, Madonna and Bernhard delighted in playing up the ambiguities of their relationship. In *In Bed With Madonna*, Madonna warns, 'Don't believe the rumours', whilst Bernhard winks at the camera and says, 'Believe the rumours.' Madonna explained that the tabloids around this time became obsessed with the idea that she must be sleeping with whichever woman was currently a friend. In fact, Madonna had recognized early on that they could be lovers, but 'I realised I could have a really good friend in Sandra', and she didn't want to damage this. Their friendship eventually fell apart, however, when Madonna became close to Bernhard's girlfriend, the model Ingrid Casares, which caused jealousy and resentment; Bernhard once turned up at Casares' apartment to find Madonna coming out of the shower in a towel. Though it has often been suggested that Madonna and Casares were a couple, there is no clear evidence that they were. Madonna's relationships with women are more mysterious, ambiguous, ephemeral; she is loudest about the ones that *seem* bisexual but actually aren't. There is little commentary from Madonna on her love affair with the American model Jenny Shimizu, for example. Jenny was dating Angelina Jolie in the early 1990s when she got together with Madonna and 'whilst the actress [Jolie] confirmed her love for the diva, the pop star never addressed her rumoured romance.' In an interview, Jenny Shimizu recalled – in somewhat tabloidy, hyperbolic prose – that 'they were both sensational lovers who got incredibly turned on by the touch of another woman.' They got together after Madonna spotted Jenny in a casting video and called her 'out of the blue', inviting her to dinner at her house. They didn't sleep together then; two nights later, at a party, there was a frisson between them and 'instantly we both knew that we'd end up in bed together.' Madonna's feelings for Jenny were more physical than emotional. Jenny became her booty call; Madonna would fly her out to various locations across the globe whenever she was in the mood for 'taking each other to heights of sexual ecstasy', a submissive role that Jenny loved playing. Jenny recalled that 'Far from the domineering, sex-crazed woman many think she is, I found her a very gentle lover.'

In 1994, Madonna met Carlos Leon, a Cuban American model and actor, when she was jogging in Central Park. The relationship lasted three years, during which Madonna gave birth to their first child, a daughter they christened Lourdes. Leon felt that Madonna's obsession with her career was challenging – he found it hard to be with a woman 'who never goes to bed before two in the morning and who then wakes up at five to see what has been published about her in some goddamn foreign country'. Madonna's ambition and artistry did result in one of the finest albums of her career, however: *Ray Of Light*, a gorgeous, magical, mystical record shaped by her experiences as a new mother, a greater sense of peace, and her interest in the Kabbalah. The album went on to recover the sales that she lost during her *Sex/Erotica* phase and won her four Grammys.

Her next serious relationship was with Guy Ritchie. He was ten years her junior, a film-maker who had just hit upon success with the black comedy *Lock, Stock and Two Smoking Barrels*. Although he spoke with a cockney accent, he had grown up in upper-middle-class privilege; his parents had divorced and each had then married into the aristocracy. Like Madonna he was talented, ambitious, driven and hard-working. Though she adored effeminate men, when it came to romantic relationships, Madonna seemed to prefer hypermasculine men; many said Ritchie reminded them of Sean Penn. They met at a party held by their mutual friends, Sting and Trudie Styler. Perhaps the first sign of trouble was Madonna's interview with *Cosmopolitan*, where she said that 'to have the right kind of man in your life, you have to be the right kind of woman.' It reminded me of a remark she made in her 'Private Diaries' for *Vanity Fair*, when promoting Evita in 1996: 'If I had known I would be universally misunderstood, maybe I wouldn't have been so rebellious and outspoken . . . I wonder if I could ever have been the kind of sweet, submissive, feminine girl that the entire world idealizes.'

Madonna conceded that she needed to make compromises for their relationship to work. Guy did not want to settle in the US, so she moved to the UK. Initially, Madonna played out in public that phase of a relationship where you're so charmed by someone that they colour your tastes and personality; whatever they like, you like. Suddenly Madonna was drinking down the local pub and being called 'Madge' or 'the Missus'; she was shooting birds and playing at being a country lady. She gave birth to their first child, a son named Rocco, in August 2000, and later that year she and Guy wed at Skibo Castle, Scotland, where the guests' activities involved the women sitting around being country ladies and the men playing at being gentleman farmers and shooting grouse.

Madonna insisted from then on that she should be known as Mrs Ritchie, sensitive to the fact that no man wanted to be Mr Madonna. There was a sense of theatricality about this, however; Madonna, the queen of reinvention, was adopting another costume, speaking in a quasi-aristocratic British accent; the accent wobbled, warning that cracks would soon appear in the persona. Madonna had clearly gone beyond compromise; she was bending herself to please her partner, reshaping her personality, even going so far as to dress more demurely because Guy didn't like her wearing provocative outfits. At the time, this shocked me far more than Madonna's wild *Sex* phase: I could hardly believe that the woman who had sung 'Express Yourself', the feminist anthem about finding a man who makes you feel like a queen on a throne, was smoothing away the thrilling kinks in her personality. Guy, meanwhile, was making no concessions in his dress, declaring that he 'will not allow Madonna to dress me like a poof'. Madonna's brother Christopher, who is gay, found himself growing distant from his sister after decades of being close, hurt by the homophobic jokes that were made at her wedding reception during the toasts.

Ritchie was certainly supportive and proud of Madonna's success. As she set off on her Drowned World tour, he attended every show. He directed a controversial video to accompany her new release, the lyrical, feminist single 'What It Feels Like for A Girl', which Madonna remarked was inspired by the fact that 'men are quite intimidated by women who accomplish a lot'. Banned by MTV, it depicted Madonna on a crime spree, smashing her car into a car of jeering men, stealing from a man at a cashpoint, winding up policemen. Even after their divorce, Ritchie said affectionately, 'Put Madonna up against any twenty-three-year-old, she'll outwork them, outdance them, outperform them. The woman is broad.' But when they split up in 2008 after eight years together, Madonna vocalized her feelings, asking, 'How much am I willing to sacrifice?' Some years later, she reflected that the marriage had left her feeling 'incarcerated' and that 'there were many times when I wanted to express myself as an artist in ways that I don't feel my ex-husband felt comfortable with.' The song 'X-Static Process', which features on her *American Life* album (2003) is the musical antithesis of 'Express Yourself'. Madonna had previously released soaring, melancholic ballads ('Live To Tell', 'This Used to be My Playground'), but the melancholy in this song feels thin and downbeat. The song captures a relationship where a woman forgets who she is, loses her sense of self, realizes her partner is special but forgets what makes her special. Whilst many of her previous videos celebrated female sexuality, her videos around this time show women fighting male aggression, such as her video for the James Bond theme song 'Die Another Day', which shows her playing a spy who is beaten and tortured.

There has been much media commentary on the ever-widening age gap of Madonna's lovers following her divorce. Aside from a fling with Alex Rodriguez, she has dated men a minimum of twenty-eight years her junior. Newspapers have tended to depict this as a vampiric craving for youth, with one reporting that 'She likes the idea of a guy being younger than her daughter. It announces her desirability to the world.' However, in a 2015 interview with the *New York Daily News*, Madonna explained why she leans towards younger partners: 'It's just what happens. Most men my age are married with children. They're not dateable. I'm a very adventurous person and I also have a crazy life. I'm a single mother. I have four children. I mean, you have to be pretty open-minded and adventurous to want to step into my world. People who are older, and more set in their ways, are probably not as adventurous as someone younger.' Madonna has argued 'The fact that people actually believe a woman is not allowed to express her sexuality and be adventurous past a certain age is proof that we still live in an ageist and sexist society.' 'Adventurous' is a good word, here; perhaps by dating younger men Madonna has avoided the power struggles of the past whereby men have wanted to tame her, control her, contain her. Her new young beaux look pleased to be with such a powerful woman, which is just the way it should be.

*

As a provocateur, Madonna has sometimes used her bisexuality to shock and titillate. At the 2003 MTV Video Music Awards, she was given free rein to mastermind a spectacle on stage; she invited Britney Spears and Christina Aguilera to join her, two artists who were often seen as pop rivals, having competed against each other as juniors in *The All-New Mickey Mouse Club*. Their set begins with 'Like A Virgin' and a mysterious figure in a white bridal dress: the woman pulls up her veil to reveal that she is Britney. Christina follows in the same guise as she launches into the chorus and they both roll around on the floor in their gowns. The centre of the stage is adorned with a huge white wedding cake; Madonna erupts out of it like a lyrical volcano, singing 'Hollywood'. In mimicry of her idol Marlene Dietrich, she is sporting black tails and a top hat, with high-heeled leather boots: a groom to the two brides. The trio flirt through song and dance; Madonna puts her top hat on Britney and ballroom-dances with Christina, before the performance culminates in her kissing each of them in turn and Missy Elliott explodes onto the stage performing a rap.

Whilst this didn't attract the outrage that Madonna's *Sex* book did, it was certainly scandalous and pictures of the kisses blazed across newspaper front pages across the world. Stevie Nicks complained to an Australian newspaper – and demonstrated her ageism in the process – that 'Madonna is too old to be kissing someone who is 22. I thought it was the most obnoxious moment in television history.' But wasn't Stevie Nicks' reaction just the sort of outraged response that Madonna was seeking? A few weeks on, she was interviewed by Oprah Winfrey, and argued, 'I've been oblivious until this moment. I had no idea that it was going to cause the ruckus that it caused. It was just a friendly kiss.' It looked like more a French kiss than a friendly kiss, and I think Madonna is being coy. It points to the contradictory impulses in her, the marketeer and the idealist, the cynic and the sincere self, which fight it out when it comes to her sexuality: she wants to cause a stir, but she also wants to normalize bisexuality; she likes to shock, but part of that is also motivated by a genuine desire to 'educate'. As Oprah pointed out, 'I don't know if most of America has [seen two girls kiss before]', and in that respect Madonna's three-way kiss was a positive spectacle.

Camille Paglia praised Madonna's MTV act as a way of 'passing the torch' on. This was the impression I got too: it was also an acknowledgement of what Madonna had endured and achieved, paving the way to enable figures such as Spears and Aguilera and Rihanna to freely express all shades of their sexuality in their music. The noughties is an era we have reassessed as a time when female stars were unfairly attacked in the media, Britney being a prime example. Madonna was ahead of her time in calling this out, no doubt recognizing troubles she had suffered herself, declaring that she was irritated by the way 'everyone beats up on' Britney. But Paglia later attacked Britney, Lindsay Lohan and co., complaining that 'these girls are lowering themselves to the level of back-street floozies.' I disagree with Paglia – sex isn't the problem here; a pop star revelling in her sexuality is fine, but they can feel like pale imitations of Madonna if they rely solely on this. People can forget that Madonna was never just about sex; she combined sex with ideas, with storytelling, with a vivid imagination, with post-modern knowingness; if she was scantily clad, it was in a Gaultier cone-shaped bra; if she satirized being a material girl in a material world, she did so whilst aping Marilyn Monroe. Like Bowie, her shows have been spectaculars that focus on theatre and set as much as the songs. On her 1993 Girlie Show tour, she once sang a rendition of 'Like a Virgin' dressed in a tux and top hat, in a faux German accent that mimicked Marlene Dietrich, paying homage to her idol whilst being ironic, playful and sexy.

Watching the Madonna video for 'Hung Up' provokes mixed feelings in me. It's a remix of her 2005 dance hit, featuring a rap from Dominican rapper Tokischa. Both Madonna and Tokischa are bi and the video features them dancing together, nuzzling, kissing, caressing. Madonna has long pink-red hair that floats like a length of silk; she's dressed like a twenty-something; and she looks simultaneously old and young, like one of those glitzy religious cards that flit between two images depending on the way you tilt it.

Here's the rub: I don't much like Madonna's recent music. Back when she was forty-two, she stated: 'I'm not a teenager anymore and I won't pretend to be one to sell records.' She used to innovate; after she teamed up with William Orbit for *Ray of Light*, pop stars flocked to him to produce their tracks until nearly every song in the charts seemed to wink with his electronic, mystical sound. Everyone chased after Madonna, but now she seems to be following the pack, to be running after youth and the styles and sounds they favour. But I do love the fact that she is refusing to conform to society's ideas of ageing, that she has carried on performing in raunchy outfits, causing scandal, and blatantly enjoying her sexuality.

Madonna has been accused of being 'too old' for her profession time and time again; from way back in 1993, when Keith Cameron in the *NME* sighed, 'one hesitates to say that at thirty-five she's too old for all this', to Lorraine Kelly declaring that Madonna's beauty treatments made her 'look like a boiled egg' in 2022. I love the fact that she is happy to defy her critics. Mick Jagger is still writhing away sexily on stage, so why should she become respectable and start putting on long skirts? At the 2015 Grammys she flashed her butt on the red carpet and later defended herself: 'I take care of myself. I'm in good shape. I can show my ass when I'm 56 or 66 or 76. Who's to say when I can show my ass? It's sexism. It's ageism.

And it's a kind of discrimination.' On her sixty-fourth birthday, her Instagram featured photos of her kissing two women in Italy, with the caption, *Birthday kisses with my side bitches.*

In an interview with five bisexuals, *Guardian* journalist Owen Jones explored the classic problems of being bi: of people immediately asking you for a threesome, or being labelled greedy, the etiquette of joining an LGBT meeting when you're in a heterosexual relationship and your queer side may appear mere theory or a pose. They are all noticeably young, in their early twenties. So often when I see bisexuals being interviewed for their opinions, this is the case. Once again, I wonder if it is *Basic Instinct* syndrome creeping in, that we want to hear from bisexuals as long as they are young, because we equate youth with glamour. Rarely do I see bis being interviewed who have grey hair or a stick or tell us what it's like being bi if you're widowed, or in an old folk's home, or how being bi might have changed over the decades. It's as though the older generation are of no interest, or the idea of older bis is less comfortable, which is probably due to the fact that bisexuality is still associated with hypersexuality and we shudder at the idea of old people enjoying sex. Madonna remains one of our few older bisexual icons.

*

In early 2023, I saw a huge display in Foyles celebrating *After Sappho* by Selby Wynn Schwartz. The book reimagines the lives of a brilliant group of feminists, sapphists, artists and writers in the late nineteenth and early twentieth century, a number featured in the bookshop display, including Virginia Woolf and Colette. It's disconcerting to consider that before 2003 a display like this would have been illegal. Section 28 prevented the publicizing of homosexuality in the public domain, and therefore libraries, museums and art galleries distanced themselves from queer-themed events. The act was repealed in 2003, and in 2006 the Equality Act (Sexual

Orientation) Regulations banned discrimination of the basis of sexual orientation. Now rainbow flags adorn tote bags, colour the traffic lights crossing in my town. Every morning on my way to work I walk over its pink and mauve and blue patterning with a smile, recognizing my colours. The bisexual pride flag was designed in 1998 by Michael Page, the pink signifying same-sex attraction, the blue different-gender, and the purple merging the two together.

Over the past two decades, huge gains have been made for queer rights. Same-sex marriage was legalized; Section 28 revoked; discrimination recognized as a hate crime; President Obama initiated Pride Month. But whilst bisexuality might have become more prominent, the same old prejudices resurfaced time and time again. The late 1990s saw an article in *Vogue* which declared that 'bi-trying' was a new fashion amongst celebrities and models; in response, the *Guardian* and the *Independent* published reproving articles, feeling that bi-triers would soon revert back to heterosexuality. Bisexual erasure still occurred over and over. In 2008, Katy Perry hit the number one spot across the globe with her bi anthem, 'I Kissed a Girl', a sweet, playful song which captures a first moment of queer experimentation. In 2017, Perry made a passionate speech at the Human Rights Campaign gala, where she accepted a National Equality Award: 'I speak my truths and I paint my fantasies into these little bite-size pop songs. For instance, I kissed a girl – and I liked it. Truth be told I did more than that . . . I was curious and even then I knew sexuality wasn't as black and white as this dress.' On the release of her song, however, the press failed to appreciate such nuances. One article declared that Perry was partaking in 'part-time lesbianism': why use such a wordy term when bisexuality is so much simpler? Of course, 'part-time' suggests Perry is moonlighting from heterosexuality, a phase that will soon be over when she gets back to full-time heteronormativity.

On other occasions, however, bisexuality has slipped into songs that haven't exactly explored the issue with much depth. In 2010,

Christina Aguilera released the song 'Not Myself Tonight' which included a line about kissing all the boys and girls. She gave the most cringey interview with *Out* magazine where she declared that her husband knew about her attraction to girls, but added the caveat: 'But I don't think I could ever really be with a woman because that's a lot of . . . estrogen and I'm a lot to deal with when it's that time of the month, so I can't imagine it times two.'

When Amber Heard came out in 2010 at the GLAAD 25th Anniversary party, she said that she had had successful relationships with men and women. 'I love who I love,' she said, 'it's the person that matters.' Heard didn't label her sexuality, declaring that she didn't want to be defined by it or hide behind it, but later clarified that she was bisexual. Yet if you come out as bi, whichever sex you're dating at the time can be misperceived as a sign of the direction you're *really* leaning. Because she was dating Tasya van Ree between 2008 and 2012, many press outlets decided that Heard was coming out as a 'lesbian'. Even when her bisexuality was eventually accepted and acknowledged, it was then weaponized against her. Following her divorce from Johnny Depp, there was speculation that Depp was jealous of her queer female friends or that she might have been unfaithful. An Australian talk show host remarked, 'It's not wise to marry a bisexual. Bye bi, Amber,' whilst Evan Rachel Wood tweeted in her defence, 'What does Amber being bisexual and having lesbian friends have to do with anything?' Later, as their trial demonstrated, it became clear that Depp and Heard divorced after shocking abuse on both sides of their relationship. If Amber's bisexuality was a factor, if Depp *was* fuelled by jealousy of her female friends, then it only serves to illustrate that bisexual women are far more prone to suffering domestic abuse. 61 per cent of bisexual women have been raped, suffered physical violence or been stalked by a partner, compared to 35 per cent of heterosexual women; and 37 per cent of bisexual men compared to 29 per cent of straight men.

Even Mary Gabriel's glorious recent biography *Madonna: A*

Rebel Life – which celebrates her as an icon and paints a rich portrait of the decades she lived through – explains the impact Madonna made on queer history without reference to bisexuals. Throughout the book, the author refers solely to 'gays and lesbians' – the 1990s are described as a time when 'gay men and lesbians became a political bloc working to end legal restrictions that kept them from living as full citizens'. I don't think the failure to mention bisexuals is deliberate, but the carelessness hurts more: bisexuals receive no mention for their part in gay history, despite the fact that Madonna is bi herself.

*

Queerbaiting is a term that was originally applied to books and films that depicted a relationship with an underlying gay frisson – such as *Sherlock* – without confirming it. But whilst I understand the anger that fuels this, it also makes me uneasy: storylines that flirt with will they/won't they can also include ambiguous heterosexual partnerships, such as Doctor Who and his assistant. Why can't bisexuality also be subtle in a narrative? Why can't it simmer rather than having to come to the boil? The term queerbaiting has evolved and is now frequently fired at public figures who are seen as capitalizing on their queer/bi sexuality, using it as a performative device to make themselves look edgy or sexy, without openly declaring their orientation. Harry Styles has received complaints because he appeared on the cover of *Vogue* in a dress, but refuses to be pinned down. Other artists who have been criticized on this front include Ariana Grande and Rita Ora. This pressure can mean they are forced into coming out before they are ready, like Kit Connor, who played a queer character in the Netflix drama *Heartstopper*. After being harassed on social media, he finally tweeted, 'I'm bi. Congrats for forcing an 18-year-old to out himself'. This kind of pressure is particularly tough for bis because statistics show that they are more likely to keep their sexuality private.

Queerbaiting accusations are a reversal of 1970s pressures, where you had to be in the closet: now, choosing to be there is a sin and sexuality must be advertised and clearly labelled. But such accusations can also reflect decades-old prejudice reincarnated in new form: rooted in the same issues that meant the 'B' was left out of LGT for too long. Bisexuality is on a spectrum. These complaints demonstrate a frustration with bisexuality's in-betweenness that can be seen as undermining gay identity; as academics Jonathan Alexander and Serena Anderlini-D'Onofrio note, bisexuality was once seen as undermining the fight for gay rights and equal marriage because it discredited the argument that 'we're born this way' and was seen as the sexuality of choice.

Madonna has been unjustly accused of queerbaiting a number of times in her career. In 2022, she made a TikTok video that went viral. Filmed in her home, it depicts her wielding a pair of hot-pink pants. She throws them at the bin, declaring that if she misses, then 'I'm gay!' Naturally, the pants land on the floor. A number of fans (mostly of a younger generation) speculated that she was 'coming out', even though Madonna has been 'out' for three decades. There were also numerous accusations of 'queerbaiting', which is odd for a woman who has been awarded the GLAAD Advocate for Change award and suffered a $1 million fine from the Russian government for speaking out for LGBT rights on her MDNA concert tour (Madonna refused to pay it). It would have taken anyone less than five minutes to google Madonna and see her history of championing gay rights, so the off-the-cuff urge to condemn her, without research, is troubling.

Madonna is far less controversial now than she was in her *Sex* era; the petty attacks she has received about queerbaiting are a sign of the times. The age of the Hollywood idol, the pop queen, the gay icon is fading. Audiences no longer attend films to see a big name but prefer the draw of a team of superheroes. Think of Marlene Dietrich in contrast, locked away in her flat in old age, refusing to let anyone see her beauty crumble because of her dedication to preserving her persona. Whilst celebrities can now avoid this fate with the surgeon and the scalpel, the persona no longer matters as much: that gap between idealized, impenetrable star and their adoring public has dissolved. Stars cannot be gods any more; they must be human. Tell-all memoirs detailing pain and insecurity, that show they suffer like the rest of us, are all the rage, such as Britney's book *The Woman In Me*. Madonna once relished her tough persona, but in recent years she has become more prone to showing her vulnerabilities. Our celebrity gods are cracking and falling like Easter Island statues. If a bisexual star does come out, the majority of bis will find inspiration in them. But the star will no doubt also suffer flak from a hardcore contingent of pious bis who love to play at policing sexuality, who may doubt them, bully them, question their authenticity. Perhaps it reflects the prevailing problem of ever-widening inequality and a mood of disillusionment; we have grown so resigned to politicians as liars, to the 1 per cent being too remote to touch, that our idols are the last people we can be disappointed by, inflict our anger on. And so we demand the impossible from them, which they can't live up to: like us, their sexuality can change or defy labels.

Although huge gains have been made for the queer community, and public opinion of gays and lesbians has improved, bis are still regarded with suspicion. Recent surveys show that the average 'straight' person's opinion on bis is that they are hypersexual, more prone to cheating, more prone to suffering STDs. I suffered prejudice first-hand back in 2015, when I co-hosted a party for the indie press I co-run. I was chatting to a male friend about the actress Seyan Sarvan, conscious of a female guest listening in. He had worked with Seyan, and I mentioned that I had a crush on her. The room was crowded and noisy, but the woman listening in seemed to overhear something she didn't like and took umbrage. After that, she blanked me, refused to talk to me, cut into my conversations with other people and turned her back on me. She seemed hurt and angry, as if warning me that my sexuality was unacceptable to her. I left my own party feeling defeated and depressed.

In 2019, there were headlines about a 'gay couple' who had suffered violence on a London bus, accompanied by stomach-churning photos of their bruised faces, a blouse stained with blood. They had been harassed by a group of four teenage boys, who learned they were a couple and pressurized them to kiss, then attacked them when they failed to comply. Most of the newspapers that reported this sickening crime decided that the couple were 'lesbians', although one of the women was bi. Even when hate crimes are being reported, bi-erasure occurs.

*

In the summer of 2020, six months into the pandemic, I started to fill my empty evenings by drawing portraits of my friends. My drawing skills were rusty, but that made it all the more fun. I sketched Nina Ellis in leopard-print with a tail; Zeba Talkhani in front of a bookcase; Stewart Home standing on his head. Then I approached Andrew Gallix, asking if I could draw him. He was enthusiastic. I knew Gallix only a little. He ran the online magazine 3:AM, one of the first literary websites; fifteen years back he'd published my first short story. We had exchanged emails from time to time and I knew a few things about him: that he was erudite, reviewed books, had championed Deborah Levy and Tom McCarthy before they achieved mainstream recognition, worked at the Sorbonne, had a son whose photos adorned his Flickr account. Just before the pandemic, he had launched the anthology *We'll Never Have Paris* at Burley Fisher Books in East London. He was a quiet, mysterious presence there. He didn't read, he didn't compere. Was he shy or shadowy? Afterwards, everyone went to the pub and I stood a foot away from him, a voice inside cajoling me to *just go and talk to him!* But I never plucked up the courage.

And now I was drawing his portrait, and it felt like a courtship. The photo he sent was of him standing next to a curtain patterned with stars; I worked hard to capture his handsome, intelligent face and the mischief in his eyes. When I sent over the picture, I commented that his lips looked like Lucian Freud's. He declared it was his platonic ideal and shouted about it on social media.

For the next six months we exchanged lengthy emails every day. The pandemic no longer felt such a lonely prison sentence. We agreed that he would come over to visit at Christmas for a week: a trial run. He came over on the Saturday evening, having drunk too much wine on the Eurostar, all a-sparkle in St Pancras. The next day, in the midst of the pandemic, everything shut down again. France introduced a blockade. It seemed that he would have to stay for Christmas.

Once upon a time, Christmas had been my favourite time of the year. But in 2011 my mother had been diagnosed with terminal cancer and that December, the hospital released her to come home to die. She lay in the dining room on a hospital bed, connected to an oxygen machine that filled the house with a monotonous sound of hissing and pumping. I dosed her with morphine; cooked her meals and fed her by hand. On Christmas Day, she managed to open a few presents before she passed away. Ever since then, the day had been doomed, fraught with bad memories and family tensions, a day to struggle through and get over as quickly as possible. But with Andrew here, I suddenly felt happy and alive. We cooked a big cake together, sharing the sieving and weighing-out and mixing; we watched movies and played board games; we went for a walk in Richmond Park in the dark and saw a herd of deer thunder past, just a foot away, a blur of beautiful flowing shapes. In Cannizaro Park, as the dark crept in and we wandered into the rose garden, a fear came over me that we weren't safe, and in reassurance he gave me our first kiss.

His fear arose a few days later. He told me that 'Women always leave me,' and became boyish with vulnerability. His last marriage had broken down after his wife kissed another woman, which made me nervous of telling him that I was bisexual. I shouldn't overplay the issue, though: him accepting my bisexuality was one of many factors necessary for our compatibility. My sexuality doesn't take the lead in my identity; it colours my actions, but it doesn't dictate them. I am many things: a writer, a carer, a cat-lover, a devourer of books, an introvert. Given that I was in my forties with many failed relationships behind me, I had plenty of baggage, a suitcase of memories, dirty and full of creases and concerns, as did he. My bisexuality made him wary at first, though over time his trust in me grew. The issue of loyalty has very little to do with being bi. If I've been disloyal in the past, it was never because I was with a man and I secretly ached to complete myself with a woman, or vice versa. I've cheated because past relationships unravelled, because I felt unloved or undervalued, or in the case of Henry, because he resented my writing addiction. The idea that bisexuals can never be satisfied is foolish, because satisfaction lies in the heart. If I see an attractive woman or a man on the street, at a party, I might register their charms, but something inside me is shut down. They can't tempt me because my heart is full to the brim with him.

*

Bisexuals do suffer from many prejudices, from erasure, phobia, misconceptions, stereotypes. I recently read a bisexual handbook that sifted through all these issues relentlessly, so that by the end I was left feeling much better informed about how much ignorance and hatred towards us exists, but also rather depressed, as to be bi was to live as a miserable victim. This is not my general lived experience, however: I feel that being bisexual is joyful, and that my love life has been greatly enriched as a result, though I recognize that this is in part due to the efforts of activists of decades past who have made life easier for us now. Whilst we should acknowledge the issues we face, we shouldn't drown in them; we shouldn't forget to celebrate being bi: to be proud. As June Jordan states: 'Bisexuality means I am free and I am as likely to want to love a woman as I am likely to want to love a man, and what about that? Isn't that what freedom implies? If you are free, you are not predictable and you are not controllable. To my mind, that is the keenly positive, politicizing significance of bisexual affirmation.'

When Ellen DeGeneres was debating whether to come out (as a lesbian) in 1997, Madonna offered her support and advice, calling her up and reading her this beautiful quote from Martha Graham, words which I love to savour:

> *There is a vitality, a life force, an energy, a quickening that is translated through you into action, and because there is only one of you in all of time, this expression is unique. And if you block it, it will never exist through any other medium and it will be lost. The world will not have it. It is not your business to determine how good it is nor how valuable nor how it compares with other expressions. It is your business to keep it yours clearly and directly, to keep the channel open. You do not even have to believe in yourself or your work. You have to keep yourself open and aware to the urges that motivate you. Keep the channel open . . . No artist is pleased. There is no satisfaction whatsoever at any time. There is only a queer divine dissatisfaction, a blessed unrest that keeps us marching and makes us more alive than the others.*

Notes

Prologue

p. 2

a terrace bathed in light and beauty, abundant in violets *A Room With A View*, E. M. Forster, 1908 (Penguin 1990), p. 89.

p. 6

'makes you seem disingenuous, like your genitals have no allegiance'.
https://variety.com/2018/tv/news/new-trailer-shows-desiree-akhavan-as-a-bisexual-in-london-in-channel-4-and-hulu-comedy-drama-1202975168/

p. 7

'It was the only physical contact I had seen men do . . .' https://www.theguardian.com/stage/2016/oct/02/michael-clark-i-still-make-the-dance-on-my-own-body-first-interview-to-a-simple-rock-n-roll-song

'I am at heart a gentleman . . .' https://www.theguardian.com/film/2017/nov/26/marlene-dietrich-androgyny-sexuality-exhibitions

p. 8

It is harder to find evidence of female bisexuality . . . *Bisexuality In the Ancient World*, Eva Cantarella (Yale University Press, 1994), pp. 3–4.

p. 9

'All great novels, all true novels are bisexual . . .' https://www.theguardian.com/books/2023/jul/12/to-be-a-writer-means-to-discover-a-truth-milan-kundera-a-life-in-quotes

In 2009, the American sociologist David Halperin listed thirteen different

definitions of the term bisexuality *Thirteen Ways of Looking at a Bisexual*, Journal of Bisexuality 9 (3–4): 451–455, July 2009.

Academic Carol Berenson notes that during the 1990s . . . *Bisexual Woman in the 21st Century*, ed. Dawn Atkins (The Haworth Press, 2002).

It's an *invisible identity* . . . it's for those of us 'who *choose not to choose*' *Bisexual Woman in the 21st Century*, ed. Dawn Atkins (The Haworth Press, 2002).

As Marjorie Garber poetically sums up, '*it's not an identity*' *Bisexuality and the Eroticism of Everyday Life*, Marjorie Garber (Routledge, 2000), p. 87.

One smart, warm and inclusive definition of bisexuality, by activist Robyn Ochs . . . https://robynochs.com/

p. 10

'Bisexuality is a whole, fluid identity. Do not assume that bisexuality is binary or duogamous in nature . . .' *Anything That Moves*, 1991.

'Still, the prejudice lingers https://www.nbcnews.com/feature/nbc-out/evolution-word-bisexual-why-it-s-still-misunderstood-n1240832

p. 11

In a recent Stonewall survey of 16–75 year olds in the UK https://www.bbc.co.uk/news/uk-63121245

In a 2021 Gallup Poll, US adults self-identifying as LGBT reached a new high https://www.losangelesblade.com/2022/02/18/gallup-poll-finds-more-americans-identify-as-lgbtq-than-ever-before/

The shift is generational, too Ibid.

Women are more likely to be bisexual than men https://www.essex.ac.uk/blog/posts/2023/02/02/women-are-more-likely-to-identify-as-bisexual-can-research-into-sexual-arousal-tell-us-why#:~:text=But%20when%20it%20came%20to,to%200.9%25%20of%20men)

Only 19 per cent of bisexuals have told the most important people in their life about their sexual preference https://www.pewresearch.org/short-reads/2019/06/18/bisexual-adults-are-far-less-likely-than-gay-men-and-lesbians-to-be-out-to-the-people-in-their-lives/

The Bisexual Resource Centre notes that bi people have statistically 'higher rates of anxiety, depression and other mood disorders' https://biresource.org/mental-health/

Research shows there's a link between these mental health issues and the phenomenon of bisexual invisibility or erasure *Australian Journal of General Practice*, Vol. 48, Issue 3, March 2019 https://www1.racgp.org.au/ajgp/2019/march/bisexual-mental-health

p. 12

Jason Epstein said that 'he wasn't unhappy about being gay'
https://bi.org/en/famous/gore-vidal

Sandra Bernhard said, 'lots of people think that bisexual means cowardly
lesbian' 'Sandra Bernhard, Acting Lesbian', Lily Burana, the *Advocate*,
15 December 1992.

p. 13

'I'd rather fall in love with a woman eventually because I think a woman
probably lasts longer than a man . . .' https://www.rollingstone.com/
feature/elton-john-lonely-at-the-top-rolling-stones-1976-cover-story-
238734/

1. Oscar Wilde

p. 16

as a gay icon, Wilde is 'flawed' 'After The Fall', Merlin Holland interviewed
by Julia Ann Charpentier, *Advocate* magazine, 19 June 2008.
https://www.advocate.com/news/2008/06/19/after-fall

'I'm not sure that because there are people who identify as bisexual there
is a bisexual identity' 'Bisexual Revolution', Carrie Wofford, *Outweek*,
1991, p. 36. http://outweek.net/pdfs/ow_84.pdf

p. 18

But earlier in the nineteenth century, the dandy . . . was associated more
with asexuality 'Redefining the Dandy: The Asexual Man of Fashion',
Daria Kent https://www.makingqueerhistory.com/articles/2018/4/7/
redefining-the-dandy-the-asexual-man-of-fashion#:~:text=But%20
before%20the%20late%20nineteenth,displaying%20traits%20
emblematic%20of%20asexuality

Neil McKenna claims that Wilde's marriage to Constance Lloyd was
'passionless' *The Secret Life of Oscar Wilde*, Neil McKenna (Century,
2003).

Richard Ellmann tries to explain what forces 'turned' Wilde's
'reorientation' *Oscar Wilde*, Richard Ellmann (Penguin, 1987),
p. 262.

p. 19

'although he was expected to talk brilliantly, he really did a great deal of
listening' *Oscar Wilde and Myself*, Lord Alfred Douglas, 1914 (Duffield
& Company), p. 38.

p. 20

'Oscar, the thing was neither right, nor manly, nor gentlemanlike in you'
 Wilde's Women: How Oscar Wilde Was Shaped by the Women He Knew,
 Eleanor Fitzsimons (Duckworth, 2015), p. 71.

'she writes as cleverly as she talks' and he was 'much attracted by her in
 every way' Letter to William Ward, August 1877, *Complete Letters*, eds.
 Merlin Holland and Rupert Hart-Davis (Fourth Estate, 2000), p. 61.

'Last night I strolled into the theatre about ten o'clock' Letter to William
 Ward, 6 August 1876, *Complete Letters*, pp. 28–9.

p. 21

'She is just seventeen with the most perfectly beautiful face I ever saw and
 not a sixpence of money' Letter to Reginald Harding, August 1876,
 Complete Letters, p. 29.

'two sweet years – the sweetest of all the years of my youth' Letter to
 Florence Balcombe, September 1878, *Complete Letters*, p. 71.

For Oscar her exquisite looks were 'a form of genius' 'Mrs Langtry as
 Hester Grazebrook', Oscar Wilde, *New York World*, 7 November 1882.

p. 22

'it is often assumed that Oscar used the adjective "Greek" to refer to
 male beauty or homosexual love' *Wilde's Women: How Oscar Wilde
 Was Shaped by the Women He Knew*, Eleanor Fitzsimons (Duckworth,
 2015).

'*And your eyes, they were green and grey*' 'Roses and Rue', Oscar Wilde, 1881.

'you must bring home the American bride' *Constance: The Tragic and
 Scandalous Life of Mrs Oscar Wilde*, Franny Moyle (John Murray, 2011),
 p. 65.

p. 23

'manhood is absent from his composition' *Lowell Daily Courier*,
 18 January 1882 https://oscarwildeinamerica.blog/2015/08/01/
 doubtful-as-men/

Thomas Wentworth Higginson, a prominent American thinker . . . crossly
 declared that Wilde's writing was 'Unmanly'. *Unmanly Manhood*,
 Thomas Wentworth Higginson, February 1882, reprinted in *Oscar
 Wilde: The Critical Heritage*, ed. Karl Beckson (Routledge, 1970), p. 51.

p. 28

Oscar wrote that American women were 'pretty whirlwinds in petticoats'
 The American Invasion, Oscar Wilde, 1887.

sleeping with a female prostitute felt like 'chewing cold mutton' *The*

Invention of Oscar Wilde, Nicholas Frankel (University of Chicago Press, 1991), p. 92.

a heart of diamonds enclosing two pearls *Constance: The Tragic and Scandalous Life of Mrs Oscar Wilde*, Franny Moyle (John Murray, 2011), p. 73.

'both are . . . charming, gifted and . . . immensely attracted to each other' Ada Swinburne-King to Lady Wilde, 30 November 1883 (quoted in Franny Moyle, p. 75).

'We are of course desperately in love' Oscar Wilde to Waldo Story, 22 January 1884.

He confided in Lillie that 'it is horrid being so much away from her' Oscar Wilde to Lillie Langtry, January 1884, *Complete Letters*, p. 224.

Robert Sherard, a close friend of Oscar's, reported that 'he was very much in love and joyous' *Oscar Wilde: The Story of an Unhappy Friendship*, Robert Sherard (Greening & Company, 1905), p. 91.

p. 29

the *Lady's Pictorial* that described them walking down the aisle – 'the bridegroom happy and exultant . . .' *Wilde's Women: How Oscar Wilde Was Shaped by the Women He Knew*, Eleanor Fitzsimons (Duckworth, 2015), p. 149.

Ada Leverson observed that: 'He was quite madly in love,' *Wilde's Women: How Oscar Wilde Was Shaped by the Women He Knew*, Eleanor Fitzsimons (Duckworth, 2015), p. 152.

'I feel your fingers in my hair, and your cheek brushing mine . . .' Letter from Oscar Wilde to Constance Wilde, December 1884, *Complete Letters*, pp. 241–2.

He wrote to the actor Norman Forbes-Robertson that his son was 'wonderful' and enthused about the joys of matrimony Oscar Wilde, June 1885, *Complete Letters*, p. 262.

p. 31

'When I married, my wife was a beautiful girl,' Oscar confided *The Era*, Frank Harris, 22 May 1886. Quoted in *Constance: The Tragic and Scandalous Life of Mrs Oscar Wilde*, Franny Moyle (John Murray, 2011), p. 114.

p. 32

'a curious mixture of ardour and indifference . . .' Oscar Wilde to Henry Marillier, December 1885, *Complete Letters*, p. 272.

'too perfect in its unity' *The Trembling of the Veil*, W. B. Yeats (Werner Laurie, 1922), p. 24.

p. 33

'one Apollonian, one Dionysian' *Oscar Wilde*, Richard Ellmann (Penguin, 1987)

'The danger was half the excitement' *De Profundis*, Oscar Wilde, 1905.

'Sodomy never took place' Letter from Lord Alfred Douglas to Frank Harris, 20 March 1925.

Douglas later explained that 'I never liked this part of the business . . .' *Oscar's Ghost: The Battle for Oscar Wilde's Legacy*, Laura Lee (Amberley Publishing, 2017), p. 37.

'there may have been post-natal medical issues on Constance's side' *Constance: The Tragic and Scandalous Life of Mrs Oscar Wilde*, Franny Moyle (John Murray, 2011), p. 123.

p. 34

Oscar 'adored his wife' and was 'still on great terms of affection' *The Invention of Oscar Wilde*, Nicholas Frankel (University of Chicago Press, 1991), p.171.

'I cannot make out whether it is my fault or Wilde's that he is so cold to me and so nice to others' *Oscar Wilde on Trial: The Criminal Proceedings, from Arrest to Imprisonment*, Joseph Bristow (Yale University Press, 2023), p. 44.

p. 35

Krafft-Ebing called bisexuality *psychosexual hermaphroditism* 'Monosexual/Plurisexual: A Concise History', Diederik F. Janssen, *Journal of Homosexuality*, 5 June 2023. https://www.tandfonline.com/doi/full/10.1080/00918369.2023.2218957

other European sexologists of this era called it 'a light form or precursor of sexual inversion' Ibid.

'the patients satisfy their perverse impulse two or three times a year, no more often' 'Monosexual/Plurisexual: A Concise History', Diederik F. Janssen, *Journal of Homosexuality*, 5 June 2023. https://www.tandfonline.com/doi/full/10.1080/00918369.2023.2218957

'which, according to Marchesini, expresses itself in girls' boarding schools as platonic love and is truly warmhearted' Ibid.

suppressed by 'careful education and willpower' . . . bisexuality showed a certain 'lack of differentiation' Ibid.

p. 36

Marc-André Raffalovich . . . wondered: is it the result of 'circumstances or . . .congenital?' Ibid.

'strong sense of man's double being' https://www.britishlibrary.cn/en/
works/jekyllandhyde/

p. 37

a doctor was asked to examine them 'for physical "signs" of
homosexuality' *Sex and Punishment: Four Thousand Years of Judging
Desire*, Eric Berkowitz (The Westbourne Press, 2012), p. 403.

'it was an early effort' at defining what characteristics a gay man might
have *Sex and Punishment: Four Thousands Years of Judging Desire*, Eric
Berkowitz (The Westbourne Press, 2012), p. 404.

'After 1886, he was able to think of himself as a criminal, moving guiltily
among the innocent' *Oscar Wilde*, Richard Ellmann (Penguin, 1988),
p. 261.

'It was the strangest book that he had ever read' *The Picture of Dorian
Gray*, Oscar Wilde, 1891 (Penguin Classics, 2003).

On his twenty-first birthday he shut himself in his bedroom, weeping at
the thought of his future 'vanished youth' *Oscar's Ghost: The Battle for
Oscar Wilde's Legacy*, Laura Lee (Amberley Publishing, 2017), p. 28.

Lord Henry Wotton in *Dorian Gray* – who is charming, witty, clever and
possessed of 'wrong, fascinating, poisonous, delightful theories' *The
Picture of Dorian Gray*, Oscar Wilde, 1891 (Penguin Classics, 2003), p. 75.

p. 38

'Basil Hallward is what I think I am: Lord Henry what the world thinks
me: Dorian what I would like to be' *Letter from Oscar Wilde to Arthur
Fish*, July 1890, *Complete Letters*, p. 440.

'I highly disapprove of them' *Oscar Wilde*, Richard Ellmann (Penguin,
1988), p. 302.

He found him 'comic looking'. It was Oscar's melodious voice that wove
its magic *The Secret Life of Oscar Wilde*, Neil McKenna (Basic Books,
2006), p. 158.

p. 39

'I am a lover of youth . . . I like to study the young in everything. There is
something fascinating in youthfulness' *The Trials of Oscar Wilde*,
2nd ed (Dover Publications, New York, 1973), pp. 202–3.

p. 40

To lose your virginity through a sexually passive role was 'a crime for
the free-born', wrote Seneca. *Sex and Punishment: Four Thousands
Years of Judging Desire*, Eric Berkowitz (The Westbourne Press, 2012),
p. 129.

the Latin term *muliebria patitur* – to be penetrated – translates as 'to have
a woman's experience' *Sex and Punishment: Four Thousands Years of
Judging Desire*, Eric Berkowitz (The Westbourne Press, 2012), p. 129.

everyone was speculating as to whether Oscar was '*passif*' or '*actif*'
14 April 1894, *The Goncourt Journal*, Edmond de Goncourt and Jules de
Goncourt (1866; NYRB Classics, 2007).

Constans and Constantinus II ordered a decree attacking those who
indulged in sex 'when a man couples as though he were a woman'. *Sex
and Punishment: Four Thousands Years of Judging Desire*, Eric Berkowitz
(The Westbourne Press, 2012), p. 133.

p. 43

a story which 'would be of interest mainly to "outlawed noblemen and
perverted telegraph boys"' https://www.newyorker.com/magazine/
2011/08/08/deceptive-picture

p. 45

'I decided that it was nobler and more beautiful to stay,' he reflected
De Profundis, Oscar Wilde, 1905.

He became 'merely the figure and letter of a little cell in a long gallery,
one of a thousand lifeless numbers, as of a thousand lifeless lives' *De
Profundis*, Oscar Wilde, 1905.

p. 46

'I have the horror of death with the still greater horror of living' Letter to
Robert Ross from Reading Gaol, 10 March 1896.

'on the day of my release I shall merely be passing from one prison into
another' Letter to Robert Ross from Reading Gaol, 1 April 1897.

Following Wilde's trial, 600 men . . . fled across the Channel. *Oscar Wilde:
Great Lives*, Radio 4, 30 November 2018. https://www.bbc.co.uk/
programmes/b01ddxcq

he 'cried a good deal' *Oscar Wilde: The Great Drama of his Life*, Ashley H.
Robins (Sussex Academic Press, 2011), p. 27.

For Wilde, 'men have gone to heaven for smaller things than that'
De Profundis, Oscar Wilde, 1905.

p. 47

he was euphoric to be free, writing that he was 'dazed by the wonder
of the wonderful world . . .' *The Unrepentant Years*, Nicholas Frankel
(Harvard University Press, 2017).

'I must remake my maimed life on my own lines' *Complete Letters*,
p. 947.

'scandalous exposure created a set of public assumptions . . .' https://www.
theguardian.com/books/2024/feb/10/beyond-oscar-wilde-the-unsung-
literary-heroes-of-the-early-gay-rights-movement

p. 48

The book was deemed 'lewd, wicked' and 'scandalous' and Ellis's editor,
George Bedborough, was prosecuted for obscenity. https://www.
thefileroom.org/documents/dyn/DisplayCase.cfm/id/852

'a common, recurrent part of human sexuality' *Coming Out: Homosexual
Politics in Britain, from the Nineteenth Century to the Present*, Jeffrey
Weeks (Quartet, 1977), p. 62.

'My feeling about Oscar Wilde is that clearly he was bisexual' *Bisexuality
and the Eroticism of Everyday Life*, Marjorie Garber (Routledge, 2000),
p. 354.

2. Colette and Bessie Smith

p. 50

the *New York Times Magazine* declared her to be 'the greatest living writer
of French fiction' https://www.nytimes.com/article/best-colette-books.
html#:~:text=In%201953%2C%20Colette%20was,Gide%20and%20
Proust%20still%20lived.%E2%80%9D

Colette presented 'a new vision of what women's lives, particularly
middle-class women's lives, could be in France in this period' *Colette's
Republic: Work, Gender and Popular Culture in France 1870–1914*,
Patricia Tilburg (Berghahn Books, 2008).

She declared that suffragettes deserved 'the whip and the harem' https://
www.latimes.com/travel/la-tr-colettequotes-20100530-story.html

p. 51

The writer Vivian Gornick reflects that: 'my friends and I read Colette
as others read the Bible . . .' https://www.bostonreview.net/articles/
vivian-gornick-feminist-icons-in-love/

She once described herself as an 'erotic militant' *The Blue Lantern*, Colette,
trans. Roger Senhouse (Farrar, Straus and Giroux, 1977).

p. 52

In France during the 1890s, bisexuals were sometimes referred to as
'*indifférént(e)s*' 'Monosexual/Plurisexual: A Concise History', Diederik
F. Janssen, *Journal of Homosexuality*, 5 June 2023. https://www.
tandfonline.com/doi/full/10.1080/00918369.2023.2218957

The word that Colette used to describe her sexuality was 'unisexuality'
  Colette, A Life, Robert Lottman (Secker & Warburg, 1991), p. 55.

p. 53

'a mental hermaphrodite' *The Pure and the Impure*, Colette (1932; NYRB
  Classics, 2000), p. 62.

'Colette's early work is a fascinating and baroque form of transvestitism'
  Quoted in *A Theatrical Feast in Paris: From Molière to Deneuve*,
  Elizabeth Sharland (2005), p. 34.

p.54

Georgie would organize a rendezvous with Colette, then Henry, in the
  same room, just an hour apart *Secrets of the Flesh: A Life of Colette*,
  Judith Thurman (Bloomsbury, 1999), p. 129.

p. 55

Le mari doit protection à sa femme, la femme obéissance à son mari was
  another https://ehne.fr/en/encyclopedia/themes/gender-and-europe/
  civil-law-a-tool-masculine-domination/civil-law-a-tool-masculine-
  domination

Looking back to Ancient Rome, we have far fewer records of female
  bisexuality *Bisexuality in the Ancient World*, Eva Cantarella (Yale
  University Press, 2002), pp. 3–4.

'the lesbian was not so much preferring women as she was fleeing from
  man, a different matter altogether' *Colette: A Biography*, Michèle Sarde,
  trans. Richard Miller (Michael Joseph, 1978), p. 228.

'The wife of a man who deceives her with another man knows that all is
  lost' *The Pure and the Impure*, Colette (1932; NYRB Classics, 2000).

p. 56

'there was no danger of pregnancy, almost none of venereal disease'
  Secrets of the Flesh: A Life of Colette, Judith Thurman (Bloomsbury,
  1999), p. 137.

'depicted Sappho as an advocate of sapphism, but also as a hypocrite who
  succumbed to heterosexual love' *Lesbian Decadence, Representations in
  Art and Literature of Fin-de-Siècle France*, Nicole G. Albert (Columbia
  University Press, 2016), p. 22.

p. 66

'Colette's Lesbos is more a comforting womb or a mid-eighteenth century
  convent than it is a debauched Gomorrah' *Colette: A Biography*,
  Michèle Sarde, trans. Richard Miller (Michael Joseph, 1978),
  p. 228.

'Two women absorbed in each other don't fear or even imagine separation
any more than they would tolerate it' *The Pure and the Impure*, Colette
(1932; NYRB Classics, 2000).

'Passion is not what creates fidelity between two women but rather, a kind
of kinship' Ibid.

'A woman enjoys the certainty in caressing a body whose secrets she
knows and whose preferences are suggested by her own' Ibid.

'I know that then you will hold me close in your arms . . .' *The Tendrils of
the Vine*, Colette, 1908, quoted in *Colette: A Biography*, Michèle Sarde,
trans. Richard Miller (Michael Joseph, 1978), p. 232.

p. 67

'A couple of women can live together a long time and be happy' . . . 'if one
of the two women lets herself behave in the slightest like what I call a
pseudo-man' *The Pure and The Impure*, Colette (1932; NYRB Classics,
2000), p. 107.

p. 68

'This book was not written for my wives, my daughters or my sisters . . .'
*Lesbian Decadence, Representations in Art and Literature of Fin-de-Siècle
France*, Nicole G. Albert (Columbia University Press, 2016).

p. 73

write homoerotic poetry about the 'bellbright bodies' of boys bathing
Epithalamion, Gerard Manley Hopkins.

p. 76

'The blues always impressed me as being very sad, sadder even than the
Spirituals . . .' *Langston Hughes: The Man, His Art, and His Continuing
Influence*, C. James Trotman (Taylor & Francis, 2014), p. 90.

Danny Barker, a jazz musician of the era, heard in Bessie's depth and
range a similarity with 'preachers and evangelists' of the Deep South
Jazz People, Dan Morgenstern (H. N. Abrams, 1976).

p. 77

'I was raised in a shit-house', Bessie would say later in life *Bessie: Revised
and Expanded Edition*, Chris Albertson (Stein and Day, 1972), p. 35.

p. 78

a 'scene whose celestial flavor and cerulean coloring no angelic painter
or nectarish poet has ever conceived' *The Young and the Evil*, Charles
Henri Ford & Parker Tyler (1933). https://americanhistory.si.edu/
explore/stories/queens-and-queers-rise-drag-ball-culture-1920s

'The thing about Bessie is that she was always herself . . .' *Bessie: Revised and Expanded Edition*, Chris Albertson (Stein and Day, 1972), p. 93.

p. 80

as Lillian Faderman terms it, a form of 'sexual colonialism' *Odd Girls and Twilight Lovers: A History of Lesbian Life in 20th Century America*, Lillian Faderman (Columbia University Press, 1991), p. 68.

'Went out last night with a crowd of my friends/They must've been women, 'cause I don't like no men' *Blue Legacies and Black Feminism*, Angela Y. Davies (Vintage, 1988), p. 41.

In 'Sissy Blues', she sang about a woman whose male lover was stolen by a 'sissy' man *Blue Legacies and Black Feminism*, Angela Y. Davies (Vintage, 1988), p. 41.

Bessie Smith's 'The Boy In the Boat' (1930) included 'When you see two women walking hand in hand . . .' https://www.collectorsweekly.com/articles/singing-the-lesbian-blues-in-1920s-harlem/

'encouraging women of her class to drink, party and have sex' 'The Life and Times of Bessie Smith: Music's First Diva', Arun Starkey, *Far Out Magazine*, 6 February 2022.

p. 81

Bessie yelling, 'I got twelve women on this show and I can have one every night if I want it' *The Famous Lady Lovers: Black Women and Queer Desire Before Stonewall* (Cookie Woolner, 2023), p. 45.

'You ain't a man but you better be like one because we're gonna have it out' *Bessie: Revised and Expanded Edition*, Chris Albertson (Stein and Day, 1972), p. 206.

'Men sure deceitful, they getting worse every day', as well as the ironic lines, 'There's two things got me puzzled . . .' *Blue Legacies and Black Feminism*, Angela Y. Davies (Vintage, 1988), p. 280.

3. Marlene Dietrich

p. 87

'Each man or woman should be able to find in the actress . . .' *Bisexuality and the Eroticism of Everyday Life*, Marjorie Garber (Routledge, 2000), p. 140.

Cocteau said that Dietrich was 'the most exciting and terrifying woman I have ever known' *Marlene Dietrich: Life and Legend*, Steven Bach (University of Minnesota Press, 2011), p. 311.

Fritz Lang complained that 'her whole life is built on a grand illusion' *Marlene Dietrich: Life and Legend*, Steven Bach (University of Minnesota Press, 2011), p. 357.

'steel orchid' *Marlene Dietrich: Life and Legend*, Steven Bach (University of Minnesota Press, 2011), p. 241.

p. 89

Dietrich once observed that, 'In America, sex is an obsession, in other parts of the world it's a fact' . . . 'It seems she didn't two-time people. She ten-timed them.' 'The Glory and the Glamour of Dietrich', Lawrence Van Gelder, *New York Times*, 31 March 1996. https://www. nytimes.com/1996/03/31/tv/signoff-the-glory-and-glamour-of-dietrich.html

p. 90

She referred to her female Hollywood lovers as her 'sewing circle', whilst the men were her 'Alumni Association' *The Girls: Sappho Goes to Hollywood*, Diana McLellan (St Martin's Press, 2000).

'I am at heart a gentleman' https://www.theguardian.com/film/2017/nov/ 26/marlene-dietrich-androgyny-sexuality-exhibitions

'a grand passion or to have sought a relationship of permanence . . .' *The Mask of Marlene*, 1 April 2000, Fergus Lineham. https://www.irishtimes. com/culture/the-mask-of-marlene-1.262542

p. 92

women 'did not seem to suffer in a world without men. Our life among women had become such a pleasant habit that the prospect that men might return . . .' https://www.encyclopedia.com/women/ encyclopedias-almanacs-transcripts-and-maps/dietrich-marlene-1901-1992#:~:text=%22Our%20life%20among%20women%20had,become %20lords%20of%20their%20households.%22

Later in life, Marlene told one of her lovers that as a child, her mother sometimes called her by a boy's name, Paulus *The Girls: Sappho Goes to Hollywood*, Diana McLellan (St Martin's Press, 2000), p. 166.

'I wanted to take the father's place—against my mother's will' *Marlene Dietrich: Life and Legend*, Steven Bach (University of Minnesota Press), p. 19.

appreciating the 'structure' that her mother's rule gave her . . . *Dietrich & Riefenstahl: Hollywood, Berlin, and a Century in Two Lives*, Karen Wieland, trans. Shelley Frisch (W.W. Norton 2015), p. 37.

'I am dying of love for her, she is beautiful like an angel . . . it's really passion, deep deep love.' *Marlene Dietrich: the Life*, Maria Riva (Pegasus Books, 2017), p. 41.

p. 93

'if she weren't married, I would do anything to win her heart and get her before her Count Gersdorf. Even now, I'd like to be him' *Marlene Dietrich: the Life*, Maria Riva (Pegasus Books, 2017), p. 42.

'Love suffers, tolerates, hopes' *Marlene Dietrich: the Life*, Maria Riva (Pegasus Books, 2017), p. 43.

'It is the kind of love I could feel for a man' Ibid.

she felt that 'all those I loved so much have forgotten me . . . I am so unhappy because I don't have anybody who loves me. I am so used to being loved' *Marlene Dietrich: the Life*, Maria Riva (Pegasus Books, 2017), p. 54.

'He groaned, heaved, panted. Didn't even take his trousers off . . .' *Marlene Dietrich: the Life*, Maria Riva (Pegasus Books, 2017), p. 57.

p. 95

Hirschfeld declared that 'Love is as varied as people are' https://www.scientificamerican.com/article/the-forgotten-history-of-the-worlds-first-trans-clinic/

Berlin is 'the most lurid Underworld of all cities, where the German . . . enjoys obscenity in a form which even the Parisian would not tolerate' *Voluptuous Panic: The Erotic World of Weimar Berlin*, Mel Gordon (Feral House, 2008).

Androgyny was celebrated; one performer, upon being asked what her gender was, replied: 'Whatever you want it to be' https://www.thesmartset.com/article04190901/

p. 96

One friend at the time remarked that Marlene told him she was 'much more interested – although not exclusively – in women' *The Girls: Sappho Goes to Hollywood*, Diana McLellan (St Martin's Press, 2000), p. 101.

'it had been instilled in me . . . that a woman's role is to complete the home with children' *Marlene Dietrich, A Personal Biography*, Charlotte Chandler (Applause, 2011), p. 46.

p. 97

whom she called 'the perfect husband' *Blue Angel: The Life of Marlene Dietrich*, Donald Spoto (Doubleday, 1992), p. 46.

As Otto Preminger, a theatre director she worked with, observed, she

was a 'free spirit' *Marlene Dietrich, A Personal Biography*, Charlotte
Chandler (Applause, 2011), p. 57.

p. 98

with 'bovine listlessness' *Blue Angel: The Life of Marlene Dietrich*, Donald
Spoto (Doubleday, 1992), p. 88.

'Not that whore!' (It is ambiguous as to whether he was referring to her
private life or her films.) *Berlin Year Zero: The Making of 'The Blue
Angel'*, John Baxter, *Framework: The Journal of Cinema and Media*
(Spring 2010), Vol. 51 No. 1, p. 164.

Marlene reflected, 'Von Sternberg had only one idea in his head: to take
me away from the stage and to make a movie actress out of me' *Blue
Angel: The Life of Marlene Dietrich*, Donald Spoto (Doubleday, 1992),
p. 88.

Declaring that his actors were 'marionettes, pieces of colour [on]
my canvas' *Blue Angel: The Life of Marlene Dietrich*, Donald Spoto
(Doubleday, 1992), p. 86.

p. 99

Each was a muse to the other, challenging, flinging down 'artist's gauntlets
like duellists'. *Marlene Dietrich: the Life*, Maria Riva (Pegasus Books,
2017), p. 180.

Von Sternberg felt that when actresses had lesbian affairs, they 'exerted a
powerful androgynous magnetism through the camera's lens . . .' *The
Girls: Sappho Goes to Hollywood*, Diana McLellan (St Martin's Press,
2000).

Ruth Bicry, writing in *Photoplay*, observed that Hollywood 'had created
a new type of heroine' *Marlene Dietrich and The Erotics of Code-Bound
Hollywood*, Gaylan Studlar; *Dietrich Icon*, ed. Gerd Gemündrn and
Mary R. Desjardins (Duke University Press), p. 217.

Kenneth Tynan observed that Marlene Dietrich 'has sex, but no particular
gender. She has the bearing of a man . . .' https://www.theguardian.
com/film/2008/jun/22/1#:~:text=Kenneth%20Tynan%20said%20'
She%20has,German%2C%20German%20in%20my%20soul

'Marlene lives in a sexual no man's land – and no woman's either' *Clothes
Make the (Wo)Man: Marlene Dietrich and Double Drag*, Rebecca
Kennison, *Journal of Lesbian Studies*, 2002.

p. 100

'there are just certain songs that a woman can't sing as a woman'
Bisexuality and the Eroticism of Everyday Life, Marjorie Garber
(Routledge, 2000), p. 141.

'In her glitter dresses, she sang to men; in her tails, to women.' *Clothes Make the (Wo)Man: Marlene Dietrich and Double Drag*, Rebecca Kennison, *Journal of Lesbian Studies*, 2002.

'In Europe it doesn't matter if you're a man or a woman,' Dietrich told her *Blue Angel: The Life of Marlene Dietrich*, Donald Spoto (Doubleday, 1992), p. 96.

'I walk around this beautiful house and you are nowhere to be found' *Marlene Dietrich: the Life*, Maria Riva (Pegasus Books, 2017), p. 128.

'The feeling is that no man looks at a woman in trousers,' she wrote to Rudi *Marlene Dietrich: the Life*, Maria Riva (Pegasus Books, 2017), p. 129.

p. 101

'a completely new concept for a Hollywood glamour star' *Marlene Dietrich: the Life*, Maria Riva, (Pegasus Books, 2017), p. 166.

'The World's Most Glamorous Grandmother' https://www.npg.org.uk/collections/search/person/mp54587/marlene-dietrich#:~:text=In%201948%20when%20her%20daughter,a%20singer%20and%20cabaret%20performer.

p. 102

'Marlene tore down Edith's panties backstage in a Berlin theatre . . .' https://www.telegraph.co.uk/culture/4720951/Ladies-who-lie-together...html

'You seem so thin and your face [is] so white', saying that she wanted to cook for her *The Girls: Sappho Goes to Hollywood*, Diana McLellan (St Martin's Press, 2000), p. 164.

'I felt you were very sad . . . I am sad too. I am sad and lonely.' *Marlene Dietrich: Life and Legend*, Steven Bach (University of Minnesota Press), p. 172.

In a letter to her husband, Marlene reflected that, 'For me, she was a relief from this narrow Hollywood mentality' *The Girls: Sappho Goes to Hollywood*, Diana McLellan (St Martin's Press, 2000) p.163

'You are the essence of the stars . . .' *The Girls: Sappho Goes to Hollywood*, Diana McLellan (St Martin's Press, 2000), p. 167.

'the house became a sort of madhouse of flowers' *Marlene Dietrich: Life and Legend*, Steven Bach (University of Minnesota Press), p. 173.

p. 103

'She always admitted to me that she preferred women to men . . .' *Bisexuality and the Eroticism of Everyday Life*, Marjorie Garber (Routledge, 2000), p. 141.

Marlene's daughter made the observation that she weaponized sex with
men *Marlene Dietrich: the Life*, Maria Riva (Pegasus Books, 2017).

whilst her affairs with women were more warm and tender *Marlene
Dietrich: the Life*, Maria Riva (Pegasus Books, 2017).

Donald Spoto suggested that it was easier at this time for two female
lovers in Hollywood to live together *Blue Angel: The Life of Marlene
Dietrich*, Donald Spoto (Doubleday, 1992), p. 174.

'You can't *live* with a woman' *Marlene Dietrich: Life and Legend*, Steven
Bach (University of Minnesota Press), p. 246.

'I haven't a strong sense of possession towards a man. Perhaps because I
am not particularly feminine in my reactions . . .' *Blue Angel: The Life
of Marlene Dietrich*, Donald Spoto (Doubleday, 1992), p. 56.

p. 104

'a woman of only moderate talent . . . needed a husband, lavender or
otherwise, or a male lover in high places to push and protect her'
The Girls: Sappho Goes to Hollywood, Diana McLellan (St Martin's Press,
2000), p. 271.

The Hays Code, introduced in 1930, dictated that 'no picture shall be
produced which will lower the moral standards of those who see it'
http://www.screenonline.org.uk/film/id/592022/#:~:text=%2D%20
No%20picture%20shall%20be%20produced,and%20entertainment%
2C%20shall%20be%20presented

'For years few adulterous women managed to escape such calamities as
prostitution or losing a child' https://www.newyorker.com/magazine/
2016/05/02/what-the-hays-code-did-for-women#:~:text=For%20
years%2C%20few%20adulterous%20women,cinema%20had%20
been%20effectively%20smothered

p. 106

suggesting she become a 'scrawny, impoverished hag' by the end of the
film *Marlene Dietrich: Life and Legend*, Steven Bach (University of
Minnesota Press), p. 194.

She was labelled 'box office poison' in a now-infamous advertisement by
Henry Brandt *The Hollywood Reporter*, 3 May 1938.

p. 107

With the release of *Song of Songs*, she was accused of taking 'prostitute
roles' in the US *Marlene Dietrich: Life and Legend*, Steven Bach
(University of Minnesota Press), p. 186.

she had 'spent so many years among the film Jews of Hollywood' that
her entire character had become 'wholly un-German' *Marlene*

Dietrich: Life and Legend, Steven Bach (University of Minnesota Press), p. 232.

Goebbels watched Dietrich in the film *Desire* and reflected in his diary that she was 'a very great actor' April 1936; *Dietrich & Riefenstahl: Hollywood, Berlin, and a Century in Two Lives*, Karen Wieland, trans. Shelley Frisch (W.W. Norton, 2015).

Goebbels a 'grotesque dwarf' *Marlene Dietrich: Life and Legend*, Steven Bach (University of Minnesota Press), p. 239.

Himmler gave a speech about homosexuals to high-ranking SS officers in Bad Tölz . . . *The Persecution of Gay Men and Lesbians During the Third Reich*, Geoffrey J. Giles, *The Routledge History of the Holocaust* (Routledge, 2010), pp. 385–96.

p. 108

Hitler also believed that Ancient Greece collapsed due to the 'infectious activity' of homosexuality *From 'Pseudowomen' to the 'Third Sex:' Situating Antisemitism and Homophobia in Nazi Germany*, Gabriel Klapholz, *The Yale Undergraduate Research Journal*: Vol. 1 Iss. 1, Article 9.

now the phrase 'sexual acts' was vague enough that it was up to a Nazi court to decide what qualified https://encyclopedia.ushmm.org/content/en/article/paragraph-175-and-the-nazi-campaign-against-homosexuality?series=200

p. 109

They rejected Hirschfeld's equation of homosexuality with hermaphroditism, finding it emasculating, and preferring to see it as an aspect of virile manliness *Gay Berlin*, Robert Beachy (Vintage, 2015), p. 116.

They also disliked his medicalization of homosexuality, which 'took away all beauty from eroticism' *Gay Berlin*, Robert Beachy (Vintage, 2015).

the lingering idea of the 'disloyal bisexual' https://aha.confex.com/aha/2019/webprogram/Paper25391.html

p. 110

Treatments were offered at the Göring Institute, which declared by 1938 that it had cured 341 of 510 patients *Queer Identities and Politics in Germany: A History 1880–1945*, Clayton J. Whisnant (Columbia University Press, 2016), p. 236.

Around 100,000 men were arrested in Germany and Austria on suspicion of homosexuality between 1933 and 1945 https://www.independent.

co.uk/news/holocaust-gay-activists-press-for-german-apology-1291337.html

Even when the war ended, homosexuals did not receive reparations; many were released from camps only to find themselves put into prison Ibid.

The 1935 law that the Nazis had introduced remained in place until 1969, meaning that many homosexuals did not speak out about the experiences they had suffered during the Holocaust Ibid.

A survey found that the programmes 'were just as devastating to German morale as an air raid' https://www.uso.org/stories/2414-marlene-dietrich-most-patriotic-women-in-world-war-ii#:~:text=The%20U.S.%20Strategic%20Bombing%20Survey,Marlene%E2%80%9D%20song%20was%20a%20hit

p. 111

'They'll shave off my hair, stone me and have horses drag me through the streets' *Marlene Dietrich: Life and Legend*, Steven Bach (University of Minnesota Press), p. 298.

Dietrich said that her war efforts were 'the only important thing I've ever done' *Marlene Dietrich: Life and Legend*, Steven Bach (University of Minnesota Press), p. 304.

p. 112

The Germans and I 'no longer speak the same language,' Dietrich said *Marlene Dietrich: Life and Legend*, Steven Bach (University of Minnesota Press), p. 406.

One front cover of 1955 depicted her with a headline in red: *The Untold Story of Marlene Dietrich* http://www.polarimagazine.com/bulletin-board/scandal-sheet-outed-marlene-dietrich-1955/

Polari magazine reports that she was outed as a 'lesbian', when in fact she was outed as a bisexual http://www.polarimagazine.com/bulletin-board/scandal-sheet-outed-marlene-dietrich-1955/

Mercedes de Acosta was described as 'a writer who favoured clothes that seemed to be tailored by Brooks Brothers' Ibid.

Confidential magazine concluded: 'In the game of *amour*, she's not only played both sides of the street . . .' https://therake.com/stories/cross-stitch-marlene-dietrich

She complained to her friend Eryk Hanut that her gay fans had turned her into 'an androgynous Madonna' – her verdict on this was 'Rubbish!' *Clothes Make the (Wo)Man: Marlene Dietrich and Double Drag*, Rebecca Kennison, *Journal of Lesbian Studies*, 2002.

4. Anaïs Nin

p. 115

'*While there are rare accounts in the unpublished diary (sometimes graphic) of her relations with women*' https://Anaïsninjournal. wordpress.com/2009/02/08/Anaïs-nin-myth-of-the-day/#comments

p. 117

'I was always living on the edge of disaster,' was Miller's summary of his life at that time *Anaïs Nin, A Biography*, Deirdre Bair (Bloomsbury, 1995), p. 122.

'the topsoil of our personalities is nothing' *Mirages: The Unexpurgated Diary of Anaïs Nin*, 1939–1947 (Swallow Press, 2013).

p. 118

'I really believe that if I were not a writer, not a creator, not an experimenter, I might have been a very faithful wife' *Henry and June*, Anaïs Nin (Harcourt Brace Jovanovich, 1986/Penguin Classics, 2017), p. 11.

'Abnormal pleasures kill the taste for normal ones' *Henry and June*, Anaïs Nin (Harcourt Brace Jovanovich, 1986/Penguin Classics, 2017), p. 5.

p. 119

she looks forward to meeting him, to an encounter between 'delicacy and violence' *The Diary of Anaïs Nin: 1931–1934* (Swallow Press, 1966), p. 8.

When Henry comes to lunch, she finds him 'flamboyant, virile, animal, magnificent' *Henry and June*, Anaïs Nin (Harcourt Brace Jovanovich, 1986/Penguin Classics, 2017), p. 6.

she has craved 'a man stronger than me, a lover who will lead me in love' *Henry and June*, Anaïs Nin (Harcourt Brace Jovanovich 1986/Penguin Classics, 2017), p. 3.

and to put herself 'under the protection, the nobility, the grandeur . . .' 1 September 1919, *Linotte: The Early Diaries of Anaïs Nin, 1914–1920* (Houghton Mifflin Harcourt, 2014).

'You fall in love with people's minds,' he warns his wife *Henry and June*, Anaïs Nin (Harcourt Brace Jovanovich, 1986/Penguin Classics, 2017), p. 10.

p. 120

'her beauty drowned me'. Anaïs sits in front of her and feels she would do anything for her, she is so dazzled: 'she was colour, brilliance, strangeness.' *Henry and June*, Anaïs Nin (Harcourt Brace Jovanovich 1986 / Penguin Classics 2017), p. 13.

men need to be 'soothed, lulled, understood, helped, encouraged' in a tender manner *Henry and June*, Anaïs Nin (Harcourt Brace Jovanovich, 1986/Penguin Classics, 2017), p .11.

'By the end of the evening, I was like a man, terribly in love with her face and body, which promised so much' *Henry and June*, Anaïs Nin (Harcourt Brace Jovanovich, 1986/Penguin Classics, 2017), p. 13.

'I will always be the virgin prostitute,' Anaïs writes in her diary *Henry and June*, Anaïs Nin (Harcourt Brace Jovanovich, 1986/Penguin Classics, 2017), p. 3.

p. 121

Hugh thinks her 'mannish' and hates her *Henry and June*, Anaïs Nin (Harcourt Brace Jovanovich, 1986/Penguin Classics, 2017), p. 16.

'I have wanted to possess her as if I were a man, but I have also wanted her to love me . . .' *Henry and June*, Anaïs Nin (Harcourt Brace Jovanovich, 1986/Penguin Classics, 2017), p. 16.

'I was at the top of a skyscraper and expected to walk down the façade of it on a very narrow fire ladder. I was terrified. I could not do it.' *Henry and June*, Anaïs Nin (Harcourt Brace Jovanovich, 1986/Penguin Classics, 2017), p. 19.

p. 122

'Over in the US, where the economic crash was blamed by many on the 'cultural experimentation'' *A Gay World, Vibrant and Forgotten*, George Chauncey, New York Times, 26 June 1994.

'Give me the perfume I smelled in your house,' June replies *Henry and June*, Anaïs Nin (Harcourt Brace Jovanovich, 1986/Penguin Classics, 2017), p. 19.

p. 123

'the beauty of her body, its fullness and heaviness' *Henry and June*, Anaïs Nin (Harcourt Brace Jovanovich, 1986/Penguin Classics, 2017), p. 20.

like 'your fingers, holding me in barbaric slavery' *Henry and June*, Anaïs Nin (Harcourt Brace Jovanovich, 1986/Penguin Classics, 2017), p. 25.

'Are you a lesbian? Have you faced your impulses in your own mind?' *Henry and June*, Anaïs Nin (Harcourt Brace Jovanovich 1986/Penguin Classics, 2017), p. 19.

'I have faced my feelings, I am fully aware of them, but I have never found anyone I wanted to live them out with, so far' *Henry and June*, Anaïs Nin (Harcourt Brace Jovanovich, 1986/Penguin Classics, 2017), p. 19.

p. 124

'he is more jealous of women than men' *Henry and June*, Anaïs Nin
  (Harcourt Brace Jovanovich, 1986/Penguin Classics, 2017), p. 23.

'She is like a man who is drunk and gives himself away' *Henry and June*,
  Anaïs Nin (Harcourt Brace Jovanovich, 1986/Penguin Classics, 2017),
  p. 24.

'too scrupulous and proud' about money matters *Henry and June*, Anaïs
  Nin (Harcourt Brace Jovanovich, 1986/Penguin Classics, 2017), p. 27.

'I had wanted to hold you and caress you' *Henry and June*, Anaïs Nin
  (Harcourt Brace Jovanovich, 1986/Penguin Classics, 2017), p. 28.

she felt, 'I am no longer woman; I am man' *Henry and June*, Anaïs Nin
  (Harcourt Brace Jovanovich, 1986/Penguin Classics, 2017), p. 58.

p. 125

Tanner argues that the *Iliad* marks the beginning of Western literature . . .
  Adultery in The Novel, Tony Tanner (John Hopkins University Press,
  1979).

'He senses uneasily that there is a certain side of you he has not grasped'
  Henry and June, Anaïs Nin (Harcourt Brace Jovanovich, 1986/Penguin
  Classics, 2017), p. 34.

p. 126

'Henry's version of her' *Henry and June*, Anaïs Nin (Harcourt Brace
  Jovanovich, 1986/Penguin Classics, 2017), p. 214.

Having 'mellowed' Henry, she observes that, 'They can talk together. I
  have changed him . . . and he understands her better' *Henry and June*,
  Anaïs Nin (Harcourt Brace Jovanovich, 1986/Penguin Classics, 2017),
  p. 214.

p. 127

'This scene in the taxi – knees touching, hands locked, cheek against
  cheek – is going on while we are aware of our fundamental enmity'
  Henry and June, Anaïs Nin (Harcourt Brace Jovanovich, 1986/Penguin
  Classics, 2017), p. 215.

'But what a superb game the three of us are playing. Who is the demon?
  Who the liar? . . .' *Henry and June*, Anaïs Nin (Harcourt Brace
  Jovanovich, 1986/Penguin Classics, 2017), p. 215.

'The love between women is a refuge and an escape into harmony. In the
  love between man and woman there is resistance and conflict . . .'
  Henry and June, Anaïs Nin (Harcourt Brace Jovanovich, 1986/Penguin
  Classics, 2017), p. 29.

'I felt like June' *Henry and June*, Anaïs Nin (Harcourt Brace Jovanovich, 1986/Penguin Classics, 2017), p. 35.

'Sinks stopped up from too much garbage. Washing dishes in bathtub . . .' *Henry and June*, Anaïs Nin (Harcourt Brace Jovanovich, 1986/Penguin Classics, 2017), p. 39.

'I have discovered the joy of a masculine direction of my life by my courting of June . . .' *Henry and June*, Anaïs Nin (Harcourt Brace Jovanovich, 1986/Penguin Classics, 2017), p. 42.

p. 128

'laugh off the jagged edges, to smooth out the discord, the ugly, the fearful, to lighten their confidences' *Henry and June*, Anaïs Nin (Harcourt Brace Jovanovich, 1986/Penguin Classics, 2017), p. 14.

'I have known three cases of "steady" home women going to pieces, for no apparent reason . . .' *The Early Diary of Anaïs Nin*, Vol. 4, 29 August 1927.

p. 129

'I cannot stay home,' she wrote in 1928. 'I have a desperate desire to know life, and to live in order to reach maturity' *Spy in the House of Anaïs Nin*, Kim Krizan (Total Global Domination, 2019), p. 59.

p. 130

'very early, primordial stages of psychic development' *Bisexuality in Psychoanalytic Theory: Interpreting the Resistance*, Esther Rapoport, *Journal of Bisexuality*, 25 November 2009, pp. 279–95.

Freud classified bisexuals as 'amphigenic inverts' (as opposed to 'absolute inverts', homosexuals) *Three Essays on the Theory of Sexuality, 1905 edition* (Verso, 2016), p. 2.

an 'originally bisexual disposition' *Three Essays on the Theory of Sexuality, 1905 edition* (Verso, 2016), p. 10.

'It is not for psychoanalysis to solve the problem of homosexuality' https://pep-web.org/search/document/PSAR.031.0253A?page=P0253

'as well as . . . feminine psychical traits, such as shyness, modesty and the need for instruction and assistance' *Three Essays on the Theory of Sexuality, 1905 edition* (Verso, 2016), p. 10.

'the sexual object is not someone of the same sex, but someone who combines characteristics of both sexes' Ibid.

Women experiencing same-sex attraction, however, 'frequently and peculiarly exhibit somatic and psychical characteristics of men' Ibid.

p. 131

'Most of those who knew her believed the diaries themselves prevented

her from becoming what she most wanted to be – a creative writer.'
'Oh, the Burden, the Anxiety, the Sacrifices', Jenny Diski, *London
Review of Books*, 20 April 1995.

'with tremendous clearness and conciseness' *Henry and June*, Anaïs Nin
(Harcourt Brace Jovanovich, 1986/Penguin Classics, 2017), p. 10.

'Would you mind if I borrowed these?' he asked, incorporating the
material into *Tropic of Capricorn Anaïs Nin, a biography*, Deirdre Bair
(Bloomsbury, 1995), p. 154.

'René Allendy, chided Nin for trying to surpass men in their work' Ibid,
p. 147.

p. 132

'with a boy's mind and a boy's heart', calling her male alter-ego Eric
Daphne du Maurier: The Secret Life of the Renowned Novelist, Margaret
Forster (Doubleday, 1993), p. 221.

Her biographer, Margaret Forster, saw du Maurier's struggle with her
bisexuality as motivated by a 'homophobic fear' *Daphne du Maurier:
The Secret Life of the Renowned Novelist*, Margaret Forster (Doubleday,
1993).

Virginia Woolf said that Coleridge thought a 'great mind is androgynous'.
She concluded that 'Coleridge . . . meant, perhaps, that the
androgynous mind is resonant and porous . . .' Ibid.

'Shakespeare was androgynous; and so were Keats and Sterne and Cowper
and Lamb and Coleridge. Shelley perhaps was sexless . . .' *A Room of
One's Own*, Virginia Woolf (Hogarth Press, 1929).

p. 133

'All great novels, all true novels are bisexual. This is to say that they
express both a feminine and a masculine view of the world' https://
www.theguardian.com/books/2023/jul/12/to-be-a-writer-means-to-
discover-a-truth-milan-kundera-a-life-in-quotes

'*It's like climbing out of a burning building into too much water*' *Bisexual*,
from the collection *Hera Lindsay Bird* (Victoria Uni Press, 2016/
Penguin UK, 2017).

p. 143

'Henry's great need of woman was due to his being such a man, a
hundred-percent man . . .' *Henry and June*, Anaïs Nin (Harcourt Brace
Jovanovich, 1986/Penguin Classics, 2017), p. 211.

'the joy when a woman finds a man she can submit to' *Henry and June*,
Anaïs Nin (Harcourt Brace Jovanovich, 1986/Penguin Classics, 2017),
p. 48.

'I cannot reach a mature control of my own life. Will I ever be free?' *Spy in the House of Anaïs Nin*, Kim Krizan, p. 59 (Total Global Domination, 2019), p. 22.

'tortured by a complexity of feelings' *Spy in the House of Anaïs Nin*, Kim Krizan, p. 59 (Total Global Domination, 2019), p. 82.

p. 144

'tired of the entire relationship to men . . .' *Spy in the House of Anaïs Nin*, Kim Krizan (Total Global Domination, 2019), p. 20.

'the status of a wife is worth nothing. If I had worked, I would be free and not afraid to stand alone' *Spy in the House of Anaïs Nin*, Kim Krizan (Total Global Domination, 2019), p. 21.

5. Susan Sontag

p. 146

'Head them off at the pass and use me for it. Use this article for it . . .' *Sontag: Her Life and Work*, Benjamin Moser (HarperCollins, 2019/UK edition Allen Lane, 2019), p. 631.

p. 147

'That I have girlfriends as well as boyfriends is what? Is something I guess I never thought I was supposed to have to say . . .' https://www.newyorker.com/magazine/2000/03/06/the-hunger-artist-susan-sontag-profile

'when you get older, 45 plus, men stop fancying you. Or put it another way, the men I fancy don't fancy me . . .' . . . 'Five women, four men' . . . 'without foundation' https://www.theguardian.com/books/2000/may/27/fiction.features

'My only wish about Sontag is that she had bothered to weather . . .' The *Advocate*, Allan Gurganus, 1 February 2005. https://www.thefreelibrary.com/Notes+on+Sontag%3A+out+novelist+Allan+Gurganus+pays+tribute+to+a+lost... -a0128102000

p. 148

'familiar code for "gay"' 'Susan Sontag and a Case of Curious Silence', *Los Angeles Times*, 4 January 2005.

The *Sydney Morning Herald* ran an indignant piece declaring that, unlike traditional news outlets, 'leading gay and lesbian news organisations announced' 'Final taboo shrouds Sontag's lesbianism', 7 January 2005, *Sydney Morning Herald*.

'beautiful young woman every male graduate student regretted . . .'
https://www.wsj.com/articles/SB10001424052748704308904576226973
164472968

'Despite occasional male lovers, Sontag's eroticism centred almost
exclusively on women' *Sontag: Her Life and Work*, Benjamin Moser
(HarperCollins 2019/UK edition Allen Lane, 2019), p. 10.

p. 149

'There are so many things in my life now that are more important to me
than my sexuality . . .' https://www.theguardian.com/books/2000/may/
27/fiction.features

'For not caring about . . . the writer and what the writer says and what the
writer knows and what the writer's life is like' Radio 4 *Free Thinking*,
'Landmark: *Against Interpretation*', 18 September 2019.

he had 'sometimes come to prefer reading about the lives of certain
writers to reading their works' https://www.theguardian.com/books/
booksblog/2015/aug/14/roland-barthes-challenge-to-biography

'I feel for the first time the living possibility of becoming a writer' *Reborn:
Journals and Notebooks 1947–1963*, ed. David Rieff (Picador, 2009),
11 November 1959.

p. 150

'unconvincing childhood' 'Pilgrimage', *New Yorker*, 21 December, 1987.

p. 151

Her 'lesbian tendencies' worry her *Susan Sontag*, Jerome Boyd Maunsell,
p. 20.

The thought of sex with a man is 'nothing but humiliation and
degradation' *Reborn: Journals and Notebooks 1947–1963*, ed. David
Rieff (Picador, 2009), p. 26.

At Berkeley, she feels exhilarated to have escaped the 'Lower Slobbovia'
https://www.nybooks.com/articles/1973/11/15/freak-show/

'one of the finest intellects I've yet come into contact with' *Reborn:
Journals and Notebooks 1947–1963*, ed. David Rieff (Picador, 2009),
p. 31.

There she meets a bookseller with a 'beautiful smile' who seems
'wonderfully, uniquely alive' *Reborn: Journals and Notebooks
1947–1963*, ed. David Rieff (Picador, 2009), p. 34.

'To love one's body and use it well, that's primary . . . I can do that, I know,
for I am freed now' *Reborn: Journals and Notebooks 1947–1963*, ed.
David Rieff (Picador, 2009). Entry for 24 May 1949.

Whatever has been cramped and blocked inside her is now released with the revelation that 'bisexuality as the expression of the fullness of the individual' *Reborn: Journals and Notebooks 1947–1963*, ed. David Rieff (Picador, 2009), p. 38.

The norms of the 1950s, with the traditional idea that you should stay chaste until the right person came along, are also something she discards Ibid.

p. 152

writing 'a couple of papers on obscure subjects nobody cares about and, at the age of sixty, be ugly and respected, and a full professor' *Reborn: Journals and Notebooks 1947–1963*, ed. David Rieff (Picador, 2009). Entry for 26 May 1949.

'tall + thin with a skeletal face + a receding hairline' *Sontag: Her Life and Work*, Benjamin Moser (HarperCollins, 2019/UK edition Allen Lane, 2019), p. 109.

p. 153

'I marry Philip with full consciousness + fear of my will toward self-destructiveness' *Reborn: Journals and Notebooks 1947–1963*, ed. David Rieff (Picador, 2009), p. 80.

'The Bi's Progress', which Moser interprets as an attempt to 'train herself into heterosexuality' *Sontag: Her Life and Work*, Benjamin Moser (HarperCollins, 2019/UK edition Allen Lane, 2019), p. 90.

in the 1950s the average marrying age in the US was twenty. https://nces.ed.gov/programs/youthindicators/

p. 154

'the leakage of talk. My mind is dribbling out through my mouth' *Reborn: Journals and Notebooks 1947–1963*, ed. David Rieff (Picador, 2009), p. 190.

She grows to dislike 'his timidity, his sentimentality, his low vitality, his innocence' *Reborn: Journals and Notebooks 1947–1963*, ed. David Rieff (Picador, 2009). Entry for 25 February 1958.

she also finds him an 'emotional totalitarian' *Reborn: Journals and Notebooks 1947–1963*, ed. David Rieff (Picador, 2009). Entry for 27 March 1957.

'not only that *I* was Dorothea but that, a few months earlier, I had married Mr Casaubon' *Susan Sontag, A Biography*, Daniel Schreiber (Northwestern University Press, 2014), p. 37.

'at least I'll know if I am anything outside the domestic stage, the feathered nest' *Reborn: Journals and Notebooks 1947–1963*, ed. David Rieff (Picador, 2009), p. 140.

she ponders if she has been herself in marriage, or 'am I myself when alone?' *Reborn: Journals and Notebooks 1947–1963*, ed. David Rieff (Picador, 2009), p. 140.

p. 155

Harriet, who feels that her 'jealousy reflex' is 'being activated big time', punches Susan in the face at a party *Sontag: Her Life and Work*, Benjamin Moser (HarperCollins, 2019/UK edition Allen Lane, 2019), p. 163.

marital wars are 'a deadly, deadening combat which is the opposite, the antithesis of the sharp painful struggles of lovers' *Reborn: Journals and Notebooks 1947–1963*, ed. David Rieff (Picador, 2009), p. 177.

an 'accelerating delinquency in her my writing of letters' and a 'growing reluctance, aversion even' to reading his letters *Reborn: Journals and Notebooks 1947–1963*, ed. David Rieff (Picador, 2009), p. 202.

'Seven years is a long time, isn't it, dear one? . . .' *Reborn: Journals and Notebooks 1947–1963*, ed. David Rieff (Picador, 2009), p. 183.

homosexuality is a 'criticism of society', a 'protest against bourgeois expectations' *Sontag: Her Life and Work*, Benjamin Moser (HarperCollins, 2019/UK edition Allen Lane, 2019), p. 231.

the end of her marriage marks the beginning of her adolescence https://www.theguardian.com/books/2002/jan/19/politics

p. 156

later she will regard those years as 'a lost decade' *Sempre Susan, a memoir of Susan Sontag*, Sigrid Nunez (Atlas Books, 2011), p. 103.

'The orgasm focuses. I lust to write . . .' *Reborn: Journals and Notebooks 1947–1963*, ed. David Rieff (Picador, 2009), 11 November 1959.

The case is reported on by the *New York Daily News*, with the headline ***Lesbian Religious Professor Gets Custody*** *Susan Sontag, A Biography*, Daniel Schreiber (Northwestern University Press, 2014), p. 60.

p. 157

'The 1950s were perhaps the worst time in history for women to love women' *Odd Girls and Twilight Lovers: A History of Lesbian Life in Twentieth Century America* (Columbia University Press, 2012), p. 157.

'The world is not to be divided into sheep and goats . . . nature rarely deals with discrete categories,' Kinsey concluded. *Sexual Behaviour In the Human Male* (1948).

p. 159

Yvonne Keller notes that Radclyffe Hall's *The Well of Loneliness*, 'Pulp

Politics: Strategies of Vision in Pro-Lesbian Pulp Novels, 1955–1965',
The Queer Sixties, ed. Patricia Juliana Smith (Routledge, 1999).
'firsthand' her 'deep and fiery need for a male' *Man Among Women*, Randy
Salem (Universal Publishing and Distributing Corporation, 1960).

p. 160

'love of the unnatural: of artifice and exaggeration . . .' *Notes on 'Camp'*,
Against Interpretation and Other Essays, Susan Sontag (Farrar, Straus
and Giroux, 1966/my edition Penguin Modern Classics, 2009),
p. 275.
'It incarnates a victory of "style" over "content", "aesthetics" over
"morality", of irony over tragedy' *Notes on 'Camp'*, *Against
Interpretation and Other Essays*, Susan Sontag (Farrar, Straus and
Giroux, 1966/my edition Penguin Modern Classics, 2009), p. 287.
'something of a private code, a badge of identity even, among small urban
cliques' *Notes on 'Camp'*, *Against Interpretation and Other Essays*, Susan
Sontag (Farrar, Straus and Giroux, 1966/my edition Penguin Modern
Classics, 2009), p. 275.
Benjamin Moser has noted that the first printing of 'Notes on "Camp"'
included the line 'I am strongly drawn to Camp . . .' *Sontag: Her Life
and Work*, Benjamin Moser (HarperCollins, 2019/UK edition Allen
Lane, 2019), p. 237.

p. 161

The *New York Times Magazine* declared that 'Notes on "Camp"' was
'potentially dangerous to society – it's sick and decadent' *Sontag: Her
Life and Work*, Benjamin Moser (HarperCollins 2019/UK edition Allen
Lane, 2019), p. 240.
'then I think our society is headed for a moral collapse unlike anything
we've ever seen' *Sontag: Her Life and Work*, Benjamin Moser
(HarperCollins 2019/UK edition Allen Lane, 2019), p. 228.
'I find New York quite different from what it was three years ago . . . every
kind of perversion is regarded as avant-garde' 'All That Gab', James
Wolcott, *London Review of Books*, 24 October 2019.

p. 162

thousands gathered 'proclaiming the new strength and pride of the gay
people' https://www.nytimes.com/2019/06/27/nyregion/pride-parade-
first-new-york-lgbtq.html#:~:text=This%20paper%20covered%20
the%20march,pride%20of%20the%20gay%20people.
To claim bisexuality at this time was dangerous, given that it supported
the idea that homosexuality was 'curable' *Bisexuality and Queer*

Theory: Intersections, Connections and Challenges, ed. Jonathan Alexander, Serena Anderlini-D'Onofrio (Routledge, 2012), loc. 170.

p. 163

'who have, as it were, been in bondage, and for whom the prison doors are now open, to show their thanks by comporting themselves *quietly and with dignity*' https://api.parliament.uk/historic-hansard/lords/1967/jul/21/sexual-offences-no-2-bill

'little boys from growing up to be adult homosexuals' https://www.bps.org.uk/psychologist/freudian-motivation-behind-1967s-sexual-offences-act

If those opposing the bill feared it would 'open the floodgates', then they were concerned about their own repressed gay desire flooding out, he argued https://www.bps.org.uk/psychologist/freudian-motivation-behind-1967s-sexual-offences-act

'a way of encouraging society to come to terms with its bisexuality . . . it was the start of opening up society to be more caring and sensitive' https://www.theguardian.com/society/2007/jun/24/communities.gayrights

In 2003, Sontag gave an extended television interview C-Span 2 TV, *In Depth*, 2 March 2005. https://www.c-span.org/video/?172991-1/depth-susan-sontag

p. 164

There's a video on YouTube that features a clip of Sontag attending the 1971 debate about feminism at the New York Town Hall https://www.youtube.com/watch?v=e2jXH-wPAfU

she was 'anti-autobiographical' https://www.pomoculture.org/2013/09/19/against-postmodernism-etcetera-a-conversation-with-susan-sontag/

p. 165

'I'd like to see a few platoons of intellectuals who are also feminists doing their bit in the war against misogyny in their own way' *On Women: A New Collection of Feminist Essays*, Susan Sontag (Hamish Hamilton, 2023).

Her son, David, noted that rather than referring to 'my work', she spoke of 'the work' *The Violet Hour: Great Writers At the End*, Katie Roiphe (Dial Press, 2016), p. 65.

'The only kind of writer I could be is the kind who exposes himself,' she wrote in 1959 https://www.nytimes.com/2006/09/10/magazine/10sontag.html

Patrick Moore has speculated that 'she may have felt that her true sexuality would limit her impact in the male-dominated intellectual elite' https://www.latimes.com/archives/la-xpm-2005-jan-04-oe-moore4-story.html

Edmund White, one of her literary contemporaries, observed, 'If Susan had been publicly identified as gay, she would have lost two-thirds of her readership' *Sontag: Her Life and Work*, Benjamin Moser (HarperCollins, 2019/UK edition Allen Lane, 2019), p. 513.

p. 166

as Jessie J discovered when she came out as a bi in 2011: 'I was honest and then BAM it took over . . .' https://www.theguardian.com/music/2014/apr/09/jessie-j-bisexuality-phase-singer-coming-out-response

'an intellectual of the first rank' who, unlike Sontag, publicly acknowledged her lesbianism *Sontag: Her Life and Work*, Benjamin Moser (HarperCollins, 2019/UK edition Allen Lane, 2019). https://www.newyorker.com/magazine/2019/09/23/susan-sontag-and-the-unholy-practice-of-biography

'I need the identity as a weapon to match the weapon that society has against me' *Reborn: Journals and Notebooks 1947–1963*, ed. David Rieff (Picador, 2009).

'The fiction comes from a deeper place and a broader place. I have much more access to myself than I do in my essays' BBC Radio 3, *Afterwords: Susan Sontag*, 20 January 2019.

portrays homosexuality as 'a playfulness with masks' *The Benefactor*, Susan Sontag (Farrar Straus and Giroux, 1963).

'Sometimes I had to forget that I was a woman to accomplish the best of which I was capable' *The Volcano Lover*, Susan Sontag (Farrar, Straus and Giroux, 1992, Penguin, 2009), p. 419.

'inhibit people from seeking treatment early enough, or making a greater effort to get competent treatment' *Illness As Metaphor*, Susan Sontag (Farrar, Straus and Giroux, 1978).

p. 167

'a narrative, it seemed to me, would be less useful than an idea' *AIDS and Its Metaphors*, Susan Sontag (Farrar, Straus and Giroux, 1989).

Jerome Boyd Maunsell argued that 'the understated autobiographical subtext . . .' *Susan Sontag*, Jerome Boyd Maunsell, p. 143.

male and female were 'dominator and dominated' *Sontag: Her Life and Work*, Benjamin Moser (HarperCollins 2019/UK edition Allen Lane, 2019), p. 231.

for women were 'raised to be masochists' *Sempre Susan, a Memoir of Susan Sontag*, Sigrid Nunez (Atlas Books, 2011), p. 73.

'the few times I saw her with men around, they seemed to relate to her as a kind of intellectually supercharged eunuch . . .' 'Desperately Seeking Susan', Terry Castle, *London Review of Books*, 17 March 2005.

p. 168

She's 'tearing her hair out' over a woman *An Interview with Benjamin Moser*, Rain Taxi, interview by Allan Vorda, October 2019.

'Oh shit . . . Now I'm just like everybody else,' she lamented. *Sontag: Her Life and Work*, Benjamin Moser (HarperCollins, 2019/UK edition Allen Lane, 2019), p. 284.

denounced by a Leningrad newspaper as 'pornographic and anti-Soviet' 'Joseph Brodsky, Exiled Poet who Won the Nobel, Dies at 55', Robert D. McFadden, *New York Times*, 29 January 1996. https://archive.nytimes.com/www.nytimes.com/books/00/09/17/specials/brodsky-obit.html?scp=38&sq=joseph%2520brodsky&st=cse

p. 169

'he made a stunning impression. He was so authoritative personally. That would register here as supreme confidence' https://wordswithoutborders.org/read/article/2008-06/thirteen-ways-of-looking-at-joseph-brodsky

a quality Susan struggled with – 'he could be very cruel' https://wordswithoutborders.org/read/article/2008-06/thirteen-ways-of-looking-at-joseph-brodsky/

Brodsky was 'so besotted with Sontag that he even asked her to marry him' *Susan Sontag, A Biography*, Daniel Schreiber (Northwestern University Press, 2014), p. 159.

she boldly declared that Communism is 'Fascism with a human face' https://archive.nytimes.com/www.nytimes.com/books/00/03/12/specials/sontag-communism.html

'I'm all alone. There's nobody with whom I can share my ideas, my thoughts' *Sontag: Her Life and Work*, Benjamin Moser (HarperCollins, 2019/UK edition Allen Lane, 2019), p. 387.

Susan saw homosexual relationships as a way of offering the possibility of 'improvising and breaking away from set conventions of the erotic relationship' *Sontag: Her Life and Work*, Benjamin Moser (HarperCollins, 2019/UK edition Allen Lane, 2019), p. 231.

p. 170

'Remember what she said the other day about finding me so different from the way I appeared at first' *As Consciousness is Harnessed To Flesh: Journals and Notebooks 1964–1980*, ed. David Rieff, Susan Sontag (Picador, 2013).

Her lover resembled her mother, 'weak, unhappy, confused, charming' *As Consciousness is Harnessed To Flesh: Journals and Notebooks 1964–1980*, ed. David Rieff, Susan Sontag (Picador 2013). Entry for 25 May 1975.

Sontag replied: 'Fuck the leaves!' *Sontag: Her Life and Work*, Benjamin Moser (HarperCollins, 2019/UK edition Allen Lane, 2019), p. 321.

'I remember going out to dinner with her and just sweating through my clothes because I thought I couldn't talk to her' www.nytimes.com/2006/10/06/arts/design/06leib.html

In their first meeting, Susan asserted a certain dominance by advising Annie, 'You're good, but you could be better' https://www.nytimes.com/2006/10/06/arts/design/06leib.html

p. 171

David Rieff remarked that 'they were the worst couple I've ever seen in terms of unkindness, inability to be nice, held resentments' https://www.nylon.com/review-benjamin-moser-susan-sontag

'sadism, hostility is an essential element in love. Therefore it's important that love be a *transaction* of hostilities' *Reborn: Journals and Notebooks 1947–1963*, ed. David Rieff (Picador, 2009).

'She was actually a very warm, outgoing person, the opposite of what you sort of expected — just so charming, even childlike in some ways' https://www.nytimes.com/2006/10/06/arts/design/06leib.html

she recognized that Susan 'was tough, but it all balanced out. The good things far outweigh the bad things. We had so many great experiences together' *Sontag: Her Life and Work*, Benjamin Moser (HarperCollins, 2019/UK edition Allen Lane, 2019), p. 623.

'the highest form of literature in the empire of the novel rather than the republic of the essay' Interview with Steve Wasserman, *Susan Sontag, A Biography*, Daniel Schreiber (Northwestern University Press, 2014), p. 189.

p. 172

Annie also bankrolled her, paying for first-class travel, a private chef and maids, spending over $8 million on her over the course of their relationship *Sontag: Her Life and Work*, Benjamin Moser (HarperCollins, 2019/UK edition Allen Lane, 2019), p. 527.

'I felt like a person who is taking care of a great monument' https://www.nytimes.com/2006/10/06/arts/design/06leib.html

Susan was finally able to focus on *The Volcano Lover*, which she fell into 'like Alice in Wonderland', working for twelve hours a day in 'a delirium of pleasure' Leslie Garis, *Susan Sontag Finds Romance*, *New York Times*, 2 August 1992.

'frustrated and upset because she was proud of the relationship' Interview with Karla Eoff, Benjamin Moser (Allen Lane, 2019), p. 627.

'in the hope that it would increase public acceptance of lesbians and gays' *Susan Sontag, A Biography*, Daniel Schreiber (Northwestern University Press, 2014), p. 184.

'called Leibovitz's studio day after day, asking her and Susan to comment on their relationship. Neither returned his calls' *Sontag: Her Life and Work*, Benjamin Moser (HarperCollins, 2019/UK edition Allen Lane, 2019), p. 520.

p. 173

'Endings in a novel confer a kind of liberty that life stubbornly denies us: to come to a full-stop that is not death' *At The Same Time: The Novelist and Moral Reasoning*, Susan Sontag (Farrar, Straus and Giroux, 2007), p. 223.

'There are still so many things I have to do, I'll never be able to forgive myself if I don't do them' *Susan Sontag, A Biography*, Daniel Schreiber (Northwestern University Press, 2014), p. 239.

Susan's son loathed the pictures, saw them as 'carnival images of celebrity death' https://www.theguardian.com/books/2008/jun/15/biography. features7

Susan once wrote that 'to photograph is to appropriate the thing photographed' *On Photography*, Susan Sontag (Farrar, Straus and Giroux, 1977).

p. 174

'It was a relationship in all its dimensions. It had its ups and downs . . . I mean, we helped each other through our lives. Call us "lovers" . . .' https://www.sfgate.com/entertainment/article/love-family-celebrity-grief-leibovitz-puts-2548168.php

p. 179

'The coming out of new debutantes into homosexual society was an outstanding feature of Baltimore's eighth annual frolic of the pansies', reported the *Baltimore Afro-American* https://time.com/4975404/national-coming-out-day-closet-metaphor-history/

'time flowed past indifferently above us; hours and days had no meaning' *Giovanni's Room*, James Baldwin (Dial Press, 1956).

'one thing that society will not tolerate' is 'that I should be . . . *nothing*, or, more precisely that the *something* I am should be openly expressed as provisional, revocable, insignificant, inessential, in a word irrelevant' Nicholas de Villiers, *Opacity and the Closet: Queer Tactics in Foucault, Barthes, and Warhol* (University of Minnesota Press, 2012).

'demanding transparency to the gaze of the interrogator' Nicholas de Villiers, *Opacity and the Closet: Queer Tactics in Foucault, Barthes, and Warhol* (University of Minnesota Press, 2012).

'If there is something self-affirming and indeed *liberating* about coming *out* of the closet . . .' David Halperin, *Saint Foucault: Towards a Gay Hagiography* (Oxford University Press, 1997).

p. 180

'I am tired of lying by omission' https://www.theguardian.com/film/2014/feb/15/ellen-page-comes-out-speech-human-rights-campaign

'it is the author naked which the modern audience demands, as ages of religious faith demanded a human sacrifice' 'The Artist as Exemplary Sufferer', *Against Interpretation and Other Essays*, Susan Sontag (Farrar, Straus and Giroux, 1966).

Sontag felt that her love life, as a whole, was a failure *Sempre Susan*, a memoir of Susan Sontag, Sigrid Nunez (Atlas Books, 2011), p. 107.

p. 181

as the academic Clare Hemmings has noticed, bisexuals are often characterized as existing in precarious geographical landscapes *Bisexual Spaces: A Geography of Sexuality and Gender*, Clare Hemmings (Routledge, 2002).

'in some way I felt the subject of female homosexuality – and whether she owed the world a statement on it – was an unresolved one for her' and 'was there some way, I wonder now, that she wanted me to absolve her?' 'Desperately Seeking Susan', Terry Castle, *London Review of Books*, 17 March 2005.

'our Sartre, our Cocteau', writing that she admired 'his courage . . . one of the most admirable being his honesty about his homosexuality in *Five Years* . . .' *Under the Sign of Saturn*, Susan Sontag (Farrar, Straus and Giroux, 1980), p. 9.

'I don't think that same-sex relationship are valid.' Karla recalled how she then 'came up with all of these things that you hear from these awful people who call themselves Christian: "The parts don't fit."' *Sontag: Her Life and Work*, Benjamin Moser (HarperCollins, 2019/UK edition Allen Lane, 2019), p. 628.

p. 182

'That must be the only thing I ever defended Susan about', arguing that, 'This is completely unfair . . .' *Regarding Susan Sontag*, 2014, dir. Nancy Kates.

'inauthenticity was the price Sontag paid for maintaining her cultural centrality' *Sontag: Her Life and Work*, Benjamin Moser (HarperCollins, 2019/UK edition Allen Lane, 2019), p. 401.

6. David Bowie

p. 184

'In Sweden, a spate of workers telephoned in sick.' https://www.tandfonline.com/doi/full/10.1080/13600826.2022.2052025

p. 185

When the *Daily Mail* ran an opinion survey in October 1965 for their readers, 63 per cent disagreed that homosexual acts in private should be deemed criminal . . . https://blog.nationalarchives.gov.uk/sexual-offences-act/#:~:text=Changing%20public%20attitudes, (HO%20291%2F127)

Queer men, therefore, couldn't chat each other up outside, couldn't exchange telephone numbers in a public place because this would be 'opportuning for immoral purposes' https://www.theguardian.com/society/2007/jun/24/communities.gayrights

'Dr Irving Bieber, for example, declared that 27 per cent of patients were 'converted' 'Queer Diagnoses: Parallels and Contrasts in the History of Homosexuality, Gender Variance, and the Diagnostic and Statistical Manual' Jack Drescher, *American Psychiatric Association*, 2009. https://www.cpath.ca/wp-content/uploads/2009/08/DRESCHER.pdf

p. 186

lesbianism was seen as 'immature' and gay men 'were trying to solve the problem with only half the pieces' *Everything You Always Wanted to Know About Sex* (*But Were Afraid to Ask)*, David Reuben (McKay, 1969).

Steven Angelides has noted, 'a particular temporal framing of bisexuality has cast bisexuality in the past or future, but never in the present tense' *A History of Bisexuality*, Steven Angelides (University of Chicago Press, 2001), p. 17.

p. 187

'blasted the closet door off its hinges' https://www.bbc.co.uk/news/entertainment-arts-21897627

p. 188

Dylan Jones recalls, 'the next day Bowie was all anyone was talking about'
https://www.bbc.co.uk/news/entertainment-arts-21897627

bisexuality offered 'a bridge between the gayworld and the straightworld'
*Bisexuality, Multiple-Gender Attraction, and Gay Liberation Politics
in the 1970s*, Martha Robinson Rhodes, Twentieth Century British
History, Vol. 32, No. 1, 2021, pp. 119–42.

p. 189

It was an interview that celebrated Bowie's sexuality and his
androgynous dress – 'camp as a row of tents', the copy cooed,
'rock's swishiest outrage'. https://www.bowiebible.com/1972/01/22/
bowie-im-gay-and-always-have-been/

Grayson Perry recalled how liberating this was, how at the time 'the social
texture was very straight'. https://www.theguardian.com/comment
isfree/2016/jan/11/david-bowie-gender-maverick-inspiration-pop-
art

'Gender bender' was the term the press affixed to him that year . . . For
example, Jon Savage interviewed Bowie for *The Face* in 1980 and called
him a 'gender bender'.

You can see this in moments such as Bowie's interview with the fusty
television presenter Russell Harty in 1973 https://www.youtube.com/
watch?v=D7L1bMtJnGE

p. 190

'I think we took it on our shoulders that we were creating the twenty-first
century in 1971. We just wanted to blast everything in the past,
question all the established values, all the taboos' *Moonage Daydream*,
directed Brett Morgan, 2022.

'There is a new vibration to spring this year. While the birds and the bees
are striking up their vernal hum . . .' *Newsweek*, 13 May 1974.

'the single major cause of the new acceptance of bisexuality was the
invention of mass birth control . . .' *TIME magazine*, 13 May 1974.

p. 191

'Bisexuality was so fashionable that it seemed that everyone I knew was
either bisexual or pretending to be' https://www.spectator.co.uk/
article/it-s-a-stupid-lie-to-say-we-re-all-bisexual/

Robertson Davies sums up the moment when he remarked that 'the love
which dare not speak its name has become the love that won't shut
up' 'Show Queen: The Musical Sublimation of Gay Romance', Sam
Biederman, *Idiom*, 14 May 2010. https://www.jstor.org/stable/43917280

In a 1979 TV appearance, Bowie is interviewed by a woman who asks him if he is bisexual Bowie interviewed by Mavis Nicholson, *Afternoon Plus*, 16 February 1979, Thames TV. https://www.youtube.com/watch?v=LwTFW4kfHl4&t=311s

'Stars are beings that partake at once of the human and divine . . .' *Madonna as Postmodern Myth*, Georges-Claude Guilbert, (McFarland, 2002), p. 11.

p. 192

'led to a terrifying confusion: for if we could not take the place of God, how could we fill the space we had created within ourselves?' *Moonage Daydream*, directed Brett Morgan, 2022.

'I believe that there was some unconscious need to create a high priest form . . .' Ibid.

Ganymede, 'the fairest of mortal men' *The Iliad*, Homer, translated Robert Fagles (Penguin Classics edition, 1992).

'the rocker and the shaman: a "traditional" rock concert functions as a mass . . .' *Madonna as Postmodern Myth*, Georges-Claude Guilbert (McFarland, 2002), p. 36.

p. 193

'What's the deal? You were gay for a while, then you were not gay, but were you bisexual, were you pansexual, were you tri-sexual?' Interview with Jonathan Ross, 2003. https://www.youtube.com/watch?v=zZdNxKkMiRE

Having once boasted to William Burroughs that he embodied 'the spirit of the Seventies' *Rolling Stone*, 28 February 1974. https://www.rollingstone.com/feature/beat-godfather-meets-glitter-mainman-william-burroughs-interviews-david-bowie-92508/

'for one thing, girls are always presuming that I've kept my heterosexual virginity for some reason . . .' https://www.playboy.com/magazine/articles/1976/09/playboy-interview-david-bowie/

He also described how, at the age of fourteen, he had slept with 'some very pretty boy in class' who he 'neatly fucked on my bed upstairs' Ibid.

the *Boston Phoenix* asserted that he was 'an authentic gay superstar . . .' Andrew Kopkind, *The Boston Phoenix*, October 1972.

p. 195

'David was a person who collected characters,' Alan Yentob reflects, 'and also because he was sort of propelled by curiosity' *Davie Bowie, A Life*, Dylan Jones (Windmilll Books, 2018).

'fans contributed more information than I put into him' https://faroutmagazine.co.uk/vince-taylor-the-real-ziggy-stardust/

'Nothing matters except whatever it is I'm doing at the moment,' he told *Playboy*. 'I can't keep track of everything I say . . .' *Playboy* interview with Cameron Crowe, September 1976. https://www.playboy.com/magazine/articles/1976/09/playboy-interview-david-bowie/

'I'm Pierrot. I'm Everyman. What I'm doing is theatre and only theatre . . .' https://www.theguardian.com/stage/2014/jun/26/david-bowie-stage-oddity-berlin-v-and-a-exhibition-theatre

p. 196

'Most people still want their idols and gods to be shallow, like cheap toys . . .' *Playboy* interview with Cameron Crowe, February 1975. https://www.bowiewonderworld.com/press/70/000275.htm

As the journalist Jon Savage sums up, 'Bowie invented the language to express gender confusion' *The Face*, November 1980.

p. 197

'Christ, I was so *young* then. I was *experimenting*' *Rolling Stone*, 12 May 1983. https://www.rollingstone.com/music/music-news/david-bowie-straight-time-69334/

felt Bowie had helped 'thousands of sexually confused kids like me, trapped in middle-class suburban high schools' The Back Page, *Body Politic*, November 1983. chrome-extension://efaidnbmnnnibpcajpcglclefindmkaj/https://notchesblog.com/wp-content/uploads/2016/01/david-bowie-1.pdf

'He was semi-straight, and semi-gay,' says Mike Berry *Starman: David Bowie, The Definitive Biography*, Paul Trynka (Sphere, 2012), p. 55.

p. 198

Wendy Leigh, one of his biographers, felt that Bowie's sexuality was 'a bisexuality of ambition' . . . Bowie only slept with him 'because it was expedient to do so' *Davie Bowie, A Life*, Dylan Jones (Windmill Books, 2018), pp. 109–10.

a promoter for the Star Club in Hamburg asked, 'Which way do you swing, Davie?' It was a residency the group were keen to get, and so Bowie replied, 'Boys, of course' *Starman: David Bowie, The Definitive Biography*, Paul Trynka (Sphere, 2012), p. 44.

p. 199

Bowie is sometimes accused of being selfish and manipulative in his career, of using people and then discarding them as he climbed ahead

See for example *Starman: David Bowie, The Definitive Biography*, Paul Trynka (Sphere, 2012), p. 38, detailing how Bowie broke up his band the King Bees, devastating his school friend George Underwood, who was the guitarist, or p. 182 for his treatment of Ava Cherry.

but others argue that he was fuelled by a passionate enthusiasm *Starman: David Bowie, The Definitive Biography*, Paul Trynka (Sphere, 2012) also details how Bowie could inspire musicians 'to reach inside themselves and come up with ideas buried deep within their consciousness' (p. 179).

p. 200

'There was something horrible permeating the air in LA in those days,' he recalled. 'The stench of Manson and the Sharon Tate murders' https://www.uncut.co.uk/features/david-bowie-remembers-berlin-cant-express-feeling-freedom-felt-98780/2/

'room to work in' https://faroutmagazine.co.uk/david-bowie-different-personas-a-complete-guide/

p. 201

One night he overdosed on coke and friends saved his life by putting him in a warm bath . . . https://people.com/music/david-bowie-berlin-trilogy-heroes-tours/ https://www.theguardian.com/books/2017/aug/12/hanif-kureishi-david-bowie-starman-new-book

p. 202

'I don't think it was a mistake in Europe, but it was a lot tougher in America' Interview with Clark Collis, *Blender* magazine, August 2002.

'that was Bowie's audience, as somehow it was more radical to be sexually ambiguous in America' *Davie Bowie, A Life*, Dylan Jones (Windmill Books, 2018), p. 153.

p. 203

'At the time, the English were very different sexually from Americans' *Davie Bowie, A Life*, Dylan Jones (Windmill Books, 2018), p. 101.

When Bowie toured as Ziggy in 1973, he faced both fan adoration and homophobic backlash, because 'for most of America bisexual just meant gay' *Davie Bowie, A Life*, Dylan Jones (Windmill Books, 2018), p. 151.

In 1976, he gave an interview to *Rolling Stone* **where he declared, 'I think everybody's bisexual to a certain degree'** https://www.rollingstone.com/feature/elton-john-lonely-at-the-top-rolling-stones-1976-cover-story-238734/

'hit a major trough . . . **and** *Blue Moves* **would be his last Top 10 album in**

the States until 1992's *The One*' David Bowie Made Me Gay: 100 Years
 of LGBT Music, Darryl W. Bullock (Duckworth, 2017), p. 150.

p. 204

'As it happens, David doesn't have much time for Gay Liberation . . . That's
 a particular movement he doesn't want to lead' Interview with *Melody
 Maker*, 1972. http://www.5years.com/oypt.htm

The academic Martha Robinson Rhodes has noted that during the 1970s,
 'rather than being an independent identity', bisexuality was often seen
 as a 'synthesis of identities' *Bisexuality, Multiple-Gender Attraction,
 and Gay Liberation Politics in the 1970s*, Martha Robinson Rhodes,
 Twentieth Century British History, Vol. 32, No. 1, 2021, pp. 119–42.

p. 206

on Tinder, for example, a guy has a 2.8 per cent chance of finding a
 match compared to 35 per cent for a woman https://roast.dating/blog/
 tinder-statistics

p. 212

'Any society that allows people like Lou [Reed] and me to become
 rampant is pretty well lost . . . [it's the] herald of western civilisation's
 terminal decline' Interview with *Melody Maker*, 1972.

'I do fall in love quite quickly. And once upon a time I used to fall in love
 quite a lot' . . . 'I think love is very important for my writing' Bowie
 interviewed by Mavis Nicholson, *Afternoon Plus*, 16 February 1979,
 Thames TV. https://www.youtube.com/watch?v=LwTFW4kfHl4&t
 =311s

'I couldn't sleep for the excitement of our first date. That she would be my
 wife, in my head, was a done deal' https://ew.com/gallery/david-bowie-
 and-iman/

'it was a beautiful ordinary life,' Iman reflected https://www.independent.
 co.uk/arts-entertainment/music/news/iman-david-bowie-never-
 marry-b1782812.html

p. 213

'they're not just experimenting' https://www.advocate.com/bisexuality/201
 8/9/30/12-bisexual-women-who-arent-just-experimenting#rebelltitem1

p. 214

Tony Visconti commented that Bowie's 'death was a work of art' https://
 www.rollingstone.com/music/music-news/david-bowies-death-a-ork-
 of-art-says-tony-visconti-33441/

Guillermo del Torro tweeted, 'Bowie existed so all of us misfits learned

that an oddity was a precious thing. he changed the world forever'
https://slate.com/culture/2016/01/david-bowies-death-inspires-tributes-
from-other-artists-on-twitter-and-facebook.html

Folk singer-songwriter Mary Gauthier said: 'David Bowie showed
this queer kid from Baton Rouge that gender outlaws are cool.
Androgyny=rock&roll, not a reason to kill myself' https://www.
sandiegouniontribune.com/sdut-bowie-lauded-as-an-artist-who-made-
it-ok-to-be-2016jan11-story.html

Kris Kneen: 'He helped me understand myself as bisexual. He helped me
accept myself' https://twitter.com/krissykneen/status/6864909643
16172289

Checkmark Becks: 'Many cis or straight folk loved Bowie but he
saved LGBT lives. He gave us a reason to keep fighting. He means
something special to us' https://www.buzzfeednews.com/article/
patricksmith/lgbt-people-reveal-why-bowie-is-so-important

p. 215

As David Bailey, who photographed Bowie on many occasions, says:
'I don't think I ever got him, not in a picture' *David Bowie, A Life*,
Dylan Jones (Windmill Books, 2018), p. 133.

7. Jean-Michel Basquiat

p. 217

'For sheer kinkiness, there has been nothing like it since the cabaret
scene in 1920s Berlin' *Basquiat: A Quick Killing in Art*, Phoebe Hoban
(Quartet, 1998), p. 47.

'Most of the reviews have been more reviews of my personality. More so
than my work' *Jean-Michel Basquiat: The Radiant Child* (2010), directed
Tamra Davis, Fortissimo Films.

In 2017, Basquiat's *Untitled (Skull)* was sold at a Sotheby's auction for
$110.5 million. It hit the headlines across the world, a record-
breaking sum https://www.nytimes.com/2017/05/18/arts/jean-michel-
basquiat-painting-is-sold-for-110-million-at-auction.html

p. 218

'a black man whose fate twisted with the whims of an all-white jury of
artistic powers' *Jean-Michel Basquiat: Hazards of Sudden Fame and
Success*, Michael Wines, *The New York Times*, 27 August 1998.

'Jean-Michel Basquiat became famous for his art, then he became famous
for being famous, then he became famous for being infamous . . .'

Quoted in *Jean-Michel Basquiat: A revolutionary caught between everyday life, knowledge and myth*, Dieter Buchhart, *Basquiat*, ed. Fondation Beyeler, Dieter Buchhart (Hatje Cantz, 2010), p. 26.

Oscar Wilde might have quipped, 'I put all my genius into my life; I put only my talent into my works' Oscar Wilde in conversation with André Gide; quoted in a letter from Gide to his mother, 30 January 1895.

p. 219

one recent *Guardian* review of *The Collaboration* contrasted the play to the Julian Schnabel biopic, comparing lines, scenes, echoes – but didn't compare it to Basquiat's actual life https://www.theguardian.com/stage/2022/feb/25/the-collaboration-review-young-vic-london#:~:text=The%20first%20half%20is%20stilted,the%20artist%20as%20a%20brand

'Basquiat is represented . . . as the stereotypical black stud randomly fucking white women,' writes bell hooks *Art In America*, June 1993. https://www.artnews.com/art-in-america/features/from-the-archives-altars-of-sacrifice-re-membering-basquiat-63242/

p. 222

the *Village Voice* runs a piece: is SAMO the work of a successful but disillusioned conceptual artist? https://www.villagevoice.com/jean-michel-basquiat-and-the-birth-of-samo/

'a tool for mocking bogusness', as Basquiat described it 'Jean-Michel Basquiat and the Birth of SAMO', Philip Falick, *The Village Voice*, 20 March 2019. https://www.villagevoice.com/jean-michel-basquiat-and-the-birth-of-samo/

Traditionally, it has been a landscape of 'white walls, with white people drinking white wine' Diego Cortez, *Jean-Michel Basquiat: The Radiant Child* (2010), directed Tamra Davis, Fortissimo Films.

p. 223

'They had a master-slave relationship and Jean would walk him around on a leash. He told me he enjoyed sex more with men' *Basquiat: A Quick Killing in Art*, Phoebe Hoban (Quartet, 1998), p. 32.

Suzanne learns that his first homosexual relationship occurred when he was about fourteen *Widow Basquiat: A Memoir*, Jennifer Clement (Canongate, 2014), p. 42.

p. 224

It was clear that his sexual interest was not monochromatic Widow *Basquiat: A Memoir*, Jennifer Clement (Canongate, 2014), p. 32.

p. 225

Once, when he was asked how he painted, he replied that it was like asking Miles Davis 'How does your horn sound?' https://www.barbican.org.uk/sites/default/files/documents/2017-12/Interview_Becky_Johnson_Tamra_Davis.pdf

Ernest Hardy captures the paradox of his art: 'Basquiat's work was about exploding formula and convention, about harnessing the energy and vision of the street' https://issuu.com/redbonepress/docs/bbv1frontmatter050206?e=4685913%2F4266438

p. 226

Basquiat as a 'wild monkey man' (his words), chained up in her basement; 'if I were white, they would just call it an artist-in-residence' https://www.theguardian.com/artanddesign/2017/sep/08/race-power-money-the-art-of-jean-michel-basquiat

or being on a date with a woman and the police asking her if Basquiat was bothering her *Basquiat: A Quick Killing in Art*, Phoebe Hoban, (Quartet, 1998), p. 79.

asked if his style was 'some sort of primal expressionism' and he shot back: 'Like a primate? Like an ape?' Interview with Mark Miller, November 1982. *Jean-Michel Basquiat: The Radiant Child* (2010), directed Tamra Davis, Fortissimo Films.

he was still being labelled 'a graffiti artist' https://www.vanityfair.com/news/1988/11/jean-michel-basquiat

Suzanne pointed out that much of his crazy behaviour seemed like that of an *enfant terrible* when it was just a normal reaction to racism he suffered *Widow Basquiat: A Memoir*, Jennifer Clement (Canongate, 2014), p. 36.

p. 227

'It could have been me,' Basquiat reflected furiously *Basquiat: A Quick Killing in Art*, Phoebe Hoban (Quartet, 1998), p. 216.

Basquiat turns up in a pinstriped Armani suit, the pants splattered with paint *Basquiat: A Quick Killing in Art*, Phoebe Hoban (Quartet, 1998), p. 90.

p. 228

'She's going to be huge' https://www.independent.co.uk/arts-entertainment/art/news/larry-gagosian-reminisces-about-the-days-madonna-was-his-driver-8446624.html

'loved the fact that she truly didn't care what people thought of her . . .'

Madonna: An Intimate Biography, J. Randy Taraborrelli (Sidgwick and Jackson, 2001), p. 82.

Madonna, in turn, finds herself waking in the middle of the night to see her lover awake and lively: 'he'd be standing, painting, at four in the morning . . .' *Life Lessons: Four Decades of Madonna and Interview*, by Mariana De Jesus Szendrey and Orson Gillick Morris, 24 June 2022. https://www.interviewmagazine.com/music/life-lessons-four-decades-of-madonna-and-interview

'I cross out words so you will see them more; the fact that they are obscured makes you want to read them,' Basquiat says https://www.moma.org/artists/370

p. 229

'They weren't choir girls, I only knew that much' *Madonna: An Intimate Biography*, J. Randy Taraborrelli (Sidgwick and Jackson, 2001), p. 85.

Klaus became a gay icon and a 'key staple of the city's new wave scene' https://faroutmagazine.co.uk/david-bowie-klaus-nomi-new-wave-vaudeville-show/

p. 230

Performance artist Joey Arias, a friend of Basquiat's, has recalled witnessing 'a naked and aroused Basquiat walking out of Nomi's bedroom' https://newyorkmusicdaily.wordpress.com/2015/08/03/joey/

Basquiat loved it when Klaus spoke German, but he gave his lover gonorrhoea and Klaus got angry he wouldn't offer any help with his medical bills *Basquiat: A Quick Killing in Art*, Phoebe Hoban (Quartet, 1998), p. 54.

When they broke up, Basquiat turned to Bowes for solace: 'He was all inside out, run ragged and raw' *Basquiat: A Quick Killing in Art*, Phoebe Hoban (Quartet, 1998), p. 107.

the two 'commiserated, finding consolation in each other' Ibid.

Interviewed by Hoban, Bowes reports that 'Basquiat was comfortable with his bisexuality', explaining that: 'He was this kind of truly exotic creature and had a kind of omnidirectional passion' Ibid.

As Ernest Hardy, *Village Voice* critic, says, critics 'turn squeamish or disingenuous when speaking of Basquiat's queerness' https://www.mandatory.com/living/950423-basquiats-relationship-contemporary-queer-black-art-explored-schomburg

which Ronnie Cutrone, an artist who was once Warhol's assistant, called 'like some crazy art-world marriage' https://www.sothebys.com/en/articles/tale-of-two-legends-warhol-and-basquiat

p. 231

'He exuded this highly sexual, highly creative energy,' she remembered. *Basquiat: A Quick Killing in Art*, Phoebe Hoban (Quartet, 1998), p. 200.

'What's Andy doing now?', 'What did he have for lunch?', 'What's he wearing now?' Basquiat would ask her 'Paige Powell on Documenting 80s New York', Grandlife interview; https://www.grandlife.com/culture/interviews/photographer-paige-powell-interview-new-york/

When Paige told Warhol that Basquiat needed help, he was uncertain – 'Well, gee, he just wants to be famous' *Basquiat: A Quick Killing in Art*, Phoebe Hoban (Quartet, 1998), p. 200.

p. 232

'Gee, I think he's better at painting than me,' Warhol wrote in his diary. And: 'He's the best' 31 October 1984, quoted in *Warhol on Basquiat* (Taschen, 2019), p. 181.

This left Paige 'hysterical' (Andy's term) and furious, declaring she'd never do anything to help Basquiat again . . . 24 November 1985, *The Andy Warhol Diaries*, ed. Pat Hackett (London: Penguin, 1989), p. 745.

Suzanne reflected that: 'Andy couldn't stand to share Jean-Michel in any way' *Widow Basquiat: A Memoir*, Jennifer Clement (Canongate, 2014), p. 144.

p. 233

'talking to himself, trying to console himself' Ibid.

'nervous breakdowns' 'Before and After' and 'Superman' – Andy Warhol, James C. Harris, *JAMA Psychiatry* 2014. https://jamanetwork.com/journals/jamapsychiatry/article-abstract/1810259

But watch Warhol and Basquiat together in 1983, being interviewed about their artistic collaboration . . . *The Andy Warhol Diaries*, March 2022, dir. Andrew Rossi, Episode 4.

American art dealer Mary Boone recalls that around Warhol, Basquiat was less inclined to take drugs *The Andy Warhol Diaries*, March 2022, dir. Andrew Rossi, Episode 4, minute 55.

p. 234

'Jean-Michel had a nice big schlong,' Warhol would tell his assistant Benjamin Liu. 'Can you imagine? That's why all those girls liked him' *Basquiat: A Quick Killing in Art*, Phoebe Hoban (Quartet, 1998), p. 214.

Over dinner, he would ask Basquiat how many times he came *Basquiat: A Quick Killing in Art*, Phoebe Hoban (Quartet, 1998), p. 215.

Warhol 'was infatuated with Jean-Michel in both a paternal and a homosexual way' https://time.com/6155980/andy-warhol-diaries-review-netflix/

Warhol famously claimed to not be interested in sex, confiding in a friend that he found it 'messy and distasteful' *Untangling Andy Warhol*, Joan Acocella, 1 June 2020. https://www.newyorker.com/magazine/2020/06/08/untangling-andy-warhol

Basquiat would tease Suzanne by saying that he wouldn't reveal if they were sleeping together *Widow Basquiat: A Memoir*, Jennifer Clement (Canongate, 2014), p. 151.

p. 235

'I wouldn't be surprised if they started putting gays in concentration camps' *The Andy Warhol Diaries*, March 2022, dir. Andrew Rossi.

p. 236

'resist the efforts of some to obtain government endorsement of homosexuality' https://www.nytimes.com/1984/08/18/us/campaign-notes-reagan-would-not-ease-stand-on-homosexuals.html

The word 'queer', once a slur, had been taken back by activists *Bisexuality and Queer Theory: Intersections, Connections and Challenges*, ed. Jonathan Alexander, Serena Anderlini-D'Onofrio (Routledge, 2012), loc. 213.

p. 237

In 1985, in the feminist magazine *Spare Rib*, an angry debate unfolded in the letters column . . . https://www.gayinthe80s.com/2019/10/the-bigotry-against-bisexuals/

Cynthia Slater, a bisexual and BDSM activist who was HIV positive, set up the first Women's HIV/AIDS information switchboard https://blog.lgbthealthlink.org/2015/01/29/the-bisexual-history-of-hivaids-in-photos/

She died of AIDS in 1989, aged forty-four, and was one of those commemorated in the AIDS memorial quilt https://www.aidsmemorial.org/quilt-history

A recurrent problem that bisexuals have faced over the decades has been a lack of proper data collected from studies; they are too often lumped in with gays/lesbians https://www.ilga-europe.org/sites/default/files/bisexual_health.pdf

David Lourea campaigned for two years for the San Francisco department of Public Health to include bi men in their official statistics for AIDS Ibid.

In 1987 *Newsweek* ran an article deeming bisexual men as the 'ultimate pariahs' of the epidemic. October 1987: https://web.archive.org/web/20191022104318/http://www.binetusa.org/bihealth.html#1987

In 1989 *Cosmopolitan* carried a piece that stereotyped bisexual men as corrupt, dishonest villains who were spreading the disease https://fujiwaradivebar.tumblr.com/post/648469012439842816/fujiwaradivebar-verilybitchie-can-someone-in

In retaliation, the New York Area Bisexual Network set up a ferocious letter-writing campaign https://blog.lgbthealthlink.org/2015/01/29/the-bisexual-history-of-hivaids-in-photos/

p. 238

Even as late as 2014, the *New York Post* ran a piece that declared three-quarters of women with new HIV infections had got it from bi men . . . https://nypost.com/2014/01/01/women-with-bisexual-partners-account-for-new-hiv-cases-study/

William Burroughs claimed that Basquiat told him that he had AIDS 'Glenn O'Brien On the Death of Jean-Michel Basquiat and Andy Warhol', *Purple* magazine, 28 February 2017. https://purple.fr/magazine/purple-25yrs-anniv-issue-28/glenn-obrien-on-the-death-of-jean-michel-basquiat-and-andy-warhol/

Basquiat was convinced he was going to die of it and friends . . . felt that this made him more reckless, treating his life more lightly, more loosely Ibid.

as well as infecting Klaus Nomi with gonorrhoea *Basquiat: A Quick Killing in Art*, Phoebe Hoban (Quartet, 1998), p. 55.

he gave Suzanne Mallouk a pelvic infection that left her unable to conceive *Widow Basquiat: A Memoir*, Jennifer Clement (Canongate, 2014), p. 166.

A *New York Times* piece asked, 'Who is using who here?' and sneered at Basquiat as Warhol's 'mascot' *Art: Basquiat, Warhol*, Vivien Raynor, 20 September 1985. https://www.nytimes.com/1985/09/20/arts/art-basquiat-warhol.html

'I asked him if he was mad at me . . .' 20 September 1985, *The Andy Warhol Diaries*, edited Pat Hackett (London: Penguin, 1989), p. 945.

'it wasn't just a father, it was also the professional approval of a white artist who was one of the masters' *Basquiat: A Quick Killing in Art*, Phoebe Hoban (Quartet, 1998), p. 223.

p. 239

'Jean Michel hasn't called me in a month, so I guess it's really over'

24 November 1985, *The Andy Warhol Diaries*, edited Pat Hackett (London: Penguin, 1989), p. 966.

'I never saw him cry before . . .' *Basquiat: A Quick Killing in Art*, Phoebe Hoban (Quartet, 1998), p. 291.

'I ran into him at a club a few days after Andy died, and it was really sad . . . He's standing in the middle of the dancefloor, crying in agony and leaning his head on a wall. He couldn't even talk' *Basquiat: A Quick Killing in Art*, Phoebe Hoban (Quartet, 1998), p. 291.

'Andy dying might have put the idea in Jean-Michel's head that you could die, even if you were seemingly immortal, because Andy always had this air of immortality about him' 'Glenn O'Brien on the Death of Jean-Michel Basquiat and Andy Warhol', *Purple* magazine, 28 February 2017. https://purple.fr/magazine/purple-25yrs-anniv-issue-28/glenn-obrien-on-the-death-of-jean-michel-basquiat-and-andy-warhol/

'You can either be a great artist or a great tragedy', to which he replied, 'Why can't I be both?' *Basquiat: A Quick Killing in Art*, Phoebe Hoban (Quartet, 1998), p. 93.

Bischofberger recalls that his drug-taking intensified, became 'the centre of his life' https://www.sleek-mag.com/article/warhol-basquiat-bromance/

Vincent Gallo, a former bandmate, said that when he saw him, 'I thought he had AIDs' *Basquiat: A Quick Killing in Art*, Phoebe Hoban (Quartet, 1998), p. 312.

p. 240

'Everyone has left me,' he lamented. She was shocked: 'It was the first time I had ever seen him feeling sorry for himself. He was usually so gutsy' *Widow Basquiat: A Memoir*, Jennifer Clement (Canongate, 2014), pp. 178–9.

'hot as a furnace' *Basquiat: A Quick Killing in Art*, Phoebe Hoban (Quartet, 1998), p. 316.

p. 241

'Greedily . . . we wonder what masterpieces we have been cheated out of by his death' https://www.smh.com.au/culture/art-and-design/keith-haring-and-jean-michel-basquiat-art-stars-who-shone-too-briefly-20191114-p53aly.html

Alexis Adler was 'horrified' by the later, declaring that 'the commercialization . . . https://www.thedailybeast.com/basquiats-close-friends-and-collaborators-speak-out-against-jay-z-and-beyonces-tiffanys-ad?ref=home

'When it comes to Basquiat, I tell some stories, and they don't wanna hear it' Kenny Scharf interview, *The Andy Warhol Diaries*, March 2022, dir. Andrew Rossi, Episode 4.

p. 242

'a brief fascination with bisexuality' 'Burning Out', Anthony Haden-Guest, *Vanity Fair*, 2 April 2014, https://www.vanityfair.com/news/1988/11/jean-michel-basquiat

Ernest Hardy has compared Basquiat with Malcolm X https://windycitytimes.com/2011/06/08/ernest-hardy-talks-hip-hop-and-sexuality/

8. Madonna

p. 246

In the UK, 100,000 copies were released and all were sold by the second day; in the US, it went straight into the *New York Times* bestseller lists *Madonna: A Rebel Life*, Mary Gabriel (Coronet, 2023), p. 573.

p. 247

Madonna had given an interview with *The Advocate*, an LGBT magazine in the US, and declared that 'Everybody has a bisexual nature' https://www.advocate.com/news/2007/07/23/madonna-x-rated-interview

in 1992 HIV infection was the leading cause of death for men aged 25–44 in the US https://www.cdc.gov/mmwr/preview/mmwrhtml/00022174.htm#:~:text=In%201992%2C%20HIV%20infection%20became%20the%20leading%20cause%20of%20death,%2C%20respectively)%20(Table_1).

'It was the first time I'd ever seen that, and it was very liberating for me,' reports one guy who had a conservative upbringing . . . *Strike a Pose* documentary, dir. Ester Gould and Reijer Zwaan, 2016.

In decades to come, Salim would go on to receive thousands of messages from people all around the world https://www.theguardian.com/artanddesign/2017/jun/16/madonna-blond-ambition-tour-1990-salim-gauwloos-dancer

'It's hard to think of another film about a nongay subject in which the presence of gay people is not only normal and accepted but treasured' https://www.advocate.com/news/2007/07/23/madonna-x-rated-interview

'They're not going to be by the time I've finished with them' Ibid.

p. 248

'The 1990s were still a time when homophobia was rife, but things were starting to change . . .' *Pride: The Story of The LGBTQ Equality Movement*, Matthew Todd (Simon & Schuster, 2020), p. 102.

Matt Cain, struggling with his sexuality as a teenager, found redemption in Madonna: he feared 'everyone would hate me if it [his sexuality] ever came out' 'Eight Ways Madonna Changed the World' by Matt Cain, 16 August 2018, *Daily Telegraph*.

'the vamp is an object of desire, but she is untouchable, like a virginal deity' *Madonna as Postmodern Myth*, Georges-Claude Guilbert (McFarland, 2002).

'the appearance of sexiness, not the existence of sexual pleasure' in women *Female Chauvinist Pigs: Women and the Rise of Raunch Culture*, Ariel Levy (The Free Press, 2005).

p. 249

'What can I say? I've been your most loyal fan. I have all your albums, all your biographies and videotapes of all your world tours . . .' *Harvard Crimson*, 6 November 1992. https://www.thecrimson.com/article/1992/11/6/an-open-letter-to-madonna-pdear/

In the 1980s, she had sold superstar quantities of her albums – 25 million copies of *True Blue* (the bestselling album of the 1980s by a female artist) https://en.wikipedia.org/wiki/True_Blue_(Madonna_album)

15 million of *Like A Prayer* https://en.wikipedia.org/wiki/Like_a_Prayer_(album)

Her *Erotica* album dived, selling 2 million in the US, a low for her https://en.wikipedia.org/wiki/Madonna_albums_discography#:~:text=Recognized%20as%20the%20world's%20best,than%20300%20million%20units%20worldwide

For the first time, she released a single, 'Bad Girl', which failed to make the Top 30 of the Hot 100 in the US https://en.wikipedia.org/wiki/Bad_Girl_(Madonna_song)

reflecting later on that she 'lost confidence in humanity' https://www.cbsnews.com/news/middle-aged-madonna-endures/

For J. Randy Taraborrelli, the book was supposed to be 'adult' but was 'childish and impetuous' *Madonna: An Intimate Biography*, J. Randy Taraborrelli (Sidgwick and Jackson, 2001), p. 230.

'as a mode of confrontation as much as eroticism'. She declares that Madonna was driven by 'white-hot anger' *Madonna: Like an Icon*, Lucy O'Brien (Bantam Press, 2007), p. 280.

p. 251

'Bisexuality is in bloom' *Newsweek* magazine, 'Bisexuality. Not Gay. Not Straight. A New Sexual Identity Emerges', 16 July 1995. https://www.newsweek.com/bisexuality-184830

In the US, the first National Conference on Bisexuality was held in San Francisco in 1990 https://robynochs.com/bisexual-movement/

'Aloha, my name is Lani Ka'ahumanu,' she started as she took the mic, 'and it ain't over til the bisexual speaks' https://www.lanikaahumanu.com/mow.shtml

p. 252

The writer Sue George notes that between 1977 and 1990 there were no titles listed in the copyright section of the British Library on the subject of bisexuality 'British Bisexual: A New Century', Sue George, *Bisexual Women in the Twenty-First Century*, ed. Dawn Atkins (The Haworth Press, 2002), p. 184.

'Women played a major role in the formation of "bisexual identity" and "bisexual politics" . . . .' *Introduction: Beauteous and Brave*, Dawn Atkins, *Bisexual Women in the Twenty-First Century* (The Haworth Press, 2002).

p. 253

in season 3, episode 4, of *Sex and the City*, a discussion on bisexuality included the line, 'It's just a layover on the way to Gaytown' https://www.satctranscripts.com/2008/08/sex-and-city-season-3-episode-4.html

p. 254

'ants were crawling over her heart', beset with worries that she will die from cancer like her mother did' 'Madonna' by David Blaine, *Interview* Magazine, 26 November 2014. https://www.interviewmagazine.com/music/madonna-1

'I know that some of my lack of inhibition comes from my mother's death,' she reflected later. *Los Angeles Times*, 5 May 1991. https://www.latimes.com/archives/la-xpm-1991-05-05-ca-2097-story.html

Her grandmother advises her 'not to go with men, to love Jesus and be a good girl' *Madonna: A Rebel Life*, Mary Gabriel (Coronet, 2023), p. 47.

both 'the male and female spirit' https://www.mojo4music.com/articles/stories/madonna-interviewed/

the concert was 'worth every minute' of the punishment https://ew.com/article/2016/01/11/madonna-david-bowie-tribute/

All of a sudden she feels as though Bowie has given her a licence to 'dream a different future' for herself https://www.mojo4music.com/articles/stories/madonna-interviewed/

p. 255

'Behind every great man is a great woman, and behind every great woman is a gay man' *Madonna: A Rebel Life*, Mary Gabriel (Coronet, 2023), p. 76.

'Oh God, I've found it,' she thinks. 'For the first time I saw men kissing men . . .' Speech by Madonna to the GLAAD media awards, 2019. https://www.attitude.co.uk/culture/film-tv/madonna-gives-moving-speech-at-the-glaad-media-awards-298838/

She realizes that until that point, she has viewed herself through 'macho heterosexual eyes' Interview with the *Advocate*, 7 May 1991. https://www.advocate.com/news/2007/07/23/madonna-x-rated-interview

she asked the taxi driver to take her to the 'middle of everything' *Madonna: A Rebel Life*, Mary Gabriel (Coronet, 2023), p. 95.

'I felt like I had plugged my finger into an electric socket' Madonna, interviewed on the Howard Stern Show, 2015. https://www.mlive.com/news/detroit/2015/03/madonna_has_unflattering_words.html

'Everyone was doing it' *Madonna: Like an Icon*, Lucy O'Brien (Bantam Press, 2007), p. 245.

'I was so miserable that I wasn't a man' *Madonna: A Rebel Life*, Mary Gabriel (Coronet, 2023), p. 74.

'I didn't feel like straight men understood me. They just wanted to have sex with me. Gay men understood me and I felt comfortable around them' Interview with *Out* magazine, 10 March 2015. https://www.out.com/out-exclusives/2015/3/10/many-heresies-madonna-louise-ciccone

p. 256

'They are looked on as outsiders, so I can relate to that . . .' https://www.advocate.com/news/2007/07/23/madonna-x-rated-interview

Boy George has described her as 'a gay man trapped in a woman's body'. https://www.forbes.com/consent/ketch/?toURL=https://www.forbes.com/quotes/10655/

in a Reddit chat, when she was asked the question, *if you were a gay man, would you be a top or a bottom*, she replied: 'I am a gay man' https://www.out.com/celebs/madonna-gay-icon

Critics debated whether she was 'arguing for gender fluidity as a road to gender equality' *Madonna's Drowned Worlds: New Approaches to Her Cultural Transformations, 1983–2003*, Santiago Fouz-Hernandez (Taylor & Francis, 2017), p. 26.

'People with AIDS – regardless of their sexual orientation – deserve compassion and support, not violence and bigotry' https://www.gaytimes.co.uk/originals/madonna-celebration-tour-hiv-activism/

p. 257

an administration, led by President Reagan, which labelled HIV a 'gay plague' https://www.bbc.com/culture/article/20201019-the-drama-that-raged-against-reagans-america

through an era when the Catholic Church condemned the use of needle exchanges and condoms 'Bishops' Panel Rejects Condoms in AIDs Battle', *Los Angeles Times*, 13 October 1989. https://www.latimes.com/archives/la-xpm-1989-10-13-mn-149-story.html

'I came home smelling like shit and vomit and death and defiance. I came home smelling like gratitude' Madonna's speech on accepting the GLAAD Media Advocate for Change, 4 May 2019 https://www.rollingstone.com/music/music-news/glaad-media-awards-madonna-andy-cohen-831408/

'Now I'm not HIV-positive. But if I were?' Madonna's award speech 10 December 1991, honoured by amfAR for her AIDS activism. https://www.gaytimes.co.uk/originals/madonna-celebration-tour-hiv-activism/

p. 258

'All of my sexual experiences when I was young were with girls' Interview with the *Advocate*, 7 May 1991. https://www.advocate.com/news/2007/07/23/madonna-x-rated-interview

'I think I've only been in love with men, because ultimately the approval I seek is my father's' Ibid.

'I suppose people would say, "You emasculate men in what you do." Well, straight men need to be emasculated. I'm sorry. They all need to be slapped around' https://www.advocate.com/news/2007/07/23/madonna-x-rated-interview

p. 259

As Madonna herself famously said: 'I wouldn't wish being Mr Madonna on anybody' https://www.theguardian.com/lifeandstyle/2008/may/18/madonna

'We split each other's split ends,' Sandra quipped mockingly, adding, 'We frighten everyone out of the room' *Late Night with David Letterman*, NBC, 1988. https://www.dailymotion.com/video/x757xgg

'I realised I could have a really good friend in Sandra' *Madonna: A Rebel Life*, Mary Gabriel (Coronet, 2023), p. 371.

'whilst the actress [Jolie] confirmed her love for the diva, the pop star never addressed her rumoured romance' https://www.koimoi.com/hollywood-news/when-angelina-jolies-former-lover-jenny-shimizu-revealed-how-madonna-used-to-call-her-for-sx-at-any-time-of-day-night-said-shes-far-from-sx-crazed-woman/

that 'they were both sensational lovers who got incredibly turned on by the touch of another woman' https://www.timeslive.co.za/sunday-times/lifestyle/2006-04-30-i-was-madonnas-lesbian-sex-slave/

'Far from the domineering, sex-crazed woman many think she is, I found her a very gentle lover.' Ibid.

p. 261

'to have the right kind of man in your life, you have to be the right kind of woman' *Madonna: An Intimate Biography*, J. Randy Taraborrelli (Sidgwick and Jackson, 2001), p. 320.

'If I had known I would be universally misunderstood, maybe I wouldn't have been so rebellious and outspoken . . .' 1 February, *Madonna's Private Diaries, Vanity Fair*, November 1996.

p. 262

'will not allow Madonna to dress me like a poof' *Madonna: An Intimate Biography*, J. Randy Taraborrelli (Sidgwick and Jackson, 2001), p. 313.

'men are quite intimidated by women who accomplish a lot' *Madonna: Like an Icon*, Lucy O'Brien (Bantam Press, 2007), p. 347.

'Put Madonna up against any twenty-three-year-old, she'll outwork them, outdance them, outperform them. The woman is broad' https://www.huffpost.com/entry/guy-ritchie-madonna-is-re_n_312360

'How much am I willing to sacrifice?' https://www.glamourmagazine.co.uk/article/madonna-talks-guy-ritchie-marriage-for-first-time

Some years later, she reflected that the marriage had left her feeling 'incarcerated' and 'there were many times when I wanted to express myself as an artist . . .' https://www.huffingtonpost.co.uk/2015/03/11/madonna-guy-ritchie-marriage-prisoner_n_6846340.html#:~:text=%E2%80%9CHowever%2C%20you%20know%2C%20I,really%20allowed%20to%20be%20myself.%E2%80%9D

p. 263

'She likes the idea of a guy being younger than her daughter. It announces her desirability to the world' https://pagesix.com/2022/09/14/since-2008-madonna-only-dates-guys-at-least-28-years-younger/

'It's just what happens. Most men my age are married with children. They're not dateable . . .' https://www.huffingtonpost.co.uk/entry/madonna-younger-men_n_6830968#:~:text=At%2056%2C%20Madonna%20says%20she's,They're%20not%20dateable

'The fact that people actually believe a woman is not allowed to express her sexuality…' https://www.independent.co.uk/news/people/madonna-claims-met-gala-dress-is-political-statement-about-ageism-a7014386.html

p. 264

'Madonna is too old to be kissing someone who is 22. I thought it was the most obnoxious moment in television history' https://nypost.com/2003/09/22/nicks-knocks-britneys-mtv-kiss/

'I've been oblivious until this moment. I had no idea that it was going to cause the ruckus that it caused. It was just a friendly kiss' https://www.eonline.com/news/1385036/lose-yourself-in-the-nostalgia-of-the-2003-mtv-vmas

p. 265

As Oprah pointed out, 'I don't know if most of America has' Madonna interviewed by Oprah, 2003. https://www.madonnatribe.com/decade/2003/madonna-tribes-year-end-review-madonna-on-the-oprah-show/

Camille Paglia praised Madonna's MTV act as a way of 'passing the torch' on https://afterellen.com/remember-when-kissing-madonna-was-the-raciest-thing-britney-had-ever-done/

by the way 'everyone beats up on' Britney *Madonna: A Rebel Life*, Mary Gabriel (Coronet, 2023), p. 742.

But Paglia later attacked Britney, Lindsay Lohan and co., complaining that 'these girls are lowering themselves to the level of backstreet floozies' https://www.theguardian.com/film/2010/jul/07/lindsay-lohan-actor-alcohol

p. 266

'I'm not a teenager anymore and I won't pretend to be one to sell records' *Madonna: A Rebel Life*, Mary Gabriel (Coronet, 2023), p. 737.

in 1993, when Keith Cameron in the *NME* sighed, 'one hesitates to say that at thirty-five she's too old for all this' *Madonna: A Rebel Life*, Mary Gabriel (Coronet, 2023), p. 605.

Lorraine Kelly declaring that Madonna's beauty treatments made her 'look like a boiled egg' https://www.independent.co.uk/arts-entertainment/tv/news/lorraine-kelly-madonna-boiled-egg-b2200804.html

'I take care of myself. I'm in good shape. I can show my ass when I'm 56 or 66 or 76. Who's to say when I can show my ass? It's sexism. It's ageism. And it's a kind of discrimination' https://eu.usatoday.com/story/life/music/2018/08/16/madonna-turns-60-revisit-her-painful-lessons-aging-while-female/982562002/

p. 267

In an interview with five bisexuals, *Guardian* journalist Owen Jones explored . . . https://www.youtube.com/watch?v=E3zYJw3jey4

p. 268

The late 1990s saw an article in *Vogue* which declared that 'bi-trying' was a new fashion amongst celebrities and models . . . 'British Bisexual: A New Century', Sue George, *Bisexual Women in the Twenty-First Century*, ed. Dawn Atkins (The Haworth Press, 2002), pp.186–7.

'I speak my truths and I paint my fantasies into these little bite-size pop songs. For instance, I kissed a girl – and I liked it . . .' https://www.nme.com/news/music/katy-perry-i-kissed-a-girl-did-more-than-that-2023048

One article declared that Perry was partaking in 'part-time lesbianism' 'Baby Dykes: The Young Girls Who Swap Their Sexuality', *Evening Standard*, 10 April 2012. https://www.standard.co.uk/lifestyle/baby-dykes-the-young-girls-who-swap-their-sexuality-6756348.html

p. 269

'But I don't think I could ever really be with a woman because that's a lot of . . . estrogen . . .' 'Christina Aguilera Reclaims The Fame', Joshua David Stein, 16 May 2010, *Out* magazine. https://www.out.com/entertainment/music/2010/05/16/christina-aguilera-reclaims-fame

'I love who I love,' she said, 'it's the person that matters.' https://www.cosmopolitan.com/uk/entertainment/a25854518/amber-heard-bisexual-coming-out-real-reason/

many press outlets decided that Heard was coming out as a 'lesbian' https://people.com/celebrity/amber-heard-coming-out-journey-lgbtq-summit/

An Australian talk show host remarked, 'It's not wise to marry a bisexual. Bye bi, Amber' https://www.smh.com.au/entertainment/celebrity/its-not-wise-to-marry-a-bisexual-peter-fords-take-on-johnny-depp-and-amber-heard-may-be-the-worst-yet-20160530-gp6wxa.html

Evan Rachel Wood tweeted in her defence, 'What does Amber being bisexual and having lesbian friends have to do with anything?' https://www.teenvogue.com/story/amber-heard-domestic-violence-psa-bisexual

61 per cent of bisexual women have been raped, suffered physical violence or been stalked by a partner, compared to 35 per cent of heterosexual women; and 37 per cent of bisexual men compared to 29 per cent of straight men https://www.nsvrc.org/blogs/Bi-phobia-series/disparities-bi-health-and-sexual-violence

p. 270

the 1990s are described as a time when 'gay men and lesbians became a political bloc, working together to end legal restrictions that kept them from living as full citizens' *Madonna: A Rebel Life*, Mary Gabriel (Coronet, 2023), p. 690.

'I'm bi. Congrats for forcing an 18-year-old to out himself' https://www.stylist.co.uk/people/kit-connor-coming-out-heartstopper/726548

p. 271

as academics Jonathan Alexander and Serena Anderlini-D'Onofrio note, bisexuality was once seen as undermining the fight for gay rights and equal marriage . . . *Bisexuality and Queer Theory: Intersections, Connections and Challenges*, ed. Jonathan Alexander, Serena Anderlini-D'Onofrio (Routledge, 2012).

In 2022, she made a TikTok video that went viral . . . https://www.newsweek.com/madonna-gay-tiktok-sexuality-lgbt-1750298

A number of fans (mostly of a younger generation) speculated that she was 'coming out', even though Madonna has been 'out' for three decades Ibid.

a woman who has been awarded the GLAAD Advocate for Change award https://glaad.org/releases/madonna-be-honored-advocate-change-award-lifetime-accelerating-lgbtq-accceptance-30th/

suffered a $1 million fine from the Russian government for speaking out for LGBT rights https://www.gaytimes.co.uk/culture/madonna-was-fined-1-million-for-supporting-lgbtq-rights-in-russia-and-didnt-pay/

p. 273

In 2019, there were headlines about a 'gay couple' who had suffered violence on a bus . . . https://edition.cnn.com/2019/06/07/europe/homophobic-attack-london-intl-scli-gbr/index.html

p. 276

There is a vitality, a life force, an energy, a quickening that is translated through you . . . https://www.theguardian.com/books/2016/oct/29/zadie-smith-what-beyonce-taught-me

Acknowledgements

Thank you to my excellent editor, James Pulford: for his faith in this project, patience whilst I grappled with various drafts, and astute editorial insights. Thank you to Erika Koljonen for taking over as my new editor. Thank you to Rachel Wright for her copy-editing and advice, and to my excellent publicist Laura O'Donnell and to Harry O'Sullivan in editorial management for being so helpful.

Thanks for love, support, and friendship: Zakia Uddin, Susan Barker, Zoe Pilger, Sam Byers, David and Leesha, Lyra, Ian Boulton, Catherine Taylor, Marina Benjamin, Anna Maconochie, Alex Spears, Venetia Welby, Thom Cuell, Susanna Crossman, Ben Pester, Seraphina Madsen, Tristan R., Cathryn Summerhayes, Will Francis, Lola Jaye, Dylan Evans, Joe Thomas, Lucy Binnersley, Jude Cook, Simon Lewis, Tom Tomaszewski, James Clammer, Harold and the Shark.

A special thanks to Stephen Gill for reading early chapters and for helpful advice.

A very special thank you to my dear Andrew Gallix.

Index